# STICKS AND STONES

## and

## Other

## Student

## Essays

SIXTH EDITION

EDITED BY
RUTHE THOMPSON
*SOUTHWEST MINNESOTA
STATE UNIVERSITY*

RISE B. AXELROD
*UNIVERSITY OF CALIFORNIA,
RIVERSIDE*

CHARLES R. COOPER
*UNIVERSITY OF CALIFORNIA,
SAN DIEGO*

BEDFORD/ST. MARTIN'S
Boston • New York

**For Bedford/St. Martin's**

*Developmental Editor:* Laura King
*Production Editor:* Bernard Onken
*Production Supervisor:* Sarah Ulicny
*Senior Marketing Manager:* Karita dos Santos
*Art Director:* Lucy Krikorian
*Text Design:* Paul Agresti
*Copy Editor:* Jamie Thaman
*Cover Design:* Donna L. Dennison
*Composition:* Textech
*Printing and Binding:* Haddon Craftsmen, Inc.,
   an R.R. Donnelley & Sons Company

*President:* Joan E. Feinberg
*Editorial Director:* Denise B. Wydra
*Editor in Chief:* Karen S. Henry
*Director of Development:* Erica T. Appel
*Director of Marketing:* Karen Melton Soeltz
*Director of Editing, Design, and Production:* Marcia Cohen
*Managing Editor:* Shuli Traub

Library of Congress Control Number: 2006926511

Manufactured in the United States of America.

2 1 0 9 8 7
f e d c b a

*For information, write:* Bedford/St. Martin's, 75 Arlington Street, Boston, MA 02116   (617-399-4000)

ISBN-10: 0-312-43103-1
ISBN-13: 978-0-312-43103-7

# STICKS
# AND STONES

# Preface for Instructors

*Sticks and Stones and Other Student Essays* is a reader designed to ac-company *The St. Martin's Guide to Writing.* Now in its sixth edition, *Sticks and Stones* continues the tradition of its predecessors: to cele-brate student writing. Following the organization of Part One of *The Guide,* it includes student essays written in each of *The Guide*'s nine genres, from "Remembering Events" to "Interpreting Stories." The introductions to the collection's chapters aim to motivate students to write in the genres, while the headnotes to readings invite them to become attentive readers of the genres. Two final sections, "A Note on the Copyediting" and "Sample Copyediting," explain the role of editing in published writing and let students see the editing process in black and white.

## NEW TO THE SIXTH EDITION

Important new features enhance this edition:

***More new essays than ever before.*** To the 16 most popular essays from the fifth edition, we have added 19 new ones. These include es-says on topics sure to excite students' curiosity (such as dragon boat-ing, zombism, and proxemics) as well as essays on topics that students will have much to say about (such as eBay, Wal-Mart, and the tobacco industry).

***Chapter introductions that motivate students to write in each genre.*** In each completely revised chapter introduction, we aim to increase stu-dents' interest and investment in the featured genre by showing them what is distinctive about it, how it relates to and builds on the others, and what they will gain academically and personally from working in it.

*Essay headnotes that invite students to become attentive readers of each genre.* Headnotes help students approach the essays as models for their own writing by spotlighting some of the writers' achievements working in the genre and by inviting students to notice other achievements. (In some cases, "as you read" sentences direct students' efforts.) Where necessary, headnotes may also supply context, such as the background information students need to understand Abida Wali's remembered event essay, set during the Soviet occupation of Afghanistan.

*Revised submission form.* To encourage students to submit their own essays, we have revised the submission form to make it less intimidating and easier to use. As an instructor, you should feel free to provide extra encouragement to a student who writes an outstanding essay. Few students have ever thought their assigned essays could be published for a national audience to read. You might work with a student on further revision and assist with filling out the submission form.

## SUGGESTIONS FOR USING
## *STICKS AND STONES AND OTHER STUDENT ESSAYS*

*Sticks and Stones* is an ancillary that can be used alongside *The St. Martin's Guide to Writing.* You could ask students to read a chapter in *Sticks and Stones,* select a favorite essay, and analyze how it exemplifies the genre as outlined in the relevant *Guide* chapter's Basic Features section. Because the essays in every chapter of *Sticks and Stones* vary so much in subject and approach, you and your students could explore essays that model the many different ways writers organize ideas, structure sentences, use vocabulary and tone, address an audience, and center themselves in a genre.

You might want to walk students through a few paragraphs of the copyedited essay at the end of the book. The editing displaces, replaces, adds, and subtracts in order to focus and speed the reading and make the relationships among ideas clearer. Students could learn from speculating about reasons for some of the edits, not all of which are so local as they seem (as you will readily recognize).

To inspire thoughtful revision and editing, you could have your students submit essays that were based on assignmens in *The Guide*—or even inspired by essays in *Sticks and Stones* itself—to be considered for publication in the campus newspaper or the next editions of *The Guide* and *Sticks and Stones*. You will find a submission form at the end of this book.

These suggestions address but a few of the numerous possible uses of *Sticks and Stones,* and we would be delighted to learn how you use this book, as well as what you would like to see in the next edition.

## ACKNOWLEDGMENTS

We are grateful to many people who made this edition of *Sticks and Stones* a reality. Most of all, we would like to thank the hundreds of students who have conceived, drafted, written, revised, and polished the essays we have received over the years. Although we cannot include every essay submitted to us, we have read each one with interest and care.

We also thank the instructors who encouraged their students to submit their work for this collection or who submitted their students' work themselves. *Sticks and Stones* would not exist without the generous efforts of these instructors.

Many thanks go to the instructors whose students' work is published in this sixth edition for the first time: Doug Anderson, Southwest Minnesota State University; Melissa Batai, Triton College; Laurie Buchanan, Clark State Community College; Amanda Callendrier, Niagara County Community College; Sandy Cavanah, Hopkinsville Community College; Rebecca Hinton, Northern Kentucky University; Joon Ho Hwong, University of California, Riverside; Irwin Oltmanns, Des Moines Area Community College; Jeff Ritchie, Lebanon Valley College; Dave Sogge, Southwest Minnesota State University; Krista Sprecher, The Catholic University of America; Erica Steakley, The Catholic University of America; Joanna Tardoni, Western Wyoming Community College; Ruthe Thompson, Southwest Minnesota State University; Jan Vierk, Metropolitan Community College; Sarah Waddle, Des Moines Area Community College; and Barbara Wheeler, Hawkeye Community College.

Many thanks also go to the following instructors, whose insightful reviews of the fifth edition helped to shape the sixth: Melissa Batai, Triton College; Kyle Bishop, Southern Utah University; Megan A. Caughron, The Catholic University of America; Bill Dynes, University of Indianapolis; Scott Hall, Anoka Ramsey Community College; Kimberly Harrison, Florida International University;

Dawn Hubbell-Staeble, Bowling Green State University; Damon Kraft, University of Missouri-Columbia; Anna M. Lang, University of Indianapolis; Cynthia Patton, Emporia State University; Deborah M. Scaggs, St. Louis University; Mary Werner, Madisonville Community College; Xuewei Wu, Century Community and Technical College; and James Yates, Northwestern Oklahoma State University.

We would also like to extend our sincere appreciation to Nathan Odell and Laura King of Bedford/St. Martin's for their thoughtful guidance, invaluable editorial suggestions, and the considerable energy and enthusiasm they brought to this project. And, of course, we thank Elizabeth Rankin, Paul Sladky, and Lawrence Barkley, whose fine work on previous editions of this book set the standards for everything that followed.

Ruthe Thompson
Rise B. Axelrod
Charles R. Cooper

# Contents

# STICKS
# AND STONES

# *To the Student* 1

The essays in *Sticks and Stones* were written by students like you in writing classes like yours across the country. If you're thinking, "I'm not like the students whose essays appear in this book; I could never write that well—or get my writing published," take heart. Truth is, the essays in this book didn't always look like they do now. They began as a few sentences of invention writing, some notes taken from a research source, a phrase written on the back of an old receipt while waiting in the grocery checkout line, a tentative paragraph in a first draft, a comment written by a classmate reading a draft. And when they began to take shape, it was a rough shape. Some essays shifted from one rough shape to the next for a long time. But the writers persisted. They tested the advice of their peers and instructors. They gathered more material, whether that meant interrogating their memories; returning to a profile place; consulting more books and electronic databases; or re-viewing a film. And they pushed themselves to think of new ways to say what they wanted to say.

There's no question that writing something good enough for publication is hard work. But there's also no question that doing so is possible for every student reading this book.

Want a tip? Here's an easy way for you to increase your chances of getting published: As you write, ask yourself, "What can I do to help the readers of *Sticks and Stones*—other students like me—understand what I am trying to say in this essay?" A metamorphosis will begin. You will no longer think of yourself as someone who is merely completing an assignment for your writing class; you will begin to think of yourself as a writer in conversation with your readers.

You will notice that the writers whose work is collected here are determined to seize their readers and provoke a response. The tone of their writing is not, "Hey, would you *mind* reading my work?"

1

nor is it that of a class assignment written for an audience of one—the instructor. Instead, these essays clearly belong to writers who have something to say, who are writing for an audience they know exists beyond themselves and those grading their work.

We can't wait to hear what *you* have to say.

# Remembering Events 2

You can't escape narratives like the ones you will read and write in this chapter, and you wouldn't want to, because they give such pleasure. In fact, your sense of who you are—your personal identity—depends on narratives: the stories told and retold in your family and among your long-time friends, the stories you tell and retell yourself in moments of reflection. These stories may calm and center you, or they may alarm and agitate you, but together they define who you are and provide the foundation for your future.

Listening to gossip, watching a film, or reading a short story are enjoyable activities. But to be on the shaping end of a story—to tell or write a story about your own life—is even more rewarding. Telling about an event might allow you to discover its particular significance in your life, for example, by writing about an event from her childhood, Cheryl Sole discovered that it marked her awareness of human duplicity, the beginning of her maturity. Or it might enable you to articulate the event's lessons: Luis Jaco's story about his first fall from a horse is also a cautionary tale about the dangers of pride. Or it might help you see more clearly how the past shapes the future: Aaron Forshier's story about a tragic accident can be seen as a case study in how an event can alter personalities and relationships.

To tell a story is to re-form an event in your mind and examine it from your current perspective, through the greater knowledge you have gained from more education and a larger life experience. As you write and revise your remembered-event essay, take advantage of this perspective: take time to see your story anew, to read each draft as if you didn't already know its details. That way you can look for contradictions and inconsistencies in your thinking, and examine and reconsider any initial, rapid conclusions you may have drawn about the experience. Sharing drafts with classmates and your instructor will

3

give you even more perspective on the event and your response to it, and will refine and deepen your insight into the event's meaning.

Whatever you do, as you cull your memory for details of a remembered event, keep an open mind. Re-seeing events can lead to self-judgment and judgment of others: "I wish I had done this," or "if only she hadn't said that!" But these reflections can be important. They allow you to notice unresolved tensions below the surface of your memory, and they teach you to reserve judgment as you struggle to understand the event.

Although language is slippery and imperfect, writing about your past is a powerful tool, allowing you to revisit remembered events, bring together your scattered thinking about them, and achieve significant insights. Your revised essay will document this voyage toward understanding.

# *Sticks and Stones*
## Nicole Ball
### *Niagara University*
### *Niagara University, New York*

This is a story about bullies. We have all known bullies; the boy in Nicole Ball's story, with his drumsticks and his taunts, is a classic example. It is also a story about words—both their power and their all-too-frequent failure. The title alludes to a familiar saying from childhood: "Sticks and stones will break my bones but words will never hurt me." As Ball's story reminds us, words *do* have the power to hurt, and the child's claim "words will never hurt me" is really a false front, thrown up to hide the very wounds that cruel words have caused. At the same time, Ball's story reminds us of the failure of words. Here the narrator's words fail, the parents' words fail, and the principal's words fail. Indeed, language harms and fails everyone but the bully, who enjoys the effects not only of his words but also of his sticks—his drumsticks.

As readers, we find this essay memorable in part because Nicole's experience denies us the story's expected conclusion: the triumph of Nicole and her brother in the banishment of their tormentor. Happy endings are like truisms, the author seems to suggest: tempting because they are easy but too often *un*true.

"Sticks and Stones" is both a challenge to common knowledge—words *do* hurt; endings are not always happy—and a coming-of-age story, a record of the narrator's dawning realization that we must all learn to rely on ourselves, both to confront conflict in the present and to evaluate and comprehend the consequences of experiences past. As a remembered-event essay, it is a confirmation of the power of words to enable the writer to challenge assumptions and strengthen the self.

---

James Nichols was short and scrawny, the smallest kid in the entire eighth grade class. But he had a foul mouth and a belligerent attitude to make up for it. And he was a bully.

1

James sat in the front seat of the school bus, relegated there by the bus driver after some infraction or other. The driver, a balding, heavy-set man who paid little or no attention to the charges he shuttled back and forth, rarely spoke and, except for that act of discipline, seemed disinclined to do anything else. The punishment, however, didn't seem to faze James; in fact, he reveled in it. Sitting in the front put him at the head of all the action and surrounded him with easy victims: those too timid or meek to trespass into the "tough" zone at the back of the bus.

I was a year older than James and, though not very tall myself, was at least a foot taller than he was. But by my last year in junior high school, I had a terrible complexion, a mouthful of braces, and a crippling shyness. I sat in the second seat on the school bus, only because I couldn't get any closer to the front.

My brother, Greg, who was a year younger, generally sat with me because while he was a bit shorter, and much more confident, he had no more desire to mix with the cigarette-toting crowd in the back of the bus than I did. And although we didn't always get along well at home, we both felt that it was nice to have someone to sit with on the bus, even if we didn't talk much.

In our junior high, as in all junior highs, skill at socializing out-ranked skill in classes. And since Greg and I were both social out-casts, we endured our share of teasing and taunts. But James Nichols set out to top them all.

At first, of course, his words were easy to ignore, mostly because they were nothing new. But as his taunts grew louder and nastier, he developed the habit of kneeling on his seat and leaning over the back to shout his unrelenting epithets down upon us. The kids in the back of the bus relished every moment of our humiliation, often cheering him on. James puffed up with pride over his cruelty. The bus driver never said a word, though he could not have helped but hear the barrage of insults. Inside, I seethed.

"Ignore him," my parents insisted. "He'll eventually stop when he realizes that you're not going to react." Their words were well meant, but didn't help. The taunts continued and even intensified when we got to school. Upon arrival, the buses lined up in front of the school building, waiting until exactly 8:10 to release their passengers. Those long moments sitting in the parking lot, staring at the red plastic seat in front of me, praying for the bell to ring so I could escape James, were pure torture.

Each morning, Greg and I would flee from the bus. "I can't take this much more," I would rage under my breath. Oh how I longed to tear James to pieces. And although I knew I would never physically attack James, I felt better imagining myself doing so. Greg, though, would never respond to my frustrated exclamations, which only added to my wrath. After all, didn't he hate James too? But more often than not, I was just too furious to care what Greg might have been thinking.

The showdown, I suppose, was inevitable.                                                    9

One morning as we sat in the school parking lot, James took his    10
taunting too far. I don't remember what he said, but I remember what he did. He pulled a long, slender wooden drumstick from his pocket. He started to tap Greg on the top of the head, each hit emphasizing every syllable of his hateful words. My brother stared straight ahead. James laughed. The kids in the back of the bus laughed. The bus driver ignored everything.

My anger boiled over. "Don't you touch him!" I shrieked, strik-   11
ing out and knocking the drumstick from James's hand. At that moment, I didn't care that my parents had advised us to ignore James. I didn't care that everyone turned to gape at me. I didn't care that even the bus driver glanced up from his stony reverie. I only wanted James to leave my brother alone. As the stick clattered to the floor, audible in the sudden silence, I bit my lip, uncertain of what I had done and afraid of what might result.

My mistake, of course, was thinking my screams would end the    12
taunts. The crowd at the back of the bus waited to see James's reaction. With his authority threatened, James turned on me like a viper. "Shut up, bitch!" he hissed. Coming from a home where "shut up" was considered strong language, James's swear word seemed the worst of all evils.

My eyes wide, I shuddered but didn't respond. Words were    13
words, and if I had done nothing else, at least I had caused the bully to revert to words instead of actions. I turned my face to the window, determined to ignore his insults for the few remaining minutes before school. But a movement from Greg caught my eye, and I looked back.

In one swift movement, Greg reached into the front seat,    14
grabbed James by the coat, yanked him out into the aisle, pulled him down, and delivered two quick, fierce jabs to James's face. Then he released him without a word and settled back into his seat. James, for once in his life, was speechless. His cheek flaming red from where the blows had struck, he stared at my brother without moving until the bus driver clicked open the doors a moment later, indicating we could go into school.

My parents heard about the incident, of course, and called the   15
assistant principal about the entire matter. When the vice principal
questioned my brother, Greg's explanation was simple: "He called
Nicole a swear word, and no one calls my sister that." Greg had
never said anything more touching.

I have heard it said that violence never solves anything, and it   16
didn't. The bus driver was advised to keep an eye on James, but no
admonition would have spurred the driver to interfere in anything.
The teasing went on, cruel as ever, until James threatened to slit our
throats with a knife he swore he had hidden in his locker at school.
After that, even though a locker search turned up nothing, my parents drove us to school every morning, and my mother talked to us
about what to do if James ever pulled a knife on us at school.

But for me an imagined weapon paled when compared with the   17
vivid memory of the complete silence on the bus, the blazing red
mark on James's face, the calm little smile that tugged at the edges of
my brother's mouth, and the click of the bus doors as they opened to
free us.

# An Escape Journey
## Abida Wali

*University of California, San Diego*
*La Jolla, California*

Some events are naturally noteworthy, dramatic, or significant. Remembering "walking backward to get one last glimpse" of her home country, Abida Wali does not need to look far—or say much—to locate and communicate the moment's significance. In "An Escape Journey," Wali tells the dramatic story of her family's flight from their native Afghanistan during the Soviet occupation of 1979–1988. The occupation had begun as assistance—military assistance—from the Soviets to the Afghani government, which was at that time Marxist. As opposition to the Marxist government and its reforms grew, however, so did the Soviet presence and authority. Very quickly Soviet troops were in control of the country, actively fighting with rebels and arresting, torturing, imprisoning, or killing dissidents like Abida Wali's uncle, who helped distribute a pamphlet called *Shabnameh*, or *The Night Letter* (a night letter is an unsigned leaflet distributed secretly). While few of us have experienced so frightening—and saddening—an event as escaping a military occupation in our own country, Wali's use of vibrant details, active verbs, and suspense-building quotes allows us to identify readily with her experience. With almost photographic recall, Wali relates what she saw, heard, and felt at each stage of her family's escape: her heart beats faster and faster; she helps her mother pack food, clothing, and the family photo album; she sheds her Western clothing for the disguise of a Chaderi—"a veil through which we could see but not be seen." Even if the most terrifying journey you have ever made was the walk into your first college classroom, read Wali's essay with the knowledge that writing about a frightening event always moves you forward, even as you look back.

---

It was 11:30 p.m. in Kabul. We were all waiting for my uncle to return from a meeting with his collaborators. Every night before the     1

9

curfew, they distributed *Shabnameh (The Night Letter)*, a pamphlet mimeographed or copied by hand and secretly left in public places. Many people had been arrested, tortured, imprisoned, and killed for the possession or distribution of antiregime night letters. Usually, my uncle got home by ten, but now the clock was about to strike twelve midnight. What could have happened? Had he been arrested? If he didn't get home before the midnight curfew went into effect, he could be shot.

Suddenly, a pounding at the door broke the silence. My heart beat faster and faster as I rushed to the door. Who could it be? Could it be my uncle—or soldiers coming to arrest my dad after having arrested my uncle? 2

"Who is it?" I asked. 3

"Open the door," a voice I didn't recognize replied. 4

"Open the door," it repeated. 5

As I turned the knob, the person pushed the door open, throwing me back against the wall. It was my uncle, who rushed into the living room. I slammed the door and ran after him. Trembling and gasping, he looked toward my dad and said, "Abdulla and Ahmed have been arrested...they could have given my name under torture...I'm next." 6

"We have to leave immediately," my dad replied. 7

I helped my mom pack canned foods, clothing, and the first-aid kit. We were told to take only the things that we would need for our journey, but Mom slipped the family photo album between the clothes. After a frantic hour of rushing from room to room, gathering our supplies in bundles, we had to wait until the curfew was lifted. At dawn, we abandoned the house forever, setting out on an uncertain journey. As Mom shut the front door, she looked for the last time at her great-grandmother's teapot. 8

We took a bus from Kabul to Nangarhar. Along the road to Nangarhar were two or three checkpoints where soldiers would search the bus for weapons and illegal documents. At the first checkpoint, a soldier got on the bus. From the hammer and sickle on his cap, I knew he was a Soviet. He wore a big army coat and held a rifle, an AK-47 Kalashnikov, to his chest. As he walked, his boots rattled the windows and the metal floor of the bus. Suddenly, he stopped, pointed his gun at a man, and signaled him to get off the bus. The man ignored him. The soldier stepped forward and tried to pull the man out of his seat, but the man clung to the seat and wouldn't let go. My heart was racing. Drops of sweat were forming on my forehead. Finally, the man 9 let go and was escorted by two other soldiers to a jeep parked beside the bus. The pounding of the boots against the bus floor started again, and this time, the soldier stopped at my dad and me.

"Where are you going?" he asked.                                                    10

"To my uncle's funeral in Nangarhar," Dad answered.               11

"Your ID?"                                                                                        12

Dad gave him his ID. The soldier opened it to see the picture. I   13
felt sweat drop from my forehead. Finally, the soldier handed back the ID. He looked around the bus once more and gave the driver permission to pass.

We made the rest of the journey in fear of getting blown up by   14
antipersonnel mines. I saw six passenger buses that had been destroyed by mines on the road to Nangarhar. Finally, after eight hours of traveling, which should have been four, we reached Nangarhar.

From the bus station we took a taxi to a friend's house and   15
waited there two days for someone to smuggle us across the border. After two days, my dad's friend introduced us to the Smuggler. His six-foot height, bushy beard, upturned moustache, and dark eyebrows made him look scary. He wore baggy trousers and heavy red-leather slippers with upturned toes, and he had a carbine slung over his back. He was a Pathan. The Pathans, an Afghan ethnic group, are warriors who obey neither God nor man. Their law is the law of the rifle and the knife. He told us that he could take only three or four people at a time. My parents decided that I should go with my aunt and uncle.

We had to dress like the Pathan peasants who lived near the bor-  16
der so that our Western clothes did not advertise the fact that we were from the capital and trying to escape. My uncle dressed like the Smuggler. My aunt and I were given very heavy dresses with colorful patterns, sequins, and dangling jewelry. In addition, outside the city, the women were obliged to wear a Chaderi, a veil through which we could see but not be seen. The Chaderi comes in three colors: yellowish brown, gray, and blue. Ours were yellowish brown.

We left the house at dawn and walked a mile or two to reach the  17
main road. The Chaderi twisted and clung to my legs. As I looked down to unwrap it, I stumbled over a rock and fell to the ground, injuring my right knee slightly. It burned, but I managed to catch up with my aunt and uncle and acted like nothing had happened. After a short time, a lorry arrived for us, and we spent the next few hours with sheep and goats, covering our faces with pieces of cloth to keep the smell and the dust out.

The sound of a helicopter approaching got our attention. It was 18 an MI-24, a kind of armored helicopter that the Soviets used to bombard villages, agricultural fields, and mosques. We feared that this time we might be its target, but fortunately it passed us. After a few minutes, we came upon the village that had been bombarded. From a small opening in the side of the lorry, I saw that the air attack had reduced the village to rubble, and those who survived it were running around shouting and screaming. An agricultural field outside the village was burned to ashes, and a pall of smoke and dust drifted over the valley. The images of those people and their ruined village haunted us the rest of our journey.

After a few hours, the lorry stopped, and the driver opened the 19 gate and called, "Last stop." Holding the Chaderi, I jumped to the ground. The desert was covered with the tracks of horses, donkeys, camels, and people. There were many groups of people traveling in caravans: young orphaned boys; a lonely man with a sad expression on his face, all of his possessions packed on top of a camel; and numerous donkeys carrying women while their husbands walked alongside. We were all on our way to Pakistan.

As we waited for our donkeys, my uncle whispered to me, "The 20 Smuggler is a government agent, a militia." My heart skipped a beat. I knew exactly what that meant—he would turn us in. The government recruits tribesmen like the Smuggler for undercover assignments. The Smuggler was talking with some other people, looking at us as he spoke. When he started to walk toward us, I thought my life was over. I wanted to scream and run. He stopped and signaled my uncle to come. As they walked toward a mud hut in the distance, my whole life flashed in front of my eyes. I saw my school, my parents, my execution.

"Did they take him for interrogation?" I asked myself. I could 21 see the hut, and I wondered what was going on inside. When my uncle came out the door, I ran to him. He had been bargaining for the price of the mules. We rented four mules and set out with the caravan.

Riding that mule was an experience that I will never forget. It 22 was hard to stay balanced with the heavy dress and the veil, especially once we began to climb a mountain. The trail was just wide enough for the mule to put down his hooves. As we turned and twisted along the mountainside, I wondered whether I should close my eyes, to try to shut out the danger, or keep them open, to be prepared when we fell down the side of the mountain. But the mule was sure-footed, and I didn't fall. I learned that if I could relax, I would not fall off.

The hot summer sun was right above our heads, and my mouth 23 was completely dry. We could see a village at the bottom of the mountain—four hours away, according to the Smuggler. After a few minutes, however, we got to a small lake. The water was yellow and covered with algae, but the Smuggler drank it and then brought me a cupful. As I looked into the cup, I was reminded of the solution that we prepared in biology class in order to grow bacteria. This lake was the main source of water for the village. God knows what micro-organisms were swimming in it.

"I wouldn't drink it if I were you," my aunt said. 24

But I closed my eyes and drank the whole cup at once. I would 25 worry about the consequences later.

We reached the village just before sunset. After eating dinner and 26 resting for several hours, we started to travel again. The night journey was magnificent. The sky was clear, the moon was full, and millions of stars seemed to be winking at the night travelers. We could hear the bells of another caravan coming from the opposite direction, getting louder and louder as it got close. The ding-a-ling of that caravan added a rhythm to the lonely desert.

Now we were in the territory of the Freedom Fighters. We knew 27 if they recognized the Smuggler, they would execute all of us as communist spies. The Freedom Fighters and the militia are enemies, and the Freedom Fighters did not trust anyone who was traveling with an agent.

At dawn we reached a small teahouse. It consisted of a large, 28 bare room with a dirt floor partially covered by canvas mats. A few small windows, with plastic in place of glass, let in a bit of light. A smoky wood fire in a tin stove served for heating and boiling water for tea. The owner brought us tea and bread, a soothing sight for weary travelers.

We walked on, and soon a signpost got my attention. As I got 29 closer, I was able to read the words: Welcome to Pakistan.

I started to cry, walking backward to get one last glimpse of my 30 beloved country.

# Without a Saddle

Luis A. Jaco

*Metropolitan Community College*
*Omaha, Nebraska*

After reading "Without a Saddle," you will better understand the old saw that "pride goeth before a fall." In this essay about the limits of an eleven-year-old boy's foresight and equestrian skill, Luis A. Jaco remembers his childhood boast that he will never fall off a horse. "I wrote this story one year after I started my first English as a Second Language class, so it was kind of hard," Jaco said. Nevertheless, Jaco's storytelling ability shines forth here. As you read, notice how Jaco builds suspense—from his announcement that he is ready to own a horse, to his excitement when his father agrees, to his wild bareback ride on a barely broken-in young steed.

———————

1   I started riding horses with my father when I was two years old. He used to take me with him everywhere on his horse, so I thought I was an expert at riding. I always said, "I will never fall off a horse."

2   My family owns a ranch outside of Ocotepeque in Honduras. It's a small but very beautiful ranch at the foot of a mountain full of pine trees, which give the air a fresh smell. I have always admired my dad because he is not afraid of anything; he thinks everything is possible. He is not a big man, but he has a big desire for working. I used to go with my dad every morning before school to help him milk the cows. He is the one who taught me everything I needed to know to work on a ranch, like how to take care of the cows and ride horses.

3   When I was about eleven, I was old enough to help my dad with the chores on the ranch, but not quite old enough to have my own horse. One day I told my dad, "I am ready to have my own horse. I know how to take care of it, and I will be responsible."

4   My dad smiled and told me, "If you think you are ready, let me know when you see one that you like and I will see if we can buy it. But you have to be very careful when you make your decision."

When he told me that, I was very happy. It was the best day of my life—I was finally going to have my first horse. I was not going to ask for the first one I looked at. It had to be perfect; I imagined it would be young, with a long tail and a black or red coat.

A few days later, my dad and I were riding two of his horses to a mountain, which was about two hours away from our town, to see some cows that my grandfather owned. Trees, mostly pines, surrounded the narrow path to the mountain. I could see a little stream where some cows were drinking water.

On the way back, we passed through a very small village that had only five houses. And there it was, the best horse I had ever seen, just as I had imagined it. It was a dark red, male horse, very young. It had a long black tail, and it was not too tall because it was still growing. That was the perfect horse; that was the horse I wanted, so I told my dad that I liked that horse and he said, "Well, we'll see."

The horse was eating outside of a small white house, and there was a boy feeding it. My dad went to him and asked him who the owner was. The boy said it was his dad and that he was inside. My dad went inside the house, and I waited outside; I was very nervous. After a while, my dad came out and said, "Let's go, son."

I was very disappointed. Then, to my surprise, my dad said, "We'll come back tomorrow to get the horse."

When we got home, I told everybody that I had a horse and that I was going to get him the next day. I couldn't sleep at all that night. I started thinking about names, and I decided I was going to name him Cometa.

The next day, my dad and I drove my dad's old, blue pickup truck to the village to get the horse. I couldn't believe it; we were going to get my horse, my new friend, the one that was going to take me everywhere I wanted. Once we got there, it took only a few minutes for my dad to close the deal, and then we were ready to go. But there was something wrong, something that neither my dad nor I had thought about. How were we going to get the horse to the ranch?

We didn't have a saddle, and it was too far away from the ranch to walk, but for my dad, nothing is impossible. He told me that I had to ride the horse home without a saddle, just with a lasso that we put around the head and mouth of the horse for me to guide it. I had done this many times before on our ranch, but not for long distances, and the ranch was about an hour away; but I decided to do it. It was going to be my first time riding my horse, Cometa; it was going to be our first adventure.

My dad had to drive home one way, and I had to take a path 13 through the mountains, which was shorter. When I got near the horse to get ready to leave, I felt the soft hair and noticed the fresh smell of the young horse.

When I got on the horse, my dad told me, "Be careful, Son; 14 don't go too fast and hold very tight." Then he asked, "Are you sure you can do this?"

I just laughed and said, "Oh please, Dad; you know I'm an ex- 15 pert at riding horses. I have never fallen off a horse, and I never will."

Then my dad said, "You must never say 'never'; there is always a 16 first time for everything."

"Not for me," I said. 17

My horse and I started on our way to the ranch. The path was 18 very narrow and rocky; it was in really bad condition. Usually when I ride a horse for the first time I am a little afraid, but this time was different. This was my horse. This was Cometa.

I was very glad to be riding my own horse; I felt that there was 19 good communication between us. After twenty minutes of going slow, I decided I wanted to get home sooner to show everybody my horse, and I wanted to know how fast the horse could run. The path was a little better because there weren't as many rocks, so I started going faster and faster. I felt very confident.

Then I saw a little hole, about the size of a small tire, on the 20 path, but I didn't give it much importance. I thought it wasn't going to be a problem for the horse, but it was for me. The horse stepped in the hole and jumped. Since I didn't have a saddle, there wasn't anything to hold on to. The horse threw me forward, and I was ejected into the air; I was flying. The landing was very painful because I landed on the hard ground and some small rocks. There I was, sitting on the grass. I couldn't believe what had happened; I had fallen off a horse—my horse.

At first I thought it was just my imagination or a dream, a night- 21 mare really. Me falling from a horse? That can't be real. But then the pain in my rear made me realize that it was real. It really did happen. I fell off of my horse, and it was entirely my fault. I wasn't careful.

My pride was hurt. I was always talking about how good I was at 22 riding horses, but there I was on the ground. I was very disappointed. In that moment my dad's words came to my mind, "There is always a first time for everything." That made me realize that everything was okay. My first time falling off of a horse had just happened, and it would never happen again. I stood up and looked back at the horse. Nothing had happened to Cometa, thankfully. He was just waiting for me to get on again.

I got back on the horse and continued on my way to the ranch, 23 this time more carefully. After a while, I regained my confidence. It seemed like the horse and I understood each other better.

When we were finally close to the ranch, I saw that my dad was 24 already there with my grandfather. They were outside of the ranch's gate talking and waiting for me. When I saw them at the front entrance of the ranch, I started going fast because I wanted to show them how good the horse was, and I also wanted to forget about what had happened before—my fall. Just as I reached the entrance, the wind blew up a black plastic bag and scared the horse. He jumped and, without the saddle, I couldn't do anything but close my eyes, fly through the air, and fall. When I opened my eyes, my dad was already standing by my side.

He helped me up, and he told me, "You must never say 'never.'" 25

# The Accident: A Grand Day Turned Tragic

Aaron Forshier

*Des Moines Area Community College*
*Ankeny, Iowa*

"I chose the subject that I did because it shows how a tragic event that lasts only a few seconds can have a profound, lasting impact on the lives and futures of the people involved," notes Aaron Forshier. Remembered-event essays often present people, and Aaron Forshier's paper about a tragic automobile accident introduces us to a very real, very complex character—Forshier's grandfather, who was profoundly affected by the crash. Forshier writes about his grandfather with the same tenderness that seems to have characterized their relationship. He refers to him not as "my grandfather" or even "my grandpa" but simply and affectionately as "Grandpa," and sketches the contours of their mutually gratifying relationship with both general examples (a list of their favorite activities) and specific ones (the events of the morning of the accident). Forshier's attitude toward his grandfather is not only tender but also non-judgmental, especially in the aftermath of the accident. When he shows, rather than tells, what his grandfather must be feeling, Forshier accomplishes a difficult feat for the autobiographer: he steps outside the personal experience of the event and examines it from a perspective unaffected by his own sorrow.

---

I began spending summers with my grandparents on their farm when  1
I was three years old. What began as three- or four-day visits gradually turned into most of the summer by the time I was seven years old. Time spent with Grandpa was always fun and exciting. Riding side-by-side in the tractor cab as Grandpa cultivated fields of beans and corn, harvested oats, or put up hay; hauling water and ground corn to the cattle in a distant pasture; repairing fences and farm equipment; helping in the garden; constructing and running his model train; fishing in the neighbor's pond; and relaxing on the

porch swing at the end of the day, laughing over the stories he told about my mom when she was growing up: these were just a few of the wonderful things that Grandpa and I did together. This all changed in the months and years following the accident; the time that I spent at the farm wasn't the same—Grandpa wasn't the same. As a result, visits to my favorite childhood place became fewer and fewer as the years passed.

I was eleven years old on that hot July day in 1999. It began as    2
many days did on the farm, with Grandpa sticking his head into my bedroom and calling, "What? There's work to be done and my best farmhand is still in bed? Rise and shine, sleepyhead." I jumped out of bed, excited for the day to begin. It was the first summer that Grandpa had let me drive a tractor by myself, and we had started putting up hay the day before. I had spent most of the afternoon proudly hauling loads of hay from the field to the farmyard and unloading them onto two growing haystacks, and I was eager to get back on the tractor and continue my first grown-up job on the farm.

Grandpa and I finished the hay by lunchtime. After devouring    3
my favorite lunch—Grandma's crispy fried chicken; creamy mashed potatoes covered with thick, savory gravy; and a big slice of juicy, sweet watermelon—Grandpa and I headed to town to deliver eight loads of bulk feed to the local Kent Feed and Supply business. Since he owned a big grain truck, Grandpa earned extra income by delivering feed to area farmers once or twice a month. We had made seven deliveries and were going back to town for the final load when Grandpa said, "It sure is hot—must be ninety-eight degrees in the shade. What do you say to stopping at the Dairy Den for an ice cream cone before making our last delivery?"

"Great idea! You always know what I'm thinking," I eagerly    4
replied. "There's nothing I'd like more right now than an ice cream cone." But I never got an ice cream cone that afternoon.

With visions of the cool, delicious treat filling my head, I was al-    5
most unaware of the passing countryside until Grandpa began slowing down. I then noticed the four hayracks parked in a single row on the right shoulder of the highway a few hundred feet in front of us. A farmhouse and outbuildings flanked the right side of the highway, and three farmers were baling hay in a field on the left side. When our truck was almost even with the first hayrack, a little girl suddenly darted onto the highway from between the third and fourth hayracks. Grandpa screamed, "Oh, God, no! Hang on, Aaron." I remember

screaming, and then everything happened so fast. Slamming on the brakes and turning sharply to the left, Grandpa tried desperately to avoid hitting the child. Sounds of squealing brakes and screeching tires filled my ears as Grandpa managed to whip his powerful stallion to the left side of the highway, but not quickly enough; the right rear wheel hit something with a heart-stopping thud that sent a chill through my body on one of the hottest days of the year. Barely missing a car approaching from the opposite direction, Grandpa continued to rein in his steed, which left the highway, stumbled across a shallow ditch, tore through the wire fence surrounding the hayfield, and was finally stopped by a huge, round hay bale.

Stunned, Grandpa and I both sat as though we were momentarily paralyzed. After a few seconds, Grandpa asked in a shaky voice, "Are you hurt?" 6

Still trying to catch my breath and waiting for my heart to stop pounding, I replied, "No, I think I'm okay, but I'm really scared. Did the truck hit that little girl?" 7

Grandpa didn't answer my question; once he knew that I wasn't hurt, he became silent and stared straight ahead, as though he were dreading what he had to face next. Without saying a word, Grandpa slowly opened the driver's door and stepped out of the truck, and I did the same. I watched Grandpa walk to the highway on trembling, jellylike legs. He collapsed beside the girl; picked her small, limp body up in his arms; and held her close. As I came a little closer, I saw tears streaming down Grandpa's face. He was sobbing softly and moaning, "No, dear God, no! What have I done?" 8

I stood frozen in my tracks, suddenly unable to move closer. This was a side of Grandpa that I was seeing for the first time; I'd never seen him cry before. Grandpa had always been so strong—an unsinkable ship. I didn't see him cry at Great Grandpa's funeral, when Grandma was very sick and in the hospital for weeks, or when he heard the news that his neighbor's son had died in a hunting accident. Seeing Grandpa break down surprised and upset me. I didn't know what to do. 9

As I continued to stand there, immobilized by what I was witnessing, the girl's mother ran onto the highway crying, "My baby, I want my baby! Please, dear God, help my baby!" 10

As the mother grabbed her daughter from his arms, Grandpa somehow choked out the faint words, "I . . . I . . . am . . . so . . . so . . . sorry." 11

Suddenly, there seemed to be people everywhere. The farmers who had been baling hay, including the girl's father, rushed to the 12 scene. Witnesses to the accident were trying to help in any way they could. A highway patrol car had just pulled up and another was close behind. Traffic was at a standstill, but police officers from town had arrived and were starting to detour vehicles onto nearby gravel roads. When I began walking toward Grandpa, a man took me by the arm and led me to his car, even though I kept telling him, "I want to be with my grandpa. Let me go."

The stranger was very persistent and insisted that I wait in his 13 car. He kindly explained, "You can help your grandpa the most right now by staying here. The highway patrol officers are here, and they need time to talk to your grandpa and everyone who witnessed the accident. The ambulance will be arriving soon. The medics need to work quickly, and they can't do that if lots of people get in their way. I promise that I will come and get you as soon as you can be with your grandpa." Finally convinced that he was probably right, I agreed to wait in the car.

As I sat and waited, I noticed that my shirt was wet; I had been 14 crying along with Grandpa and hadn't even realized it. Tired and concerned about Grandpa, I closed my eyes and tried to push both the picture of him crying and the accident out of my mind. I heard people talking and crying, the muffled voices of officers questioning witnesses, a siren blaring to announce the arrival of the ambulance, tractors idling impatiently in the hayfield, and the distant, lonely howl of a dog. Mixed with these sounds were the pungent aroma of freshly cut hay, the overpowering odor of a nearby hog farm in ninety-degree temperatures, and the smell of hot rubber from smoldering tires that had left their outer layer of skin on the highway in a desperate attempt to stop the truck in time. The combination of the sounds and smells, along with the intense heat, had almost lulled me to sleep when a loud wail of despair suddenly brought me back to reality.

When the stranger finally came back to his car, he said, "The am- 15 bulance is almost ready to leave, and the police officers are finished with their reports, so you can go to your grandpa now."

I immediately ran over to Grandpa, who was still sitting beside 16 the highway, and gave him a big hug. At the same time, I asked, "Grandpa, are you all right? Can we go home now?" When he didn't answer, I looked at him more closely and saw that he seemed to be in some sort of trance. I sat down beside him and held his hand, waiting for him to return to me from wherever he had gone. Watching the ambulance slowly leave, I remember wondering why it wasn't speeding away from the scene with its siren blaring or its lights flashing.

Even though I knew in my heart that the girl probably would not survive, I wondered why the medics weren't rushing her to the hospital. Wasn't that their job? I learned later that the girl had died in her mother's arms shortly before the ambulance arrived. It had been the mother's wail of despair that I heard while sitting in the stranger's car.

Grandpa and I walked to his truck and sat beside it, but he still 17 didn't give me any indication that he knew I was there. I said, "Grandpa, I'm here. Can you hear me?" Although he didn't answer me, he did squeeze my hand to let me know that he heard me and knew that I was there. I was worried about Grandpa. Even with a summer tan, he seemed too pale, as though the life had been drained out of him. His eyes looked hollow and distant, giving me the eerie feeling that he was in a place shut off from the rest of the world—a place where I could not be with him. Pain and guilt glazed his eyes, from which tears continued to ooze and trickle down his cheeks, etching mournful trails through layers of dust and sweat. Not knowing what else to do to help Grandpa, I sat silently beside him, holding his hand and resting my head against his arm while he dealt with the pain in his own silent way. I had my own pain to deal with— what had happened to the Grandpa I'd always known? Why wasn't he talking to me?

After we had been sitting beside the truck for a while, my mom, 18 grandma, and uncle arrived. Grandpa rode home with Grandma, and my uncle drove the truck home. Before leaving, Grandma took me aside and said, "I'm sorry that you were with Grandpa this afternoon. Are you okay?"

With trembling lips, I replied, "I guess I'm okay, but Grandpa 19 won't talk to me. Did I do something wrong?"

Grandma returned my question with a hug and said, "Why 20 would you think that? You did nothing wrong. Grandpa is hurting very deeply right now, but he still loves you very much. Go home with your mom, and I'll call you in a few days and let you know how Grandpa is doing. Don't worry; he'll be okay."

I gave Grandpa a good-bye hug and said, "I love you, Grandpa." 21 He managed to give me a weak hug but still didn't say a word. He seemed to be drained of every ounce of strength he had. It had been a long, horrible afternoon for both of us.

I cried myself to sleep that night, not only for the little girl and her 22 family, but also for Grandpa and me. Grandpa had always been so strong and full of life, but today he reminded me of a deflated balloon.

Even so, I truly believed that everything would be better in a few weeks—but it wasn't. The grandpa that I'd bonded so closely with for more than eight years never really came back to me; a special part of who he'd always been died with that little girl. He lost interest in most of the activities that we had always loved doing together, such as fishing, farming, and model railroading. His truck collected dust in the machine shed for two years before he finally sold it. He changed from a man who had enjoyed every moment of life to a man unjustly imprisoned by guilt.

Nearly six years have passed since the accident occurred, and I've come to realize that Grandpa will probably never be able to forgive himself for what happened that day. Unable to forgive himself, he has become unable to reach out to others like he once did. I still have a grandpa, and I know that he still loves me; that will never change. But a part of him is missing—the part that made the two of us such a special team. I continue to spend time with Grandpa now and then, but we never recaptured the close bond that we once shared. Today, I cherish many unforgettable memories of the summers I spent with Grandpa, and I am grateful for the powerful bond we shared. Yet at the same time I feel cheated out of what could have been. Fate—that invisible something that brought Grandpa's truck and a little girl to the same place at the same moment in time—cheated me out of many more special years with Grandpa and cut short a wonderful chapter in my life.

# A Lesson Learned

Cheryl Sole

*Niagara County Community College*
*Sanborn, New York*

In the first sentence of this remembered-events essay, Cheryl Sole invites readers to enter the "hot sunny summer morning" of her childhood. In the first paragraph, she captures that mix of freedom and boredom that children, out of school and out of chores, so often enjoy—or suffer. We feel transported; we are drawn into the scene and the story. How does Cheryl do it? In part, it is the clear-eyed simplicity of her writing: she seems to have put on the observant, unjudgmental eyes of a child. What's more, she isn't just playing with her readers. No, she has a reason for transporting us. Cheryl, who composed this first assignment of her college career upon returning to school after raising a family, writes, "My intended audience was my classmates, who are all much younger than I, and while I wanted to entertain while recalling this event, I also wanted to show them how important it is to forgive a child who does something as wrong as I did." As you read, notice how—and where—Sole communicates this insight.

——————

It was a hot sunny summer morning. I loved just lying around under our big old maple tree. My best friend was away on vacation, and I couldn't decide what I wanted to do. My mom was inside trying to get my baby brother to sleep, so I had to be quiet. The birds were chirping, and I could see a nest high up in the tree. I missed watching the mother bird feed her new babies worms. My mom said the babies had all left because they were old enough to fly off on their own. How I wished I was older. Then I could go to day camp with my older sisters and brother. It just wasn't fair. I was stuck home while they were off making molds. Next summer, I'd be old enough to go. But that seemed so far away.

My mom had just bought me some new play dishes and told me that if I was good, she would make me a picnic lunch and let me eat

24

outside. I wanted to invite my friend Nancy Blake over to eat with me, and my mom said maybe. I knew "maybe" usually meant "no," but I was still hoping she'd say yes. I didn't think my mom liked Nancy because I had heard my parents talking one night when I was in bed. I heard my dad say that some people weren't meant to have kids and that the Blakes' house looked like a junkyard. The Blakes lived next door, and I loved going over there. They had nine kids, and there were always bikes and toys scattered all over their driveway and yard. It wasn't like my house, where we had to put our toys away. And her mom didn't care if they ate ice cream right before lunch. Nancy's little sister Cindy was always running outside in her underwear, and her mom would scream out the door at her to get in and put some clothes on. My dad said Nancy was a bad influence because whenever I was with her, we'd get into trouble. She was a whole grade ahead of me and sometimes mean. All the kids in school were afraid of her. One time she put a thumbtack on her teacher's chair and had detention for a week. She was always doing cool stuff like that.

I saw her outside and called her over. I told her about lunch, and   3
she wanted to see my dishes. I snuck in and got them and brought them outside. She said, "Let's make our own play lunch." We started picking grass to fill the bowls and poured water in the teapot. There were some big fat mushrooms growing on our lawn, so we picked some of them. We cut them up with the play silverware and added them to the bowls. Nancy's bratty sister Cindy saw us and came over. We told her to go home, but she begged us to let her play too.

Nancy whispered in my ear, "I know how to get rid of her. Tell   4
her the mushrooms are candy. After she eats them, she'll get sick and go home."

"No," I whispered back. My parents had told me never to   5
eat anything I picked unless I showed it to them first. We had berries growing on a bush in our yard, and my dad said they were poisonous.

"Chicken. You're as big of a baby as she is."   6

"Okay, but if she gets sick, I'm not taking the blame."   7

I pretended I was eating them.   8

"Mmmmm, these are soooo good."   9

We got Cindy to eat the whole bowl.   10

A few minutes later, my mom called me into the house, so   11
Nancy and Cindy went home. My mom said I had been good so I could have my picnic. As she started to make my lunch, the phone

rang. It was Mrs. Blake. Cindy was sick, and Nancy had told her I had forced Cindy to eat the mushrooms. She was really upset because they might be poisonous and now she had to bring Cindy to the hospital. My mom was really mad and told me to go to my room and stay there until my dad got home. I tried to tell her what had happened, but she wouldn't listen. She said this was very serious, and we could have killed Cindy. I had never seen her so mad at me.

I stormed upstairs, not knowing if I was madder at Nancy or my mom for not listening to me. Oh, I wished Nancy had eaten them instead! She deserved to be the one with poison in her stomach. As I sat there pouting on my bed, my brother came home for lunch, and I could hear him outside talking with Kenny, Nancy's brother. I looked out my window and saw him riding his bike up the driveway. 12

He looked up and saw me and yelled, "Oooooh, you're gonna get it. Wait till dad gets home. He's gonna get out his big thick belt." 13

"Shut up," I said. "I hope you fall off your bike and break your leg." 14

Now I was getting scared. My dad always told us he had a big thick belt, and if we didn't behave, he'd bring it out. We had never actually seen the belt, but why would he lie? 15

The day dragged on, and I was getting really nervous. What if Cindy died and I was sent to jail? Would I be fed only bread and water? By now I was crying so hard I had the hiccups. I heard the phone ring and heard my mom talking. She called me downstairs and told me to stop crying. Cindy was okay; they had pumped her stomach and were bringing her home. She told me I had to go over and apologize when they got back. I begged her not to make me, so she said she'd go with me. When they got home, my mom took my hand and practically dragged me over there. I knocked on the door and Mrs. Blake answered. She looked really mad as I told her I was really sorry about Cindy. Mrs. Blake told my mom I should be spanked so hard that I wouldn't be able to sit for a week. To my surprise, my mom stuck up for me and told her that her daughter was just as much to blame. Mrs. Blake shook her head and slammed the door. My mom was really mad, and as we walked home, she told me I couldn't play with Nancy anymore. I didn't care. I was sick of getting into trouble. 16

When we got home, she told me to go back to my room and wait for my dad to get home. The day dragged on forever as I stared out my window and waited. When I saw my dad's car pull up, my heart started racing. Would he get out the belt and spank me like 17

Mrs. Blake said? I could hear him and my mom talking as they went into their room while he changed his clothes. I wished they'd hurry up so he could get the spanking over with. I knew it was time for their cocktail. Every night he would sit in his chair and watch my mom as she cooked dinner. My sisters and brother and I would beg him for the cherry in his drink and whoever was really good that day would be the lucky one and get it. I knew it wouldn't be me that night. I could hear the spoon clinking in the glass as my mom stirred their drinks.

"Cheryl, would you come down here, please?" he said. 18

"OK, Daddy." I knew he was mad because he never called me 19 Cheryl unless he was really mad. He always called me his little peanut pusher. As I walked down the stairs, my legs shook. My brother was in the living room and was pretending he had a belt and laughing. Now I was really afraid. I walked into the kitchen with my head hung down and stood by the wall.

"Your mother tells me you had quite a day today." 20

I nodded my head because I knew if I talked I would start cry- 21 ing. My lip was trembling hard as I stood there trying not to cry.

"Come over here." 22

I stood in front of him, looking at the floor. The next thing I 23 knew I was on his lap.

"Look at me. Did you learn anything today?" 24

"Yes, Daddy. Never play with Nancy again; she gets me in too 25 much trouble."

"Did you learn anything else?" 26

"Uh-huh. Never ever make anyone eat stuff that will hurt them, 27 and I'm really sorry for what I did."

By now the tears were falling down my face, and to my amaze- 28 ment, my dad wiped my tears.

"Listen, my little peanut pusher. What you did today took a lot 29 of courage, going over there and saying you were sorry. And I know you learned your lesson. Now give me a hug and stop crying, and go out and play until dinner is ready."

I gave him the biggest hug and kiss, and as I was climbing off his 30 lap, he gave me his cherry! "He isn't mad at me," I thought! As I went to my room to get my sneakers, I saw my brother. I stuck my tongue out at him as I ran by, making sure he saw the cherry in my mouth.

# *Writing Profiles* 3

The essay you write for this chapter will almost certainly be the one you least expected to write in this class. It will not draw you back into memory, as the remembered-event essay did (chapter 2), nor will it lead you to the library, as the other kinds of essays in this book will likely do. Instead, it will take you off-campus to see someone else's place of work or play and—stranger still—require you to ask that person about it and capture what he or she says as a primary source for your essay.

It may seem daring or even reckless to walk into some unfamiliar place and ask strangers about their activities. Countless students given this assignment have done so nevertheless, gaining self-confidence and satisfying their curiosity about some unfamiliar corner of the everyday world—such as the soup kitchen, supermarket, glass studio, disc golf course, and dragon boat festival visited by the student essayists in this chapter. The biggest surprise for many profilers is how willing strangers are to talk about their work and other interests.

You may find your expectations about the people and place confirmed, but more likely you will be surprised or even astounded by what you learn—so surprised you may need to make a second visit to gather more information and to figure out how it all fits together. What you need in this special situation of observing and writing is an open mind—or better, a curious mind. Cultivating and stocking a curious mind should be a major goal during your college years, for curiosity is a defining characteristic of a civic-minded citizen in a democracy and a requirement for thinking productively in any writing situation you encounter in college and later in your career. Anticipate that you will be surprised at what you see and hear in your visit and interviews. Embrace that surprise, use it in your essay, and continue to cultivate the curiosity that inspired it.

# Our Daily Bread

## Linda Kampel

*Pennsylvania State University, York*
*York, Pennsylvania*

A two-room cinder-block building in York, Pennsylvania: It's the center of the world for the nearly three hundred people who depend on Our Daily Bread soup kitchen—people like tall, heavyset Andy in his dark cap, who yells at an unseen companion while waiting for lunch in the food line; and Carol, who thinks of Our Daily Bread as more of a social club than a breadline, though that perspective seems optimistic if not distorted when contrasted with her "worn-out clothes" and her admission that she has frequented the soup kitchen for about two years. Colorful characters like Andy and Carol surprise us and engage our attention, but they are not the focus of Kampel's essay. Instead, Kampel's spotlight is reserved for Joe and Marie, the self-described "business manager" and "inventory-control specialist" of Our Daily Bread—in short, the operation's human backbone. To diners "so lost that they can't find themselves anymore or have accepted this daily routine as the reality of a bad hand they've been dealt in life," Joe and Marie provide not only hot food but also a daily portion of hope.

———

1    To anyone who has the luxury of regular meals and a safe place to call home, walking through the entrance of Our Daily Bread soup kitchen is like stepping into a different world. Our Daily Bread operates out of a two-room cinder-block building in York, Pennsylvania, that has been transformed into a kitchen and dining area, where nearly three hundred poverty-stricken people come every day to eat. The front doors open at 10 a.m. on a large room with rows of six-foot metal tables, dim lights that cast gray shadows, and walls that are painted in 1970s "harvest gold," which has dulled with time.

2    In the back of the room there is a stainless-steel, cafeteria-style serving counter, where people line up to be served hot coffee and

29

donuts. As gloomy as the surroundings may sound, the majority of the people in the place seem to be comfortably familiar with the daily routine of standing in line, waiting for a meal. Occasionally, someone tells a joke or a funny story and one or more people laugh, making the atmosphere seem almost cheery.

A tall, heavyset black man wearing a dark cap suddenly starts yelling at an invisible companion who has obviously upset him. "F— you! I'll do what I want!" he yells. Everyone else in the room goes on with their business. "I said I'm going to do what I want. Just leave me alone!" 3

At first, it seems like this man could be a real threat, but when I ask him what his name is, he very calmly says, "My name's Andy." 4

There is something sad about the look in Andy's eyes, and within a few minutes, he's arguing again with whomever it is that has made him so unhappy. 5

At 11 a.m., the crowd grows to about 80 people, and volunteers are preparing to serve lunch. By 11:30, the number increases to 120, and by 12:15, there are close to 250 men and women, and a handful of children, making their way into the line that moves like a well-rehearsed act in a play. Today's meal consists of vegetable soup, broccoli, bread, and tuna-noodle casserole, with a choice of either lemonade or coffee to drink. People of every age, gender, and race move through the line. No one is turned away. 6

Carol, a thirty-five-year-old black woman dressed in clean but worn-out clothes, says that she has been coming here for about two years. "Most people who come here aren't homeless," she says. "We all have a place to live and all. It's just that sometimes meals are a problem. Some people come here because it's a social thing, you know. You take a break from whatever you're doing. You come in here and have some food and talk to people you know." 7

A tall white man, about sixty-five years of age and dressed in dirty, old clothes, walks past us. He has donut powder all over his mouth and chin. "That's so sad," Carol says. "He doesn't even know it's there. That poor man. Now *he* needs help. At least he's here in a place where he'll be taken care of." 8

At first it's easy to think that Carol's problems aren't all that bad, perhaps because she has become so good at convincing herself that this way of life is normal. I fall right into her train of thought. But later, thinking back, I can't help realizing that the majority of the people who come to Our Daily Bread do need help of some kind or they wouldn't be there. They're either so lost that they can't find 9

themselves anymore or have accepted this daily routine as the reality
of a bad hand they've been dealt in life.

Around 12:30 p.m., a volunteer worker walks over to a micro-
phone at the end of the serving counter and asks, "Has everyone gotten the food they need to eat?" No one says a word. "If anyone
needs more to eat, please come up and get as much as you want." ⟨10⟩

A few people return to the counter for second helpings, but
most people are beginning to leave. They've been well fed and
maybe somehow given the boost they need to make it through
the day. ⟨11⟩

At the helm of this well-run operation are two people, Joe
McCormick and Marie Rohleder, both of whom seem to have a genuine and unconditional interest in making sure that for at least two
and a half hours a day anyone who needs a hot meal or emotional
support in a warm, dry place can find it within these walls. ⟨12⟩

Joe McCormick, the business manager, is a tall, white-haired,
sixty-year-old man whose smile lets you know right away that he is a
very special human being, the "real thing." Joe cares about every
inch of this place and about the people who come here for help. Joe
is semi-retired now, but he still takes care of all the expenses of Our
Daily Bread, keeps track of the donations, and sends out thank-you
notes to all those who contribute food or services. Every Monday,
Joe is in charge of food preparation and serving. ⟨13⟩

"We've been here for seven years now," he says. "We're open
Monday through Friday from 10 a.m. to 12:30 p.m. You should
have seen the place we were in before we moved here. It was hell on
earth, in the basement of Cristo Salvador, a local Spanish church.
The kitchen was about a third of the size of this one here. There was
barely enough room for a dishwasher and a stove. That place used to
get about 150 degrees in the summertime when we were making
food, and there were times when the water on the floor from rain-
storms was six inches deep. We were afraid to use anything electric."
Joe lights a cigarette. "Back then we were serving about 107 people
a day. Now we're serving around 300. It used to be 400 before
September House started its senior citizen outreach program, but I'll
let Marie tell you about that later." ⟨14⟩

Cartons of pastries arrive through the back door, so Joe goes
over to help bring them in. When he returns, he leans against a stack
of crates. ⟨15⟩

"Last Thanksgiving we were really sweating it out because we
supply Helping Hands with their turkeys, and we hardly had any ⟨16⟩

turkeys at all. Then right after the holidays, we got a call to come and pick up fifty of them. It's feast or famine around here. When Chuck E. Cheese closed down last year, I got two truckloads of pizzas and birthday cakes. Boy, were they good. People still come in here and ask, 'Do you have any more of those birthday cakes?' We're never at a loss for resources for food, it seems. It's not always the greatest, but it's out there. York County is a very giving place."

Joe tells me, "Just a second," and when he returns, he is with a dark-haired woman about thirty-five years of age, wearing a blue nylon jacket. She has the same welcoming smile that Joe has, and I can't help thinking how lucky everyone here is to have these two people on their side. Joe introduces the woman as Marie, who is, by her own definition, the inventory-control specialist. 17

"In other words, I make sure that all the food gets put in the freezer, which explains the jacket. I also rotate the food on the shelves so that nothing stays around too long." 18

Marie also takes on the responsibilities of food preparation and serving on Thursdays and Fridays. 19

"There's a guy named Charlie who takes care of Tuesdays and Wednesdays, but he's not here right now. Anyway, an organization called September House started an outreach program a couple of years ago. They go and pick up our senior citizens and take them for meals at their senior citizen center. They're much better off over there because they get the attention they really need. That's why the number of people we serve here has dropped off slightly. It's a wonderful organization. It's hard not to get involved sometimes. There are some people you can't help but get involved with. They need that. And there are some people who come and go. We just found out today that one fellow we get involved with *a lot* just got sent to jail last night. Busted for drugs. It's heartbreaking sometimes because you know how hard they've been trying. There was one guy who used to do dishes for us. Lester. He tried *so* hard to stay sober, and he just couldn't do it. Eventually he died from alcohol poisoning." 20

"That's the hardest kind," Joe says. "You see these people and you know that no matter what the hell they do, they're in a hole. And they're never gonna get out." 21

One of the volunteers comes over and asks where to put a tray filled with pumpkin bread. 22

"That's Pat," Marie says after she points her toward a storage shelf. "She's one of our regular volunteers. She comes in almost every day, along with the volunteers from at least one church group. 23

We get about fifty volunteers a week. The only problem is that no one wants to clean up—everyone wants to serve or cook, but as soon as 12:30 hits, *boom,* they're out the door. York College is sending over a group of students this Saturday to paint these walls. And the group Up with People is coming in tomorrow, I think, to help out. I'm glad they're coming because Fridays are the worst. For some reason, that's the day when the people who really are in desperate need come in, so that they can load up for the weekend. We always have extra bread, so we can give out a couple of loaves to everyone."

When 12:45 arrives, the volunteers are finished serving lunch. 24
There is clean-up work to be done, and Joe and Marie take their place among the volunteers so that they will soon be able to call it a day.

# *True Worker*

## Erik Epple

*Bowling Green State University*
*Bowling Green, Ohio*

Many grocery store department managers would probably avoid the graveyard shift, but Larry Harshman prefers it. Harshman, the subject of Erik Epple's profile essay, takes great pride in his efficiency and energy, which allow him to fill pallets with groceries faster than the stockers can unload them—and then step in to help the stockers when they fall behind. Following Harshman through one of his all-night shifts, Epple witnesses both the man's mythic on-the-job performance and his more vulnerable human side—his loneliness and regret at the end of his twenty-five-year marriage, and his fierce pride in his old-fashioned work ethic, which is in danger of crumbling beneath fatigue (after all, Harshman has spent a quarter century moving up the Kroger employee ranks in physically demanding positions). As you read, notice the range of writing strategies that Epple uses to illustrate his perspective that "Larry Harshman is a far more complicated person than my coworkers would have me believe." For example, he *contrasts* Larry Harshman with his coworkers. He *narrates* a sequence of tasks that Larry performs: first unloading a delivery truck with a pallet jack, then slitting box tops. He explains the *causes* of Larry's preference for the night shift, and reveals the *effects* of his years of hard work—his failed marriage, his bad back. These strategies help Epple give readers a complete and nuanced picture of Larry Harshman, and a very unusual behind-the-scenes look at a very usual place.

---

I've been working at Kroger supermarket in Springville, Ohio, for  1
two weeks now, and my coworkers keep mentioning Larry Harshman, head of the store's grocery department. Depending on whom I talk to, Larry is either the most solitary, antisocial person on staff, or some kind of mythic hero, like Paul Bunyan or Pecos Bill.

34

I decide I want to meet Larry for myself. The mystique around    2
him only grows when I learn he works the graveyard shift. I head back
to the supermarket at 11:00 one Thursday night and introduce myself
to Larry. As we talk, I begin to realize that Larry Harshman is a far
more complicated person than my coworkers would have me believe.

The chattering of mechanical devices, the smashing of falling    3
crates, and the ripping of cardboard would cause most people to
cover their ears. Larry welcomes the noises, though. They prove to
him that he is working hard and also ease his loneliness.

Sitting across from Larry in the dimly lit break room, I am inspired    4
by his work ethic. Over twenty-seven years, Larry has worked his way
up from a bagger to head of the grocery department. Clark Carr, the
store manager, has nothing but praise for Larry: "He is a very reliable
worker, one that I go to every time I need something done."

Larry, however, is beginning to feel his age: "It's my back; I just    5
can't move as quick anymore."

Other Kroger employees, however, believe that no one there can    6
outwork Larry, even with his disadvantage of a fifty-year-old body.
Whether he is cutting open boxes or unloading a truck, he seems to
defy his limitations and works in a flurry of activity, in an environment of ordered chaos. *Efficient, practiced,* and *precise* are words that
best describe Larry.

Larry's days are exact: arise, go to work, return home, sleep. The    7
routine is periodically interrupted when he goes out to eat with a
friend, but such interruptions are rare. And while Larry works nine to
five, he does not go to work in the morning, like most other Americans, because his workday begins at 9 p.m.

"I've never been much of a social person," Larry states with    8
downcast eyes. "That's why I work third shift." Larry prefers to work
alone and would rather have just one good friend than many. He
likes those nights when only he and Carol—a night cashier and close
friend of his—work the shelves. His obsession with work and desire
for solitude have destroyed his home life. His wife of twenty-five
years filed for divorce, leaving Larry totally dispirited.

"I like being alone," he comments, "but alone doesn't mean    9
without anyone to care about you. She was always that one special
person in my life and was always there when I needed someone to listen to me. Now she is gone, and all that I have left are my friends at
Kroger."

After a moment's quiet, I ask Larry to explain his job. He sips his    10
Pepsi and responds: "After my break, I'll show you."

Fifteen minutes later, he hauls himself out of the metal chair and   11
nods toward the door. Following him into the backroom, I am surprised by his change of mood. His eyes narrow, and cursing under
his breath, he falls into step with another employee as they survey the
work left undone by the day crew.

"Looks like another long night for us, Oscar," Larry proclaims   12
to his companion, cursing again.

"Just once," Oscar growls, "I'd like to see those lazy bastards   13
work a night shift."

Grabbing the handle of a pallet jack—a large machine that re-   14
sembles a miniature forklift—and rolling the jack toward him, Larry
begins speaking to me over his shoulder.

"First, we unload the truck, which usually isn't too bad but can   15
be a pain in the ass at times," he declares, as the twin prongs on the
jack slide under the first pallet of groceries.

I watch Larry repeatedly maneuver the forklift in and out of the   16
semi's trailer, each time appearing with another pallet stacked with
boxes; within a half hour the sixty-foot trailer is empty. When all of
the pallets are lined along the back wall, Larry pulls a box cutter out
of his rear pocket.

I watch as Larry mechanically slits the tops, one by one, off of   17
each box. Although working at a frenetic pace, he never cuts into the
groceries inside. After removing each top, he places the open boxes
on cartlike devices called wheelers. Four workers appear from the
front of the store to take the now-filled wheelers inside. As the night
continues, I discover Larry always has a wheeler filled before someone comes back for a new one.

Everyone agrees Larry is the key to a successful night.   18

"It worries me sometimes, watching him gimp around the break   19
room, but his age never shows through his work," comments Rita,
an employee who works the wheelers.

"He gets six weeks out of every year for vacation. During those   20
weeks, Oscar loads up the wheelers and Spencer unloads the truck,
and everything just goes to hell," complains Mark, another worker.

Returning the box cutter to his pocket, Larry calls break over the   21
loudspeaker. As everyone else begins shuffling toward the break room
for a few smokes or a snack, Larry heads for the front of the store,
buys himself a can of soda, then sits down on one of the register belts.

"It's just not like it used to be around here," Larry mumbles.   22
"Clark takes away all of our help, and the ones who *are* working
don't take it seriously. It's all a big joke these days. Some of the

workers spend most of their time on the clock talking on the telephone to God only knows who. Others just joke around and never go beyond what is expected of them. The spirit of working and earning your pay is gone. That gets to me sometimes."

Glancing around me, I see exactly what Larry means. Empty 23 boxes are scattered up and down the aisles, left on the floor for the morning crew to pick up. The six workers unloading the wheelers inside the store cannot keep up with Larry, the only person working in the back on the dock. Not only are wheelers spread around the store, still loaded, but many more are choking the back; I weave my way through a narrow canyon of wheelers to reach the break room.

"He just takes his job too seriously. He needs to lighten up, 24 enjoy himself," remarks a cocky, tall worker, whom I later find out is Greg. "If you want my opinion," he continues, "he needs a woman."

As if to add gloom to the picture of Larry's personal life, Rita 25 chimes in: "Oh, you know old Larry will never get himself another woman; he doesn't even know how to act around one anymore."

The crew falls into its own private thoughts. Through the 26 canyon of wheelers, I can see Larry still sitting by himself in the front. Half an hour later, everyone is back at work.

"No reason to keep stacking up the wheelers," Larry growls, as 27 he stares at the many wheelers waiting to be taken into the store and unloaded. "They'll just get so backed up that no one can get into the back."

Larry turns and begins stacking the now empty pallets and cleaning 28 up the docking area. When he is satisfied that everything is in order, he takes the remaining wheelers out to the front. Instead of leaving the work to the other employees, Larry begins to help them stock the shelves. With Larry helping, the others finish in less than an hour.

"Now is when I slack because all the work is done," Larry states. 29 "There is nothing left to do, even if anyone wanted to. It makes no sense to slack before the work is over."

Driving away that night, I realize that Larry Harshman is neither 30 mythic hero nor recluse but someone who represents a time when how well a person performed his job was a measure of that person's worth. It is an attitude that his coworkers, both those who see him as Superman and those who don't, do not seem to perceive or understand. But in just one night, I learned not only to appreciate him as a hard worker but also to respect him as someone who refuses to let unenthusiastic coworkers or his own physical decline stand in the way of getting the job done.

# The Dance with Glass

**Brenda Crow**

*Front Range Community College, Larimer*
*Fort Collins, Colorado*

In this profile of a glassblower who is also a lively storyteller and an inspiring teacher, Brenda Crow skillfully blends explanation, description, and narration. Using a narrative plan, she threads information about the creative and technical process of glassblowing through an entertaining account of her visit to the artist's studio and a detailed portrait of the artisan himself. Thoughtfully made and sparkling with detail, her essay bears a likeness to the dazzling, highly colored ornaments Dan Daggett produces by hand in his studio. In fact, the artist's work might be taking place right before our eyes, thanks to Crow's meticulous reportage: We see Daggett and his studio, hear him speak, learn some of the terms and history of glassblowing, and—perhaps most memorably—experience Daggett's movements, which Crow reproduces using rhythm and repetition. After reading the essay, we can picture the glassblowing process and the glass pieces almost as clearly as we can see Dan Daggett, and we have come to share Crow's respect for his work.

---

The door to one of the ovens is opened. Inside, the light is intensely bright, glowing brighter than a volcano's lava. Four feet away, it feels as though going any closer would surely melt flesh from bone. Clear glass is being heated to a Day-Glo bright 2,150 degrees Fahrenheit.

The glassblower pushes one end of a five-foot-long stainless steel rod, called a *punty*, a couple of inches deep into the molten glass. He picks up the lump of molten glass and twirls the rod continuously as he closes the door of the oven and moves over to a metal worktable. He then lays the punty on the tabletop and begins rolling the molten glass along the table's surface. "This is *mavering*," he tells me.

On the right side of the table he has laid out three rows, each five inches long and a half-inch wide, of tiny, colored glass chips,

38

poured from a collection of clear plastic bags and an odd assortment of coffee cans and Styrofoam cups that surround the table's edge. "*Frit,*" he says.

From oven, to table, to *glory hole*—a kilnlike oven with no door— 4
the glassblower moves the molten glass. Glowing. Hot, hot, hot. The glassblower lays the punty on a small metal stand with two small rollers on the top. The opposite end of the punty is in the glory hole, reheating the glass.

"*Glory hole* got its name because that's where all the glory hap- 5
pens. That's where all the colors come together," he says.

The glassblower is constantly turning, always turning, and mov- 6
ing, always moving the punty inside the glory hole. Right to left, left to right. "*Flashing,*" he says.

Back to the table, more mavering. He then lays the liquid glass, 7
which is suspended on the end of the punty, into the frit. He then lifts the punty, rotates it a half turn, and again lays the liquid glass into the frit. He repeats the process yet again. He works quickly, the punty always moving, always spinning. Back to the glory hole, reheating the glass and melting the frit into the core of clear, molten glass. More mavering, again to the glory hole. Spinning, turning, spinning, rotating.

Quickly he lays the edge of the punty on one of the metal brack- 8
ets, pushes it forward into the glory hole, slides in behind it, and sits with his back toward me. The pressed-wood bench he sits on sags slightly from his weight. He pulls the punty back, bringing the end with the molten glass closer to him. In swift, fluid movements, he lifts a wet, wooden block from one of the murky, water-filled, five-gallon buckets on either side of the bench. The blackened cup-shaped block on a long wooden handle has a section of the side cut away. With the punty resting on the bracket, he touches the glass with the cup-shaped block; steam rises, water hisses. He rounds the molten glass with it.

Up, off the bench, moving, always moving, glory hole, more 9
flashing, spinning, more spinning, back to the bench in fluid movement, this is the dance with glass. He lifts a pair of shears, places them an inch from the far end of the glass, and applies pressure. Turning, always turning the punty, slower now, pulling with the shears, extending the softened glass and causing a swirl pattern to form from the frit he had embedded into the clear glass moments earlier. Waiting now, gauging the temperature of the glass, he squeezes the shears harder, then pinches off a round piece of glass the size of a baseball. "Christmas ornament," states the glassblower.

A sign, in royal blue letters four feet by two feet on a white back- 10
ground to the left of the door on the old brick wall, reads, "Daggett
Glass Studio—Hand Blown Art Glass." The studio is housed in an
old, nondescript building in downtown Loveland, Colorado. The
studio is somewhat cluttered, but a couple hundred beautiful and
delicate pieces of blown and hand-shaped glass line the wall on my
right. Some pieces are hanging from strands of nearly invisible fishing
line; others sit on cloth-covered tables and display cases. The glass is
in every shade of green, blue, red, purple, orange, and yellow and in
every conceivable shape I can imagine. Vases; bowls; paperweights;
perfume bottles; candy dishes; "witch balls," which, when hung in a
window, are supposed to keep evil spirits at bay; Christmas ornaments; icicles; candy canes; fruit; and fish are on display. As are solid,
dome-shaped pieces of clear glass with mother-of-pearl powder suspended in them, pieces the glassblower calls "Ice Fog," which he
created one day as he was "playing."

The studio has one exposed brick wall, on which the glass is dis- 11
played. The other walls are paneled on the bottom one-third of the
wall and painted white on the upper two-thirds. The ceiling is covered
with old Victorian pressed tin tiles that have been painted a rust color.
The floor is old and wooden, worn from the passage of many years
and many feet. Heavy sheets of metal, which squeak when walked on
and are joined together with what appears to be scuffed-up duct tape,
cover the floor between the ovens and the worktables. The back of
the studio is four-feet deep in clutter; I imagine only the owner knows
what resides there. To my left are the ovens. The annealing oven is
at 950 degrees. It holds finished pieces of glass and is set to cool at
60 degrees per hour in order to limit stress on the cooling glass. Glass
cooled too quickly shatters. Beyond the annealing oven is the oven
that holds the molten glass. Between the two, glowing bright yellow-
orange, is the glory hole. Discarded pieces of worked glass line the
floor under the annealing oven. Covered in dust that only partially
obscures their beauty, they look like discarded jewels.

As I draw nearer, the man sitting behind the desk at the far end 12
of the studio bounds out of his chair and strides toward me as he says
hello. Dan Daggett is a tall, rotund man with a warm, friendly de-
meanor. He has pleasant brown eyes; curly, somewhat frizzy, brown-
ish gray hair, which he often runs his fingers through; and a graying
mustache, which completely covers his upper lip. He is casually
dressed in an untucked white T-shirt, khakis, and tennis shoes. I feel
immediately comfortable in his studio and begin asking questions

and commenting on the wonderful pieces of art glass he has created. Dan holds up one of his many multicolored, iridescent swirled glass icicles: "A woman from a magazine called me and asked if I would mind if they featured these in an article of fun things to buy. Would I *mind*? I would be delighted," he smiles.

From the glory hole, Dan grabs a *blowpipe,* a hollow punty. After    13 he has picked up a dab of molten glass, mavered it, reheated it in the glory hole, mavered it again, picked up some frit—this time shards of flat dichoric glass, which is dark on one side and looks like metallic foil on the other—flashed it and mavered it yet again, he lifts the blowpipe and blows into the end. Because of the liquid state of the glass, Dan needs only to blow gently: "Not at all like blowing up a balloon," he says. I stand at the opposite end of the blowpipe and see the air bubble come into the molten glass and stay suspended there. He is quickly moving away, spinning always spinning the blowpipe, working the glass. Back to the glory hole, flashing more flashing, turning always turning.

Clear glass comes in a surprising form: small, chalky-looking    14 pebbles that are then thrown into the oven. Clear glass is inexpensive, "Twenty-eight cents a pound. It costs me as much to ship it as it does to buy the glass itself. Colored glass is more expensive. Red, especially, because gold is needed to produce the color," Dan says. He doesn't make his own colored glass because of the chemicals involved. Arsenic and cyanide are two he mentions. He purchases rods or canes of colored glass, which are solid tubes of varying circumferences, from Kugler, a company in Germany. "There is a wide variety of colors with varying amounts of transparency or opaqueness available," Dan informs me. "Some glass comes as twisted multicolored canes called *latticino.*"

Interesting effects are produced by layering different colors of    15 liquid glass and by introducing colored glass by different methods. Adding salt to molten glass produces an iridescent quality on the finished piece's surface. "*Millefiori* is a type of floral-patterned cane class," Dan tells me. "It was first made in Murano, an island not far from Venice, Italy. The methods used for making it were kept secret for over four hundred years, by threat of death! Once an apprentice learned how to make *millefiori,* he had to stay on the island." These small canes, a quarter of an inch in diameter, are broken into three-eighth inch pieces and added to the layers of molten glass.

As it turns out, Dan is somewhat of a storyteller, and I could    16 have stayed for hours watching him work and listening to him talk. I comment to Dan that it is obvious he is a happy man. "I am blessed," he says. "I get to come here every day and play. Every night I go home and thank the Lord that I get to do what I do. I knew from the very first time I worked with glass that this was what I wanted to do for the rest of my life. I fell in love with it, the romance of it, the beauty of the colors, the immediacy of working with it." As he works, Dan shares stories rich in glass history: the story of Muhammad and his armies building a fire in the desert at night and discovering in the morning light that the heat had melted the sand into glass. Some say this event marks the discovery of glass. Or the story of a glassblower named John Booze who made bottles to store whiskey in.

Dan speaks of the loss of many old skills due to the lack of apprenticeships in today's workforce. On that note, Dan shares yet another story about an old glassblower from Niwot, Colorado, whose craft was making prosthetic glass eyes for people. The old craftsman bemoaned to Dan his regret at not being able to pass his skill on to anyone before he died.    17

"Duck!" my brain shouts, a split second after I hear the first sharp ping, followed by the sound of glass breaking and the sense of it shooting across the studio. I cannot locate the source, and I ask Dan what caused the noise. "As the small amount of glass that is left on the punty or blowpipe begins to cool, it shatters and pops off, sending pieces shooting across the floor of the room," Dan informs me. While it is a startling occurrence, the second time it happens, running for cover seems a bit dramatic; instead, I stay seated and continue to watch Dan work his glass.    18

Dan is a craftsman, an artisan, and a teacher. As we speak of the classes he teaches, he tells me of high school students he is working with: "I was worried about working with high school kids, but it's been wonderful." Dan shows me a clay mask that has a resemblance to his face, mustache and all. "I came to work one morning, and this was on my desk," he says. "A student made it for me." The pride on his face and in his voice is no less brilliant than the shine on the multiple pieces of glass that are in front of us. Dan is touching lives not only by the beauty he creates but also by passing on the skills of his craft to others. He is an inspiration, a mentor.    19

# Disc Golf

## Christine Tandrup

*Northern Kentucky University*
*Highland Heights, Kentucky*

Christine Tandrup gives readers a new perspective on two familiar pastimes—Frisbee and golf—in this profile of disc golf, a sport played with golf rules on a golflike course with a Frisbee-like disk. Disc golf originated with the "object courses" of the 1970s, which were built around ordinary city fixtures like lamp poles and fire hydrants. The first real disc golf course was built in California in 1976 by "Steady" Ed Headrick of the Wham-O Corporation, the company that invented the Frisbee. In this hands-on presentation of the hybrid sport, Christine Tandrup introduces readers to Chris Ruttel, a computer programmer who plays disc golf professionally (and whose house—which Chris shares with two fellow enthusiasts—is filled with disc golf equipment). As a participant narrator, Tandrup goes out on the course with Ruttel, discovering that the game "is not as easy as it looks." As you read, notice Tandrup's perspective—which might be described as respectful but not overly serious—and her use of dialogue, which serves both to reveal Clark Ruttel's personality and to inform readers about disc golf.

---

1 When someone says "professional athlete," most people think about pro-basketball, pro-baseball, or pro-football players. Someone might think of pro golfers, but not the kind of pro golf that Clark Ruttel plays professionally. His golf involves a disc (more commonly known as a Frisbee), not a ball. He is not aiming for a hole in the ground but a large metal basket sticking out of the ground. The money involved is also quite different; instead of hundreds and thousands of dollars, a disc golf pro might hope for a few hundred—and that is on a good day. But any disc golfer will tell you that he or she is not in it for the money.

2 Clark Ruttel, a twenty-eight-year-old computer programmer with Mentor Technologies, plays for his health and to relieve stress.

"It may not be physically hard, but it's a sport that requires a lot of walking. After all, some exercise is better than none. It also helps me relax and forget about my worries at work." Clark lives with two fellow disc golfers. "It's great to live with people who also play. Then we can have long conversations about how we played last weekend, about our mistakes, and about when we are going to play next."

I am interviewing him in his house, and as I look around, I notice that the room is full of disc golf equipment. There are professional disc golf discs and large disc golf posters on the walls. In the corner of the room, there is a miniature basket with miniature discs in it. I ask what the little basket is for, and he responds, "For practice!" I go over to the basket and take out a small disc, then go about twenty feet away and try to make the basket. I fail miserably. It's not as easy as it looks. We decide to continue the interview on a disc golf course.                                                                            3

It's a rather crisp Saturday morning, but Clark is wearing shorts   4
and a T-shirt. A T-shirt, of course, with a disc golf logo. He is carrying a bag made specifically for professional golf discs. We get to hole one at Mount Airy Forest, and he reaches into his bag and pulls out a disc.

"Nah, it's a bit windy; I think I'll go with this," he says, reaching   5
back in for a different disc. I look into his bag, and there are about ten discs inside.

I ask, "Do all the discs do different things?"                          6

He responds, "Yes, some are drivers and some are putters. There    7
are discs I use for approach shots. I'm going to throw a Cyclone now, which is good for distance."

He goes up to the tee pad and tees off. As he releases the disc,     8
you can hear it rip through the air. The disc flies perfectly, not a wobble, under the low ceiling of the trees. It flies straight down the narrow fairway. As it slows, it turns a little to the left and lands about ten feet from the basket.

"I parked it!" he says.                                                 9

"How far did you just throw that?" I ask.                            10

"About three hundred feet, which is OK. The world record in    11
length with a golf disc is somewhere around seven hundred feet. I can throw about four hundred to four hundred and fifty feet."

We walk down to the disc. He sets a tee marker down, takes a   12
putter out of his bag, putts, and makes it.

Clark has been invited to the 1996, 1997, and 1998 World   13
Championships, but has never placed in the top ten. He says he's not

disappointed with himself. "If I play good solid rounds, what is there to complain about?" The 1998 World Championships were held in Cincinnati. "We tried to get some news coverage, but only got five-minute segments here and there. We were also on ESPN 2. We need as much publicity as possible to get some new players, especially women." On a good day, about 10 women will show for a tournament, as opposed to about 100 to 150 men.

When asked about travel, Clark responds, "Disc golfers travel a   14
lot. Almost every weekend, during the spring through fall, there are tournaments. I've been to Texas, Florida, Michigan, and North Carolina, to name a few. Since there are only about ten courses in the near vicinity, it's fun to get out and play some different courses." At the World Championships in 1998, there were players from Sweden, Germany, Japan, and other countries as well. He is excited about a new course coming soon to Burnett Woods. He helped design it with a couple of friends. "It's a little scary designing a course, especially with the limited amount of space we have at Burnett. It's a great location, though. Hopefully we can get some new players, since it's so close to UC."

As we reach hole six, Clark suggests I try to play some. He hands   15
me a disc and says, "This is a good beginner's disc." I go up to the tee pad and throw the disc. I throw about 150 feet, which he says is really good for my first try. We finish the hole. I have taken six shots; he has taken three. In disc golf tournaments, all holes are played as par three no matter how long they are or how difficult. As we walk up to the next hole, I see Clark reach down and pick up some garbage and put it into his bag. I ask him why, and he says, "Well, it reflects poorly on disc golfers if their courses are littered with garbage. We want to be on good terms with the park district so that maybe we can get some more courses in other parks." A disc golf course can be put on land that other sports cannot use. Most sports require a large, flat, nonwooded area. For disc golf, woods and hills are often essential for having a good and fun course.

As we reach hole ten, Clark says, "This hole is called the Green   16
Monster. It's called this because if you throw your disc in the rough to your right, you'll probably never find it again." To the right are huge bushes that could very well swallow up a disc. We both throw very cautiously. The rules and terms used for disc golf are almost the same as regular golf. There are no handicaps, but the rest is comparable.

Clark and I finish up at hole eighteen, and we are right where we   17
parked. We decide to sit on a bench and continue the interview. I ask

him what other sports he plays. He says, "I play ball golf, ultimate Frisbee, and tennis, and occasionally I run a couple of miles." I am confused about what ball golf and ultimate Frisbee are, so I ask him. "Ball golf is regular golf. Disc golfers have to differentiate between the two because we call disc golf just golf. Ultimate Frisbee is a game kind of like football with a Frisbee, except there is no tackling. It's really fun, too. You should try it. We have about ten people come out, and we play five on five. There are usually two girls and three guys to a team. It's really great."

As we are sitting there talking, some other disc golfers drive up.   18
They come out and talk to us. Clark knows everybody's name, and everybody knows him. They seem to be like a tight-knit family, yet I feel completely welcome. Clark tells them what I am doing and that I played today. They are all very enthusiastic. I decide to ask them why they play. They all basically say the same thing—"For fun!" I ask about tournaments and winning money and they all say, "Most of the time you don't win any money, but you always have to pay an entry fee. Most of the time we end up losing money."

The other disc golfers leave to go play. Clark asks me how I liked   19
playing, and I say, "I liked it very much. I think I might come out and play again." He thinks that is a good idea. He hands me some pamphlets on the upcoming tournaments and tells me when they play ultimate Frisbee. He says I should come out and play. I feel he is being sincere, not just trying to be nice by inviting me to play. He also gives me the two discs I had been using while we played and tells me I can keep them. I feel bad taking them; after all, a couple of discs would cost fifteen to twenty dollars, but he insists. We get in our cars, and I follow him out of the park. As we are stopped at a red light, I look at the back of his van. There are about six or seven stickers plastered on his bumper all having something to do with disc golf. I laugh to myself.

# "Paddlers Sit Ready!" The Enduring Sport of Dragon Boating

### Katie Diehm

*The Catholic University of America*
*Washington, D.C.*

Katie Diehm's profile of dragon boating differs from the other essays in this chapter in an important way. While the other profile authors do occasionally insert themselves into their essays—reflecting on an interviewee's comment, for example, or briefly joining the scene they are describing—for the most part they are detached observers, reporters instead of participants. Diehm, on the other hand, takes us through a brief, action-packed race from the seat of her boat. Diehm's participant-observer role allows her to offer readers not only the look and sound of the race, but also its feel. Readers experience the tug of the water as the paddlers struggle to hold their boats at the starting line; their rush of adrenaline at the command "Go!"; and the strain on their arms, stomachs, and backs as they paddle through the rainy, windy weather. Diehm's essay brings readers not just into the race but into the bodies of the racers.

--------

As we bob up and down in the river, our arms begin to shake in anticipation. Our hands grip our paddles tighter as we hold them down straight into the water, bracing the boat and willing it to stay still despite the rain blowing into us. From my seat on the left side of the fifth bench, I can see the call boat over the heads of my nervous teammates. The timer watches us intently until that exact moment when all four teams are lined up and he can give us the go. [1]

Over the sound of water hitting the sides of the boats, we can hear cheering from the excited spectators on the shore. From the other side of the river, the spectators appear as a long streak of moving color lined up in front of perhaps the most colorful of festivals. Tents with various Chinese wares, food, and music cover the lawn, all part of this joyous celebration of the dragon boat tradition. [2]

Dragon boats first originated more than two thousand years ago    3
in China when, as legend has it, disgruntled Chinese poet and scholar
Qu Yuan committed suicide by jumping into a river after his village
was overrun with enemies. As *Washington Post* journalist Paul
Schwartzman tells us, "local fishermen searched for him in their boats,
pounding drums and beating the waters furiously to ward off the water
dragons they feared might eat him" (2). Dragon boat racing soon developed in honor of this event, often as part of the Chinese Festival of
the Dragon Boat, meant to honor and appease the dragon ruling over
the river. Today's dragon boat races are often accompanied by a festival, which generally begins with a flag-raising ceremony the day before
the races. This ceremony, in which the Chinese flag is raised over the
river, symbolizes China's lasting importance in the event. A far cry
from the fishing boats of Qu Yuan's era, today's dragon boats are
forty-five feet long and made of fiberglass, complete with a dragon's
head and tail at either end. Sixteen paddlers line both sides of the boat
and paddle in synch in a way unique to dragon boating.

"Boat Three draw left!" the timer yells over the wind, and the left-    4
side paddlers on the boat in the third lane begin to work hard, paddling sideways to move their boat further away from the second lane.

"Boat Four hold! Paddle back!" the timer yells as the wind shifts    5
and their team begins to pull forward past the starting line. The paddlers strain to hold their paddles down in the water, keeping the boat
still, and then slowly and steadily begin to paddle backwards.

The beginning of a dragon boat race is often the hardest due to    6
elements like wind and the river current. Getting lined up often takes
the better part of ten minutes—an ironic beginning for a race that
lasts approximately three—and is grueling for the paddlers as they
sometimes paddle constantly just to stay in one place. As the boats finally pull into place, the timer wastes no time in barking out orders.

"Paddlers sit ready!" he calls, signaling the time for all paddles to    7
be removed from the water and proper grip on the paddle—the
upper hand gripping the top of the paddle as if in a fist, the lower
hand gripping the lower section of the paddle, directly above the
wide part—to be assumed.

"Attention!" At this call the teams lean forward, arms extended    8
and paddles raised about five inches above the water, ready to plunge
with all intensity into the river. Mike Dojc, a dragon boat enthusiast,
explains that the paddlers stretch their backs out straight, ready to pull
at the paddle with the muscles from their arms, stomach, and back by
twisting their bodies and keeping their arms straight (Dojc 1).

"Go!" Instantly the teams spring into action. Simultaneously, my    9
teammates and I drop our paddles down and forward and pull back
with all our strength. The start time in dragon boat racing is extremely important—it's a thirty-second chance to gain additional
speed that will last even when the paddlers fall back into a slower and
more constant pace. The tiller—the person in charge of steering the
boat—stands at the back and grips the till, willing through long
strokes or skillful dips of the till that the boat stay on course. The
caller, standing on the front of the boat and struggling to keep her
balance despite the surging of the boat, beats out a fast rhythm on a
drum, shouting the counts over the beat.

"One! Two! Three! Four! Watch-your-lead! Two! Three! Four!    10
Keep-it-up! Two! Three! Four!"

As the boats leave the beginning of the race, the quick-start pace    11
subsides and the paddlers begin to pace themselves. At ninety strokes
a second, however, the pace is hardly relaxing. As arms begin to go
numb, the paddlers begin to focus all their energy on keeping up
with the rest of the paddlers in the boat, as they know that even the
slightest delay on their paddle's entrance into the river can mean a
demerit of a couple of seconds. Suzanne Ma, a journalist from the
*Hamilton Spectator,* tells us that the aim is for the "rhythm of the
boat to be like one collective heartbeat" (1). Each team has a unique
way of keeping everyone in time using some division of the paddlers.
My team divided the sixteen paddlers into two groups. The first ten
paddlers (two per bench) watch the two paddlers in the front (called
the lead strokes), the left side paddlers watch the lead on the right,
and the right side paddlers watch the left. The paddlers on the fourth
bench, called the mid-strokes, serve as pacers for the back half of the
boat as they watch the lead strokes and are then watched in the same
way by the back paddlers. From my left-side fifth bench position, I sit
directly behind the mid-strokes and am dubbed a part of the "engine
room," the part of the boat that is relied on for constant, steady paddling. The front of the boat is made up of paddlers who have long,
solid paddle strokes. These paddlers must also be very strong, as they
are paddling dead water. The rear three benches are made up of powerful paddlers called rockets. These six paddlers are perhaps the most
important on the boat, as it is their strength that propels the boat
forward. Some describe the feeling of paddling in rhythm as entering
a Zen state, and Schwartzman tell us that "if the boat is in tune, you
can feel it gliding" (2). Paddling in unison with proper technique
and a tailwind, our boat can get up to 6 mph.

As the boat reaches the end of the five-hundred-meter race, 12
adrenaline kicks in to counteract our fatigue. At one minute to go,
our designated flag catcher, chosen for her light weight and gymnast-
like frame, gets up, climbs behind the tiller, ties her feet into a strap
secured from the neck of the dragon, and lies down prostrate over the
dragon's head until she is extended a good two feet off the dragon's
nose. Her outstretched arm directs the tiller toward the flag that she
must catch or the team will receive a hefty demerit on its time.

The last thirty seconds of the race are often the hardest. Clearly 13
fatigued and struggling to maintain the pace, the paddlers rely solely
on adrenaline to get to the finish line. The pace accelerates to the beat
of a drum, and the caller urges the paddlers to "Finish-it-now!"—a
signal to paddle faster and firmer than before. As soon as the boats
speed through the finish line and flags are caught, the callers waste no
time in yelling, "Hold the boat!" We thrust our paddles straight down
into the water and attempt—despite the speed of the boat—to hold
them still. Our boat comes to a stop about eight feet away from the
grassy shore, and the tiller rapidly begins to spin the boat around and
back to the docks. With now-shaking arms and pounding hearts we
slowly make our way back, where we unload and trade places with the
next team waiting to go out. The races continue all day and into the
next, tournament style, until only four teams are left. These last four
compete against each other in one final race—the last of the season.

As the teams narrow down, the festivities increase, and teams 14
that are out of the running return to the shoreline to cheer for the
teams that are still competing. The smell of Chinese foods cooking
fills the air, and ethnic music explodes from all corners of the
grounds, reminding the participants just how unique an experience
the Chinese Festival of the Dragon Boat really is.

## WORKS CITED

Bradley, Theresa. "Students Revel in Asian Tradition: Dragon Boat Race."
     *Miami Herald* 29 Sept. 2005: 1–3. Lexis-Nexis. The Catholic U of
     America Mullen Lib. 13 Oct. 2005 <http://web.lexis-nexis.com>.

Dojc, Mike. "Blazing Paddles: Q&A with a Dragon Boat Enthusiast."
     *Toronto Sun* 26 June 2004: 1–3. Lexis-Nexis. The Catholic U of America
     Mullen Lib. 13 Oct. 2005 <http://web.lexis-nexis.com>.

Ma, Suzanne. "Pulling Together: Dragon Boat Racing Soothes the Mind,
     Energizes the Body." *Hamilton Spectator* 7 July 2005: 1–4. Lexis-Nexis.

The Catholic U of America Mullen Lib. 13 Oct. 2005 <http://web
.lexis-nexis.com>.

Schwartzman, Paul. "In Dragon Races, Team Spirit Sinks In, and That's Not
All: Ancient Chinese Tradition Grows with Fourth Year of Competing
on Potomac." *Washington Post* 29 May 2005: 1–3. Lexis-Nexis. The
Catholic U of America Mullen Lib. 13 Oct. 2005 <http://web
.lexis-nexis.com>.

# Explaining a Concept 4

You've noticed a phenomenon: Many of your friends don't think twice about downloading commercial music from the Internet or burning CDs for one another, even though some of your college instructors have lectured that this practice is unethical or illegal or both, and your parents or employers have discussed installing software on your computer that prevents you from joining in the fun. This phenomenon or other phenomena that have intrigued you or that you've participated in but never thought seriously about may provide just the concept you need for this assignment. Once you have identified a phenomenon, your next step is to gain a quick orientation to it. Let's say you've heard about "participatory culture" and would like to know more. A bit of Web surfing reveals that the term *participatory culture* names the universe of file sharing networks, blogs, wikis, and other platforms that enable ideas and content to flow among peers; the shared values of these participants; and the participants themselves. Voila: a concept you could learn more about and write about. (A concept is a phenomenon or process like participatory culture, academic failure among college athletes, the dowry system in India, jihad, secular humanism, zero-based budgeting, short-term memory, federalism, mitosis, null space, gravity, seasonal affective disorder, ozone depletion, run-and-shoot offense, the hit-and-run play, bankruptcy, the lemon law, or machismo.)

Writing that explains a concept is not so personal as narrating a remembered event (chapter 2) or profiling a place or activity you have observed (chapter 3). It need not be so accommodating to readers' expected resistance as arguing to support your position on an issue (chapter 6) or proposing to solve a problem (chapter 7). But it does invite you to attune yourself to your readers, precisely measuring what they will already know about the concept: you aim neither to bore them nor to strain them, but to enable them to learn about your concept without too strenuous an effort. No showing off is allowed: of course you know more than your readers about your concept-subject, but to win their ear, you must remain tactful and modest throughout, authoritative yet never talking down.

Every academic discipline, profession, career, sport, kind of work, governmental or political organization, local community, or religion has its concepts. Through concepts, we define, understand, and manage our world. We can't live without them. These are not just big words—they are required words. As a college student, you'll add hugely to your concept hoard. In doing so, you'll gain a wider understanding of the myriad aspects of your life and times, and you'll have the precise words—the concept names—to help you organize and deploy your new knowledge.

# Proxemics: A Study of Space and Relationships

## Sheila McClain

*Western Wyoming Community College*
*Rock Springs, Wyoming*

---

We all understand the power of personal space: someone standing
closer than we expect seems to be invading, while someone giving
us a wide berth seems rude, literally "standoffish." But did you
know that the use of personal space to communicate is the subject
of an academic field called proxemics? Sheila McClain discovered
proxemics while researching body language. When body language
proved too broad a topic for a focused concept essay, she returned
to proxemics in part because "it was a little known term and I felt it
would prove interesting and easy for readers to relate to." As you
read, notice how McClain moves between the two concepts, allowing the larger, more familiar subject (body language, or "nonverbal
communication") to lead her into an explanation of the smaller,
less familiar one (proxemics).

---

Every day we interact and communicate, sometimes without even say- 1
ing a word. Body language, more formally known as nonverbal communication, speaks volumes about who we are and how we relate to
others. As Lester Sielski, an associate professor at the University of
West Florida, writes, "Words are beautiful, exciting, important, but
we have overestimated them badly—since they are not all or even half
the message." He also asserts that "beyond words lies the bedrock on
which human relationships are built—nonverbal communication"
(Sielski). A group of pscyhology students at the University of Texas
recently demonstrated just how profound an effect nonverbal communication can have on people. The students conducted an experiment to test the unspoken rules of behavior on elevators. Boarding a
crowded elevator, they would stand facing and grinning at the other
people on board. Understandably, the people became uncomfortable;
one person even suggested that someone call 911 (Axtell 5–6). Why

54

all the fuss? Unspoken elevator etiquette dictates that one should turn and face the door in a crowded elevator, being careful not to touch anyone else and honoring the sacred personal space of each individual by staring at the floor indicator instead of looking at anyone else. Although they are not written down, strict rules govern our behavior in public situations. This is especially true when space is limited, as on elevators, buses, or subway trains (Axtell 5–6).

Patricia Buhler, an expert in business management and associate 2 professor at Goldey-Beacon College, confirms the large role nonverbal communication plays. She asserts that as little as 8 percent of the message we communicate is made up of words. We communicate the rest of our message, a disproportionately large 92 percent, with body language and other nonverbal forms of communication (Buhler). While researchers have long known that nonverbal cues play a large role in communication, for many years they made no effort to learn more about them (Sielski). Amid rising public interest, several scientists pioneered new research in the field of nonverbal communication in the 1950s. Among these experts was anthropologist Edward T. Hall. He focused on a specific type of nonverbal communication called *proxemics*. Proxemics is the study of how people use space to communicate nonverbally. Whether we are conscious of it or not, our use of space plays a major role in our everyday interactions with others.

A review of some of Dr. Hall's main terms will help us better understand proxemics and appreciate just how much our use of space affects our relationships. For example, according to Dr. Hall, in our everyday interactions, we choose to position ourselves to create either "sociopetal" or "sociofugal" space. Sociopetal space invites communication; sociofugal space is the opposite—it separates people and discourages interaction (Jordan). A student in a school lunchroom may sit alone at an empty table in a corner, away from the other students (creating sociofugal space), or directly across from a person he would like to befriend (creating sociopetal space).

Dr. Hall identifies three kinds of general spaces within which we 4 can create either sociofugal or sociopetal space. These are "fixed-feature space," "semi-fixed feature space," and "informal space" (Jordan). Fixed-feature spaces are hard, if not impossible, for us to control or change. For example, because my college English class is too small for the number of students attending, we have a hard time positioning ourselves so that we can all see the overhead projections. We cannot make the walls of the classroom bigger or the ceiling higher, and the overhead screen is likewise "fixed" in place. We must work within the constraints of the space. A semi-fixed feature space is usually defined by mobile objects such as furniture. The couches and chairs in a living room, for example, may face only the television, thus discouraging conversation and relationship building. But we are able to reposition the furniture to create a more social environment. Informal space is by far the easiest to manipulate. We each control our personal "bubble," and we can set distances between ourselves and others that reflect our relationships with them. Take for example the way that people approach their bosses. A man who is afraid of or dislikes his boss may communicate with her from as far away as possible. He might stand in her doorway to relay a message. Conversely, a woman who has known her boss for many years and is good friends with him might come right in to his office and casually sit down in close proximity to him. Individually, we have a great deal of control over our informal space, and how we use this space can speak volumes about our relationship with others.

After observing many interactions, Dr. Hall broke down informal    5 space further, identifying four distances commonly used by people in their interactions with others: "intimate distance," zero to one and a half feet; "personal distance," one and a half to four feet; "social distance," four to twelve feet; and "public distance," twelve feet and beyond (Beebe, Beebe, and Redmond 231). Intimate distance, as the name suggests, is generally reserved for those people closest to us. Lovemaking, hugging, and holding small children all occur in this zone. The exception to this rule comes when we extend our hand to perfect strangers in greeting, allowing them to briefly enter our intimate space with a handshake. Personal distance, while not as close as intimate, is still reserved for people we know well and with whom we feel comfortable. This zone usually occupies an area relatively close to us. It can at times be applied, however, to include objects we see as extensions of ourselves. For instance, while driving, we may feel our personal space being invaded by a car following behind us too closely. We see our own car as an extension of ourselves and extend our "personal bubble" to include it. Social distance is often considered a respectful distance and is used in many professional business settings as well as in group interactions. There is a public distance between a lecturer and a class, or someone speaking publicly from a podium and his or her audience.

As we have seen, in positioning ourselves in relation to others—    6 especially in choosing nearness or distance—we communicate respect or intimacy, fear or familiarity. We can improve a friendly relationship simply by using a warm, personable distance, or drive potential friends away by seeming cold and distant, or getting quite literally too close for comfort. We can put people at ease or make them uncomfortable just by our proximity to them. The study of nonverbal communication, and specifically proxemics, demonstrates the truth of the old adage, "Actions speak louder than words."

## WORKS CITED

Axtell, Roger E. *Gestures: the Do's and Taboos of Body Language around the World*. New York: Wiley, 1998.

Beebe, Steven A., Susan J. Beebe, and Mark V. Redmond. *Interpersonal Communication: Relating to Others*. 2nd ed. Boston: Allyn, 1999.

Buhler, Patricia. "Managing in the 90s." *Supervision* 52.9 (1991): 18–21. *Business Source Premier*. EBSCO. Western Wyoming Comm. College, Hay Lib. 29 Sept. 2004 <http://web29.epnet.com/authHjafBrowse.asp>.

Jordan, Sherry. "Embodied Pedagogy: The Body and Teaching Theology." *Teaching Theology and Religion* 4.2 (2001): 98–101. *Academic Search Premier*. EBSCO. Western Wyoming Comm. College, Hay Lib. 29 Sept. 2004 <http://web29.epnet.com/authHjafBrowse.asp>.

Sielski, Lester M. "Understanding Body Language." *Personal and Guidance Journal* 57.4 (1979): 238–42. *Academic Search Premier*. EBSCO. Western Wyoming Comm. College, Hay Lib. 29 Sept. 2004 <http://web29.epnet.com/authHjafBrowse.asp>.

# Digital Plastic Surgery

Sara Snyder

*University of Minnesota, Twin Cities*
*Minneapolis, Minnesota*

What phenomenon has intrigued you lately? When graphic-design major Sara Snyder asked herself that question, she had a ready answer: the use of digital retouching to perfect the images of female celebrities and models that appear on magazine covers and in ads. Casting about for a name for this concept, she came upon *digital plastic surgery*—a term that neatly combines two facts about the practice: that it is computer generated and that it is motivated by superficiality. The concept of digital plastic surgery is inherently interesting, and Snyder's breezy tone and cascade of vivid examples make it even more so. As you read her essay, notice where it especially piques your interest, and why.

---

Forget plastic surgery. Today, makeovers are only a click of the mouse away. With digital imaging software, it is possible to remove blemishes and other skin imperfections, change hair color, and even alter body shape. Once viewed as the magazine industry's dirty little secret, digital altering is now so rampant that virtually every celebrity image circulated today has undergone some modification. With advancements in imaging software, the manipulation of digital images is easier and faster to do and more difficult to detect. What once took hours to airbrush or consolidate can now be done in a matter of seconds by a well-equipped and savvy art department (Kennedy). As a result, digital retouching has become the norm in fashion and entertainment magazines, and has created a myth of perfect beauty—especially female beauty.

Using digital retouching, the fashion industry creates images of women so perfect that their real-life counterparts look ordinary by comparison. Cindy Crawford has said, "I wish I looked like Cindy Crawford" (qtd. in Kilbourne). Computers and digital photography

58

have ushered in a whole new era in the construction of the ideal image. In the past, photographers used cosmetics, camera angles, lighting, and airbrushing; today, that magic takes place on the computer screen. Moreover, digital retouching goes far beyond airbrushing, making it possible to dramatically alter faces and bodies or even to rearrange them.

Kate Winslet is known as a celebrity advocate for healthy, natural    3
bodies. In the British *GQ* magazine, however, her legs and torso were digitally slimmed down, and her breasts were made to appear more pert (McNear). Although the actress had approved the original photos, she was not consulted about the digital changes. Winslet was rightfully upset about the editing. She said:

> The retouching is excessive. I do not look like that, and more importantly, I don't desire to look like that. I actually have a Polaroid the photographer gave me on the day of the shoot. I can tell you they've reduced the size of my legs by about a third. For my money it looks pretty good the way it was taken. (qtd. in "Retouching Is Excessive")

The editor of the magazine eventually admitted the photos were    4
altered, but to no greater extent than other photos normally featured in the magazine (McNear).

Kate Winslet is not the only celebrity to go through digital plastic    5
surgery without her consent. Julia Roberts was outraged to discover that in the poster for the 1990 film *Pretty Woman,* a photograph of her head had been placed on the body of a more slender model (McNear). Nor was that poster Roberts' last experience with digital manipulation. According to Jean Kilbourne in "The Murky Road of Digital Retouching," a July 2003 *Redbook* cover featured a grinning—and out-of-proportion—Julia Roberts. As it turns out, the cover pose was constructed from separate photographs: a shot of Roberts' head was placed on an entirely different photograph of her body.

*Redbook* had treated Jennifer Aniston similarly on the previous    6
month's cover. The June 2003 cover image, a composite of three separate photographs of Aniston, made the actress look so disjointed that she considered legal action (Kilbourne). Phil Tsui—principal retoucher and partner at Resolution, a New York–based photo-retouching firm—says such composites are used far more often than the public imagines. "So many shots are pieced together; it's only when they screw it up that it becomes an issue" (qtd. in Grossman).

Editors of the British magazine *FHM* were not happy with singer    7
Nelly Furtado's stomach, so they gave her a flatter, more muscular

replacement before featuring her on their cover. To emphasize their handiwork, they shortened Furtado's shirt to just below her breasts. "I don't like being misrepresented to my fans," Furtado said. "You work hard to represent a certain thing and have a certain image, and somebody can take it all away with the cover of a magazine" (qtd. in Cobb).

After her release from prison, a beaming, fresh-faced Martha Stewart appeared on the cover of *Newsweek*. Well, at least her head did. The body was that of an unidentified model (Kingston). *Newsweek* responded to criticism by hiding behind the caption: it was clearly labeled as a false image; if readers assumed otherwise, it was their mistake. 8

Mark Kennedy's article entitled "Photo Retouching: It's a Question of Ethics" in the August 29, 1997, issue of *Greensboro News* lists several more examples of digital retouching. Oprah Winfrey's up-and-down weight struggle took a bizarre twist when the talk-show queen's face was superimposed on actress Ann-Margret's hourglass figure for a *TV Guide* cover in 1989. Actress Mira Sorvino complained when photographer David La Chapelle digitally altered her eyebrows, added a scowl, and superimposed another figure over part of her body for a photo spread in *Allure* magazine. Kathie Lee Gifford was given an electronic manicure in *McCall's*. *Premier* realigned Jodie Foster's belly button, digitally moving it a full three inches. In 2003, Kate Beckinsale asked for her breasts to be digitally altered for the *Underworld* poster because she felt they were not big enough (McNear). In *USA Today,* Tyra Banks said people are sometimes disappointed when they meet her because she looks so different from her photos (James). Virtually every picture in any magazine has been digitally manipulated in some way. 9

"Several of the celebrities who we retouch require quite a bit of work. In certain cases even the texture of their skin is completely rebuilt," says Phil Tsui of Resolution. "They are certainly not the perfect images you see in the final product" (qtd. in Grossman). Some media go as far as to create completely fictional images. *Mirabella* magazine put a computer-generated woman on its cover. In another instance, a Swedish animator created a "model" named Webbie Tookay for a cell phone advertising campaign (Kilbourne). Some say this development marks the wave of the future, and that computer-generated models will begin to replace real people on magazine covers and in advertisements. 10

The CBS News program *48 Hours Investigates* produced a special entitled "Extremely Perfect" to cover an unusual photograph on 11 the cover of *More* magazine, a publication geared toward women over forty. The magazine featured an unretouched photo of actress Jamie Lee Curtis wearing next to nothing. "I said, 'Let's take a picture of me in my underwear. No lighting, nothing. Just me. No makeup. No styling. No hair. No clothing. Pretty brutal lighting," Curtis says (qtd. in "Extremely Perfect"). Curtis' motive was to demonstrate that the women who smile at us from magazine covers, billboards, and TV commercials never look so good in person (Kilbourne). "The whole goal for me with this was just that people would look at it and go like this, 'Oh, I get it. She's real. She's just a person like me,'" Curtis said (qtd. in "Extremely Perfect"). In the interview printed along with the photo, Curtis told readers:

> I don't have great thighs. I have a soft, fatty little tummy. I don't want the unsuspecting 40-year-old women of the world to think that I've got it going on. It's such a fraud. [ ... ] No matter how beautiful or thin the model, she's often retouched in some way to make her even more beautiful and thinner still. What the magazines are selling is beauty that is largely unattainable. People don't look like this. People are flawed. It's why we're people. We're flawed. (qtd. in "Extremely Perfect")

In "Extremely Perfect," *More* magazine editor Susan Crandell   12
said the public's reaction was 100 percent positive. "We got hundreds of letters from women saying 'Thank you,' and they were saying 'You look like me' or 'I look like you.'"

Fashion magazine editor Leanne Delap states, "Retouching has   13
permeated the industry both in advertising and editorially. Photos were always retouched for such things as skin tone or a crease in a skirt, but with new technology the temptation is to do more" (qtd. in Cobb). Current technology makes image-enhancing possibilities almost endless. "A good retoucher can basically make the person in the picture look better, enhance the way they look," says Kate Betts, a former top fashion editor at *Vogue* and editor-in-chief of *Harper's Bazaar*. "They can do anything. They can open eyes wider, make them brighter, change the shape, contour the face a lot" (qtd. in "Extremely Perfect").

Jane Tallim—education director of the Ottawa-based Media   14
Awareness Network, an educational group funded by major Canadian media companies—says the challenge is to help readers understand that most images in entertainment or fashion-oriented magazines do not reflect real people:

> Only a small percentage of the population can meet the physical demands of a super model. But now, apparently, even they can't reach the

necessary standard of perfection. If Kate Winslet can't meet the standard for a magazine cover, what chance do the rest of us have? It's daunting. (qtd. in Cobb)

Models employed to sell products in magazine ads, or in the glossy flyers inserted in our morning newspapers, are rarely as perfect as they appear.

*Harper's Bazaar* editor Betts remarks that "we do live in a culture   15 that is about display, and I don't just mean the red carpet. I mean everybody is concerned about their image, whether they're Nicole Kidman or Jane Doe on the street. And I think image has become a big part of our culture" (qtd. in "Extremely Perfect"). Once viewed as the industry's dirty little secret, digital altering is now so rampant that virtually every celebrity image circulated today has undergone some modification (Kennedy). Digital manipulation has become the norm in fashion and entertainment magazines and has created a myth of artificial beauty. In the words of Pascal Dangin, the digital retoucher for Hollywood's fashion and celebrity photographers, "This world is not reality. It's just paper" (qtd. in Hitchon et al.).

## WORKS CITED

Cobb, Chris. "Digital Fakery: Happy, Healthy, and Fat." *Ottawa Citizen* 2 Feb. 2003. *ProQuest.* 10 May 2005 <http://proquest.umi.com>.

"Extremely Perfect." *48 Hours Investigates* 2 Aug. 2003. 10 May 2005 <http://www.cbsnews.com/stories/2003/04/28/48hours/main551362.shtml>.

Furtado, Nelly. "Powerless (Say What You Want)." *Folklore.* S.K.G. Music, 2003.

Grossman, David Michael. "It's A-Listers versus Art Decorators in a Showdown." *Folio: The Magazine for Magazine Management* 1 Aug. 2003. 10 May 2005 <http://preview.foliomag.com/design/marketing_alisters_vs_art/>.

Hitchon, Jacquelin Bush, Sung-Yeon Park, Sheila Reaves, and Gi Woong Yun. "If Looks Could Kill: Digital Manipulation of Fashion Models." *Journal of Mass Media Ethics* 19.1 (2004).

James, Renee A. "In Interviews, Celebrities Are Just Like Us. Sure!" *Morning Call* 10 Aug. 2003. *ProQuest.* 10 May 2005 <http://proquest.umi.com>.

Kennedy, Mark. "Photo Retouching: It's a Question of Ethics." *Greensboro News Company* 29 Aug. 1997. *ProQuest.* 10 May 2005 <http://proquest.umi.com/>.

Kilbourne, Jean. "The Murky Road of Digital Retouching." *Darwin* Dec. 2003. 10 May 2005 <http://www.darwinmag.com/read/120103/manipulation.html>.

Kingston, Anne. "Now You See It, Now You Don't." *National Post* 2 Feb. 2002. *ProQuest.* 10 May 2005 <http://proquest.umi.com>.

Leach, Susan Llewelyn. "Seeing Is No Longer Believing." *Christian Science Monitor* 2 Feb. 2005. *ProQuest.* 10 May 2005 <http://proquest.umi.com>.

McNear, Ramsey Edwards. "Photo Retouching for the New Century." *The Student Life* 116.19 (2004) <http://www.tsl.pomona.edu/index.php?article=679>.

"Retouching Is Excessive Says Slimline Covergirl Kate Winslet." *Hello!* 10 Jan. 2003. 10 May 2005 <http://www.hellomagazine.com/film/2003/01/10/katewinslet/>.

Sheringham, Sam. "The Camera Never Lies? Well, It Can Clearly Bend the Truth a Little." *Daily Post* 3 April 2003. *ProQuest.* 10 May 2005 <http://proquest.umi.com>.

# Battered-Woman Syndrome

**Hobi Reader**

*Southwestern College*
*Chula Vista, California*

How much do you know about battered-woman syndrome? How much *don't* you know? Hobi Reader doesn't ask these questions directly, but she might as well have. The tone of Reader's essay is challenging. With its early momentum—one statistic and then another and another—it seems bent on sweeping us out of our own ignorance. As you read, notice how aware Reader is of her audience—not only early on, when she engages us by challenging our knowledge and then startling us with statistics, but throughout the essay. For example, watch how she logically unfolds information about battered-woman syndrome—first explaining why women stay in violent relationships, then exploring the psychological triggers to an abuser's explosive temper. Notice how, when she comes to a term her audience might not know ("learned helplessness"), she explains it simply and thoroughly. She never lets her readers off the hook—not even in the last paragraph, where, in describing the value of education and action in preventing spousal abuse, she brings us back to the challenge of the essay's beginning, reminding us of our own ignorance, our own silence.

---

Battered-woman syndrome. This is the current name for spousal abuse. Before that it was called wife beating. Before that it was called okay. For eons, a woman was considered the possession of a man. Not only was beating a woman accepted, but it was also expected in order to keep her under control, to show her who was the boss, and to allow a man to prove his superiority and manliness. 1

The term *battered-woman syndrome* was coined by Lenore Walker and described in her book *Terrifying Love*. In an earlier book, *The Battered Woman,* she identifies three phases of abuse. The first is a tension-building phase, when minor battering occurs. This is followed by an 2 acute battering period, when intensity or frequency increases. The third phase is a calm period, often with the batterer begging for forgiveness and offering gifts and kindness. This is when he usually promises never to hurt the woman again. Even with professional help, however, the abuse usually continues (Walker, *Battered* 49).

Battered-woman syndrome is a very misunderstood concept. 3 Many people are not aware of its widespread existence. Others are not even sure what the term means. Once statistics are reviewed, many are shocked. According to the National Organization for Women, there are more than four million women beaten by their husbands or boyfriends every day in the United States, although most assaults are not reported to law-enforcement agencies. One out of seven women has been repeatedly raped by her partner (United States 3). The statistics for divorced women who no longer live with their abusers show that more than 75 percent of these women are still being battered. The most shocking fact, perhaps, is that there are three times as many animal shelters in this country as there are battered women's shelters.

Many behaviorists compare a battered woman's emotional state 4 to the Stockholm syndrome, the state of mind of hostages and prisoners who sometimes undergo a bonding with their captors. The hostages become complacent and withdrawn and are often suspicious of anyone who comes to their rescue (Hickey 9).

The battered woman is, in effect, brainwashed into believing 5 whatever her captor/husband says. She becomes distrustful of outsiders and increasingly relies on the husband's truths as her own. The woman is a creature created by the batterer. She has been told lies for so long about who she is that the lies become part of her beliefs about herself. She comes to believe that she is stupid, worthless, unable to make decisions for herself, a bad mother, etc. She is so used to being controlled and beaten into submission that she becomes the perfect victim. Everything is her fault. Nothing she does is good enough. And, to make matters worse, the abuser is often so inconsistent with his beatings that the woman lives in a constant state of fear, never knowing what might set him off. This fear creates an incredible amount of stress, and the psychological damage that results creates a prison for the battered woman (Walker, *Terrifying* 49). As one battered woman said, "The bruises and slaps would eventually heal and go away, but I'll never forget the awful things he said about the way I look, the way I cook, and how I take care of the kids" (qtd. in Spouza 1).

Many an abuser will not let his wife out of his sight. The woman 6 is confined to the home and not allowed contact with family or friends. The abuser is suspicious of everything — phone calls, mail, looks from other men — even a gesture or look by his wife might mean something is amiss. The man controls all aspects of the woman's life — what she wears, whom she speaks to, where she goes, how much money she gets. The woman comes to feel trapped and powerless as the man asserts his control.

Often the abuser was himself abused as a child. Many never learned how to deal with their anger. Underneath all this aggressive behavior, there is often a scared and insecure man venting the feelings he has about his own lack of self-esteem. The abuser may never have learned how to feel or express anger without associating his anger with violence (United States 5). Or, he may have seen his father beat his mother. A man may also batter because of socialization and the belief that it is a man's role to dominate the family by any possible means. Although these stereotypical "macho" characteristics are more prevalent in certain cultures, wife beating knows no ethnic boundaries. It is also blind to age, wealth, social standing, religion, and any other diversity of humankind. 7

Why would a woman enter a relationship such as this? There are many reasons. The first is that the man often doesn't show any violent behavior during the courtship period. He is an expert at manipulation and is often very romantic — the last man she might think could be violent. Another reason is that the woman might think she can change the man if he has already become violent with her. "Once we're married, he'll be nicer," she may tell herself. "When the children start coming, he'll be better." Or: "He's just stressed out now. If I stop talking back so much, he won't have to hit me." The battered woman usually makes excuses from the very beginning of an abusive relationship. Often, she has been in a violent home before and knows the signs but chooses to ignore them. In this way, she becomes trapped in a cycle of abuse, feeling she deserves it. She may actually be comforted that she is getting attention from a man, even if it is negative. And so the cycle of abuse continues. 8

Sexual abuse and degradation are common in violent relationships. Rape is very common, and forced copulation with friends of the abuser also occurs. These acts are more than sexual; they are in fact about control, with the abuser acting from the need to control every aspect of a woman's life. 9

Why do women remain in these abusive relationships? Many times they remain because they are terrified. They have become the victims of abusers. Walker borrowed the term *learned helplessness* to 10 describe the emotional state of a battered woman. The term was originally used by Martin Seligman to describe the condition of dogs that were electrically shocked at repeated but irregular intervals. The dogs eventually became so broken in spirit that they didn't use opportunities given them to escape (Walker, *Battered* 40).

The physical injuries suffered by a battered woman are often so severe that they cause bruises, strangle marks, black eyes, broken bones, internal bleeding, miscarriage, brain damage, and death. The emotional injuries are just as severe, if not more so, even if not physically visible. In desperation, a woman may resort to self-defense in order to survive. Sometimes this means that the victim kills her abuser. Unfortunately, many of these women who do retaliate against their abusers end up in jail for first-degree murder because of our criminal justice system's lack of understanding. The children of these women become orphans, their husbands become victims, and, as always, the woman is guilty. 11

When there are children in the home, there is a 300 percent increase in physical violence by male batterers. These children suffer from a variety of symptoms as well, including psychological and physical harm that is irreparable. Many grow up to become batterers themselves or the victims of batterers (NiCarthy 32). 12

Society has begun to change its views on battered women. Once, the cycle of violence was viewed as the woman's fault, just as it was considered the man's right to beat his wife. Through education and public forums, however, the general public is becoming more informed about battered-woman syndrome. This may be the first important step in stopping the cycle of abuse. 13

## WORKS CITED

Hickey, Cheryl. "Battered Woman Syndrome—License to Kill or Self Defense?" *California Now News* Apr. 1992: 9.

NiCarthy, Ginny. *Getting Free.* Seattle: Seal, 1982.

Spouza, Valerie. *Domestic Violence Info Guide.* San Diego: Junior League of San Diego, San Diego Domestic Violence Council, n.d.

United States. Dept. of Health and Human Services. *Plain Talk.* Washington: GPO, 1993.

Walker, Lenore. *The Battered Woman.* New York: Harper, 1979.

———. *Terrifying Love.* New York: Harper, 1989.

# Existentialism: A Philosophy of Existence, Time, and Freedom of Choice

Stefan Sapoundjiev

*Western Wyoming Community College*
*Rock Springs, Wyoming*

*Existentialism:* You may have heard the term before, but have no real understanding of its meaning or its influence on the lives of its originators and students. Perhaps you have even been assigned to read Albert Camus' classic existentialist text *The Stranger*, but could not pin down what the French novelist was trying to communicate. In this essay, Stefan Sapoundjiev simplifies the complicated notion by describing three of its essential ideas and explaining why existentialism developed, who conceived of it, and how a follower of existentialism might conduct his or her life. Sapoundjiev begins with the historical underpinnings of the philosophy, describing existentialism as a response to "the harsh reality of life in Europe during and after World War II." He continues to provide historical context throughout his essay, even pointing out one of existentialism's echoes in late twentieth-century America—the phrase "stop and smell the roses," which revisits the existentialist idea of "consciousness of time present." While existentialism "no longer contributes to contemporary philosophy," an understanding of the twentieth century requires a basic grasp of the concept, and Sapoundjiev offers just that.

The twentieth century was marked by two world wars, the Korean    1
War, the Vietnam War, the Cold War, and many ethnic conflicts.
It seemed at times that humanity was on a path of self-destruction.
Offering a philosophical resolution, a new school of philosophy—
existentialism—arose during the latter half of the twentieth century.
This philosophy echoed the harsh reality of life in Europe during and
after World War II—that human beings are unique individuals isolated in a hostile, indifferent universe. Existentialism's most famous
adherents are Søren Kierkegaard, Karl Jaspers, Martin Heidegger,

Gabriel Marcel, Simone de Beauvoir, and Jean-Paul Sartre, who coined the term *existentialism* to describe his own philosophies. It would be virtually impossible for a brief essay to succinctly summarize the ideas of these philosophers, but there are a few essential ideas for understanding existentialism: (1) existence before essence, (2) the consciousness of time present, and (3) the inevitable freedom of choice and the responsibility that comes with that choice.

The phrase "existence before essence"—the "main premise that all or most existential philosophers seem to agree on" (Dolhenty)—was coined by Jean-Paul Sartre, one of the more prominent figures of existentialism, in his "Existentialism and Humanism." To existentialists, *existence* is the actual "human reality of experience," and *essence* embodies the qualities—reason, justice, and dignity, for example—deemed essential to human beings (Christian 249). To understand this important distinction, one can consider the difference between a robot and a human. The first robots were initially conceived and designed in the minds of scientists and engineers for a special purpose, long before any single robot was produced. In other words, the robot's essence, all the component parts of its structure and operation, came before its existence, its actual manufacture. While this idea is relevant to all created objects, it is not relevant to people because, as Christian remarks, existentialism promotes the idea that people were not projected on a "drawing board" or formed in any mind, divine or otherwise, to attain a special goal, and then created to achieve this goal. Unlike created objects, people create themselves from within (250). Or, stated another way, "You are what *you* make of yourself" (Moore and Bruder 512). And since no two humans create themselves the same way, no two humans are alike. No human has essence until the individual creates who he or she is. That is why existence precedes essence only for people (Christian 250). A robot is ready to take on its repetitive tasks as soon as it is assembled. A person develops human characteristics—for example, trust and love—gradually after birth and goes on to develop more complex characteristics, such as justice and dignity, throughout a lifetime.

Another important existentialist idea is the idea of the consciousness of time present. Being a philosophy of time, existentialism urges us to fully experience life, to live for the moment (Christian 250). We are required to change our routine existence within the present. This change is possible only when we realize that it is up to us to choose how we create consciousness, the self-awareness of who we are as individuals. If we let our consciousness be invaded by moods, recollections, or

2

3

habits from our past, our consciousness determines the meaning of our present. Also, if our consciousness overwhelms us with concerns and expectations about future events, we deprive our present of its uniqueness and suspense. Thus, our "now" can lose its vitality (Christian 250). But we can still recover the intensity of our personal existence; we only need to realize that, as Christian asserts, "we can make decisions as to how we shall live the only thing that, in the final analysis, each of us actually possess—namely, consciousness of time present" (250). The mid-1970s platitude "Stop and smell the flowers" is a pop-culture resurrection of this aspect of existentialism. Instead of photographing the flowers, identifying the species by Latin and common names, noting in one's journal where and when the flowers were discovered—that is, instead of processing the experience to present to others—existentialism asks the individual to truly experience the flowers: to touch them, to smell them, to wander through them, to make the flowers a part of one's own consciousness.

The third idea—that freedom is an attribute of man—is of great importance for understanding existentialism. Free choice and individual responsibility are the distinguishing characteristics of humanity (Stallknecht and Brumbaugh 476). Existentialists do not share the belief of the followers of Spinoza and Kant—that freedom itself is the archachievement of human life. Instead, Jaspers, Heidegger, Sartre, and Marcel argue that people are inevitably free and that, therefore, freedom is not a valuable asset of our life but the state of it. Newton P. Stallknecht and Robert S. Brumbaugh, in *The Spirit of Western Philosophy,* state that people's "inalienable and unavoidable freedom" (477) results in their perceiving that they "cannot choose not to choose" (477). However, and here is an irony, when people recognize freedom as a duty, from which they cannot be discharged, they begin feeling anguish or distress. People may then try to "escape" from freedom and its responsibility by justifying their actions with moral and social criteria established in society (Runkle 124). For example, during the Nuremberg Trials of 1945–1946, a number of Germans being tried for their war crimes attempted to defend themselves by saying they were only following orders when they participated in arresting and killing Jews. But humans are accountable for all their actions and even for their emotions. As Stallknecht and Brumbaugh point out, "for the Existentialist, the man who undertakes to argue himself out of responsibility, who denies his freedom, is deceiving himself and thus, by falsifying his humanity, falling into what Spinoza would describe as human bondage" (482). But the existentialists argue that no matter to what

extent we misinterpret our freedom, we continue to be free and responsible for all other human beings.

Existentialism originated in Europe at a time when people felt    5
alone and could not explain or justify their existence. And while a
number of different schools of existentialism developed (for example,
French, German, Danish, atheistic, and theistic), existentialism never
truly developed as a philosophical movement. But authors such as
Samuel Beckett, Albert Camus, Eugene Ionesco, and Ingmar Bergman
gave voice to existentialism as a literary theme in their works. And
while existentialism's themes remain embedded in the world's litera-
tures, existentialism no longer contributes to contemporary philosophy
(Dolhenty). It does, however, exist to remind us of a time when the
world, despairing, sought answers to its sense of hopelessness.

## WORKS CITED

Christian, James L. *Philosophy: An Introduction to the Art of Wondering.* 4th
  ed. New York: Holt, 1986.
Dolhenty, Dr. Jonathan. "Subject: Re: Existentialism." E-mail to the author.
  15 June 1998.
Moore, Brooke Noel, and Kenneth Bruder. *Philosophy: The Power of Ideas.*
  2nd ed. Mountain View, CA: Mayfield, 1993.
Runkle, Gerald. *Theory and Practice: An Introduction to Philosophy.* New
  York: Holt, 1985.
Stallknecht, Newton P., and Robert S. Brumbaugh. *The Spirit of Western
  Philosophy.* New York: David, 1962.

# How to Survive a Zombie Attack: A Guide for the Living

**Brian Reed**

*Southwest Minnesota State University*
*Marshall, Minnesota*

Long a fan of horror films, Brian Reed says that anytime he can liven up a writing assignment by combining his pet interest with outside-of-the-box thinking, he'll do it. In "How to Survive a Zombie Attack," Reed uses the format of a survival guide to explain zombism, a concept that movies like *Night of the Living Dead* have rooted in our cultural imagination. Of course, zombism is not entirely a Hollywood creation. Zombies are a part of Haitian folklore, and according to one theory, the idea of the zombie may have originated during the Haitian slave uprising of the late 1700s, when voodoo priests used a drug made in part from the toxic puffer fish to debilitate and control slaves who betrayed the cause of the revolution. Perhaps it is no surprise that the concept of zombism has migrated from Haitian folklore to American fiction; after all, wandering—zombielike—from one mind to the next is what concepts do best.

---

It's happened—gruesome, late-night horror flicks have become gruesome, late-night reality. Fiction has become truth, black has become white, and—worst of all—your dearly departed grandmother is gumming at your scalp like a bowl of prunes. That's right: the dead walk the earth.

"How could this happen to me?" you might ask. "I'm a headstrong, obstinate young person; I'm supposed to live forever!" If your first reaction to the crisis is to ask this sort of question, chances are you *will* live forever—as a shambling, reanimated corpse. Zombies won't be interrogated; you had better buckle down and get your head straight if you hope to keep your head at all.

Look around you; let it all sink in. You don't have forever to sit and ponder, but take the time to figure out just what has happened.

You'll come to discover the shocking reality that very strange things are going on. Fires are blazing all around you, thieves are looting hastily abandoned shops, haunted-house monsters are guzzling down human flesh, and you're all alone without a chainsaw. Get over the shock; this is big. You need to know just what these zombies are. And, for that matter, you need to know how to handle your new-found nemeses, what you're going to do, where you're going to do it, and what happens when all of this business blows over.

All right, first things first. What exactly *is* a zombie? Try walking     4
up to one. Is it friendly? You'll find that no, it isn't. Have you tried poking the zombie? You'll find that it is quite dead and, again, very unfriendly. These two bits of information are best summed up by Soren Andersen as "an animate cadaver that has returned from the grave to wreak havoc on the living." He goes on to explain that zombies are limited by the condition in which they were originally slain (such as a missing arm, leg, chunk of torso), as well as that they're driven by the basic need to feed. However, you won't see a zombie at an Arby's; they're thinkin' brains.

OK, so you're up against innumerable hordes of walking, moan-     5
ing, brain-munching corpses—what now? Max Brooks' ground-breaking 2003 tome, *The Zombie Survival Guide,* offers some basics for zombie preparedness:

1. Organize before they rise!
2. They feel no fear; why should you?
3. Use your head: cut off theirs.
4. Blades don't need reloading.
5. Ideal protection = tight clothes, short hair.
6. Get up the staircase, then destroy it.
7. Get out of the car; get onto the bike.
8. Keep moving, keep low, keep quiet, keep alert!
9. No place is safe, only safer.
10. The zombie may be gone, but the threat lives on. (5)

At this point, armed with Brooks' ten commandments of the un-     6
dead, you're in high hopes with a slim chance of making it home for Thursday tea. But since crumpets are of no use against the living dead, you still need to know a little more than the rookie rules. In fact, just how the living dead do, indeed, live is almost inescapably dependent on what movie you happen to hold more stock in. The most widely accepted hypothesis is that "zombism" is caused by a virus. Such viruses are portrayed in films (or documentaries, rather)

such as *Resident Evil* (2002) and *28 Days Later* (2003). And although that theory is touched on in George A. Romero's original *Night of the Living Dead* (1968), the actual cause of zombism in this classic that started it all is stated, "When hell is full, the dead will walk the earth." (If hell was full in 1968, when the movie that brought the threat of zombies to widespread public attention was made, it must be even more crowded by now.)

Now that you know just what you're up against, we need to go    7 over where to escape to and what to bring. Remember the Boy Scout motto: Be Prepared. The same motto applies to flesh-eating monsters. First, you're going to need something to fight with, both for long-range offense and hand-to-hand defense. For long-range attacks, think guns. However, a firearm of *rational* firing rate is recommended—you're not out to make a big mess. Remember: the faster, the bloodier. (If you *are* out to make a mess, this author suggests a chainsaw—although better suited for close-range combat—because it needs no ammunition, only fuel. And as you'll see, gas-station attendants won't necessarily be watching the pumps.) As for shorter ranges, any long or rather blunt object, such as a hammer or a baseball bat, should do the trick. Be sure to pack two or three. Also, it would be to your benefit to practice up on your Whac-a-Mole skills; you'll see why later on.

As for a place to go, movies such as the recently filmed remake    8 *Dawn of the Dead,* directed by Zack Snyder, subtly suggest the large, supply-laden refuge of a shopping mall. However, keeping in mind Soren Andersen's highly respected writings on zombie behavior, we know that zombies retain limited memory; and in our consumer-based populace, a shopping mall is the first place a mass of brainless zombies (not necessarily the undead) would flock, so if you choose this option, beware.

Simply put, bring your weapons and common supplies (food,    9 water, Game Boy, etc.) to a secure place—such as the Statue of Liberty—and, according to an interview with zombologist James McNeese, "always have a back-up escape plan cuz [the zombies are] a little unpredictable."

Weapon in hand and haven on mind, you'll set out. Seems easy,   10 doesn't it? Well, it isn't, so read on. Next, we'll go over the precise reason why only one or two out of a handful of people survive when this sort of thing happens: it isn't in the nature of a zombie to give a warm welcome. Let's face it: zombies don't come toward you with open arms, kiss you on the forehead, and tell you everything's going to be okay. They hobble toward you with outstretched arms, bite you on the forehead, and utter unholy moans into the evening. Chances are you're going to see some of your closest friends and family transmogrified into undead enemies. It's not a comforting thought, but you don't have time to cry. Your job is to make sure these kinds of horrible things don't happen often—even when you're surrounded.

Almost all reputable zombologists agree that destroying the 11 brain or severing the head of a zombie is the only sure way of ridding yourself of said creature. This is where your Whac-a-Mole skills come in handy. Pick up your blunt object and get to work. Don't hesitate, McNeese observes, for "once you're found out, they come in herds." This is quite a sobering thought. Don't let a "scout" zombie alert another—or another twelve. When you're in the open, keep moving, keep smashing; and don't forget that these things are mindless; do not, under any circumstances, attempt to reason with a zombie. You'll find yourself rationalizing toward a brick wall—a brick wall that wants to eat you.

So you've followed this advice and you're still alive. Good work. 12 But your troubles aren't over yet. No vigilante undead warrior in history, fiction or non, has managed to rid the world entirely of the undead. It won't happen. However, sooner or later the sun will rise upon the night of the living dead, and the chaos will subside. This isn't to say that things will go back to normal. No shade of white is perfect. Weeks, months, or even years after Z-Day, you may be shocked to find yourself in a variety of possible situations, including nearly complete human genocide, nuclear winter, or the less extreme prospect of a relatively undistorted civilization, festered, but still growing. Whatever the outcome may be, keep your blunt object handy and be on the lookout for any place containing vital necessities (food, water, batteries, etc.)—if you're lucky, the pandemonium will have emptied a Wal-Mart or two of managerial supervision. Who knows what might happen in the aftermath of the Zombocaust? Just be prepared to begin a new life.

So, you've read through this guide, and now you're ready for the 13 worst. "This could never happen," some might say; "you're wasting your time." Well, when they see casket lids begin to creak open, they'll be coming to you. Follow my advice: get your facts straight, pick up a hammer, get somewhere safe, and ride it out. Don't be left in the dark—the zombies like it there.

# WORKS CITED

*28 Days Later.* Dir. Danny Boyle. Fox Searchlight Pictures, 2003.

Andersen, Soren. "Soren Andersen's Guide to the Movies." *News Tribune* [Tacoma, Washington] 16 Sept. 2005: F33.

Booth, W. "Voodoo Science." *Science* Apr.–May 1988: 4.

Brooks, Max. *The Zombie Survival Guide: Complete Protection from the Living Dead.* New York City: Three Rivers, 2003.

*Dawn of the Dead.* Dir. Zack Snyder. Universal Studios, 2004.

McNeese, James. Personal interview. 26 Oct. 2005.

*Night of the Living Dead.* Dir. George A. Romero. Elite Entertainment, 1968.

*Resident Evil.* Dir. Paul W. S. Anderson. Sony Pictures, 2002.

# *Explaining Opposing Positions* 5

Every day, high-stakes issues fill the air and the Internet and crowd the pages of newspapers and magazines. Most issues we only glance at, while a few may engage us deeply—either because we are curious or because we recognize that the outcome of these issues is important to us personally: Should prayer be permitted in public schools? Should a married woman be required to get her husband's permission to have an abortion? Should search engines like Google or Yahoo release individuals' search records to researchers or businesses? Should phone and cable providers be able to charge Web users differently for different levels of service?

By definition, an issue is unsettled, unresolved. A debate swirls around it. As we read or listen to this debate, we may want to be persuaded to take sides. Often, however, we merely want to understand the debate. We are looking not for an argument on one side but for an impartial explanation of both sides. Adam Hood's essay illustrates this kind of impartial explanatory writing. Hood read two essays that take representative positions in a debate, identified the essays' shared topics, and then used these topics to explain—not to take a position on—the issue. (In chapter 5, we use the word *topic* to refer to a one-time or recurring element in an essay, such as the use of analogy to define an issue, a set of references to moral values that supporters of a position share or should share, or a call to action.)

In chapter 4 you read essays explaining a concept. The essays in chapter 5 explain a debate, relying on many of the same basic features and writers' strategies illustrated in the chapter 4 essays. In chapter 6 you will join the position takers on an issue you care about and take a position yourself, arguing vigorously and responsibly to support it. These three assignments—explaining a concept, explaining opposing positions, and arguing a position—build on one another. Together, they give you a valuable foundation for presenting or taking sides on the issues you will encounter in college and in your career.

Explanations of debates can be informative to readers who want to understand issues of the day. They can also clarify and even help resolve immediate dangers or crises in a business or corporation; inform debate in an elected governing body, like a city council or the United States Senate; or introduce newcomers to an ongoing debate among experts over an important academic discipline, like those from which you choose your college courses. You will encounter these disciplinary debates in your textbooks and other assigned reading, sometimes as an introduction in a chapter in disciplines like sociology, anthropology, cosmology, education, philosophy, botany, geology, aeronautical engineering, or history.

This assignment will increase your confidence as a reader and writer. It will engage you deeply in the debate on one issue, teach you a strategy for analyzing a debate comprehensively, and guide you in presenting the debate in an impartial way to your readers. It is work for any serious, ambitious student to embrace.

Note: This type of writing is new to the eighth edition of *The St. Martin's Guide to Writing*. In this chapter, the single student essay by Adam Hood was written in a class trying out an early version of this chapter. Because we need more essays explaining opposing positions for the next edition of *Sticks and Stones*, we hope you will consider sending us your essay to consider. You will find guidelines for doing so on p. 207.

# File-Sharing: A David and Goliath Debate

## Adam Hood

*University of California, Riverside*
*Riverside, California*

In this essay, Adam Hood explains the debate over Internet file-sharing of published, copyrighted music. As you read, notice how Hood presents the debate and debaters to his readers in paragraphs 1–4 and avoids even a hint of which position he favors. Hood then goes on to explain differences between the two positions in terms of the ethics of file-sharing, definitions of music itself, and consequences of attempting to prevent file-sharing. He ends with a prediction about the future of the debate. No mysteries here—just impartial comparison and contrast of the major, in-common topics he has identified in two opposing positions.

Just six months after eighteen-year-old Shawn "Napster" Fanning created the Internet file-sharing program that would rock the music world, his small start-up company was sued by the Recording Industry Association of America, whose claim was later backed by the United States 9th Circuit Court of Appeals (Ante). From the beginning, the file-sharing debate has been a battle waged between the little guy and the big guy. Both sides see it this way, but in slightly different terms. From the standpoint of those who defend the practice of swapping files, the fight is between the "industry" and the common listener. From the perspective of those who oppose the practice, the fight is between defenders of justice and lawbreakers. 1

The debate also pits the young and the old. According to the Pew Internet & American Life Project, it is young adults and full-time students who are among the most likely to download or share files—and the least likely to say they care about copyright. And it is college administrators and professors who have ended up joining forces with the courts and the music industry to control these file-sharing upstarts. 2

Enter Matthew Scrivner, a little guy (DOB 1976), and Graham    3
Spanier and Cary H. Sherman, big guys (and graybeards). Scrivner,
author of "In Defense of Music Downloading: Why Internet File-
Sharing Is Necessary for the Survival of Music," does tech support by
day and spends the rest of his time "hanging out"—reading, listening
to music, watching movies, and playing Dungeons and Dragons—by
his own account. Spanier and Sherman, coauthors of "Thou Shalt
Not Pirate Thy Neighbor's Songs," are presidents: Spanier of Penn
State University and Sherman of the Recording Industry Association
of America.

The little/big, young/old split is not just a surface divide—it    4
also extends to argumentative styles, if Scrivner's "In Defense" and
Spanier and Sherman's "Thou Shalt Not" can be taken as representative approaches to either side of the debate. Scrivner argues as an underdog would, wrestling every point to the ground and seeming to
make himself breathless with the effort to get his points across.
Spanier and Sherman, on the other hand, argue from the secure van-
tage point of righteousness: They devote more time to convincing
their audience of university professors and administrators to take action against file-sharing on campus, and to showing them how, than
to arguing explicitly against file-sharing. Much of their argument is
implicit.

Whether file-sharing is unethical is central to the debate. Both    5
Spanier and Sherman on the one hand and Scrivner on the other acknowledge the question's importance by addressing it right away,
with Spanier and Sherman saying essentially, "of course it's unethical," and Scrivner protesting, "not so fast." Spanier and Sherman
treat the question with cool confidence in their first paragraph, asserting that there has lately been "a new level of clarity"—the impli-
cation is moral clarity—on the issue of file-sharing. They present
their case evenly and without embellishment: Thanks to a new (June
2005) ruling from that ultimate arbiter of ethics, the Supreme Court,
the "message" on file-sharing is now more "straightforward" than
ever: file-sharing is "wrong," plain and simple (para. 1).

Recognizing that the appeal to ethics is one of his opponent's    6
strongest hands, Scrivner sets it up and knocks it down right away.
His first two sentences get right to the point: "The record industry is
lying to you. At the 46th Grammy Awards this month they an-
nounced a new initiative that would promote an 'ethical viewpoint
about music downloading'" (para. 1). Notice how Scrivner locates
the ethical stance not in the ruling of the highest court in the land, as

Spanier and Sherman do, but instead in the mouth of the record industry, where the "message" suddenly seems nothing other than a public relations line. With this tactic, and by relating the industry to concepts such as "power" and "control" and pitting it against the average music listener ("you"), Scrivner manages to portray the music industry as a control-hungry behemoth with questionable motives. We would do well to have a healthy suspicion of its message, Scrivner seems to be saying.

With the underdog's typical all-out effort, Scrivner sweats to establish a definition of music, stringing example to example and scenario to scenario in an attempt to communicate that music is just information, that tunes are just memes—germs of "intellectual infection," as he puts it, passing through networks of people. Gathering momentum, he asks:  7

> A hundred years ago, if I heard a song at church, and rode my horse home and found myself humming it, I was stealing? And fifty years ago, if I heard a song on the radio, and it was so catchy that I found myself singing it out loud later on while I cooked dinner, I committed theft? And ten years ago, when I waited hours for the top 40 count down to play that one song just so I could tape it to cassette for my girlfriend, I was taking something that wasn't mine? (para. 6)

In establishing his definition of music (both here and elsewhere), Scrivner keeps the focus on the listener, and avoids mentioning those behind the music—composers, songwriters, singers—thus skirting the question of creative authorship.

Spanier and Sherman also avoid addressing the question of creative authorship. Instead, they assume that the question of creative authorship has already been settled. When they assert that "Stealing intellectual property is wrong" (para. 1), they assume that readers have already equated music with intellectual property. When they speak of the necessity of fostering "an environment that respects all creative work" (para. 6), they assume readers already think of music as a form of creative work. They acknowledge no other viewpoints. Like soft-spoken lecturers who hold sway over their students by sheer self-possession, Spanier and Sherman quietly bully their readers into sharing their definition of music.  8

When it comes to the consequences of cracking down on file-sharing, Scrivner becomes a doomsayer: "[Music] cannot be contained or controlled. Doing so, kills it, and leaves us in nothing but silence" (para. 7). Spanier and Sherman meanwhile frame  9 crackdowns at individual colleges as a way for university professors and administrators—their readers—to protect creative environments like their own by protecting copyright: "[Fostering disdain for copyright protection] is unacceptable in any instance but should be particularly disturbing at colleges and universities, where creators and inventors thrive" (para. 6).

It is telling that the debaters seem to drop out of conversation with one another here, with Scrivner focused on the future of music—the "future of sound," he says—and Spanier and Sherman more concerned about the future of copyright. In the end, the file-sharing debate won't be resolved until each side acknowledges what matters most to the other. Maybe then both sides will stop overcompensating with prophecies of the end of the world as we know it. 10

## WORKS CITED

Ante, Spencer E. "Shawn Fanning." *Business Week* 15 May 2000. 3 Sept. 2006 <http://www.businessweek.com/2000/00_20/b3681054.htm>.

Madden, Mary, and Amanda Lenhart. "Music Downloading, File-Sharing and Copyright: A Pew Internet Project Data Memo." 31 July 2003. *Pew Internet & American Life Project.* 3 Sept. 2006 <http://www.pewinternet.org/PPF/r/96/report_display.asp>.

Scrivner, Matthew. "In Defense of Music Downloading: Why Internet File-Sharing Is Necessary for the Survival of Music." *2 Walls Webzine* 15 Feb. 2004. 2 Sept. 2006 <http://www.2walls.com/Music/defense_of_downloading.asp>.

Spanier, Graham, and Cary H. Sherman. "Thou Shalt Not Pirate Thy Neighbor's Songs." *Chronicle of Higher Education* 2 Dec. 2005. 2 Sept. 2006 <http://chronicle.com/weekly/v52/i15/15b02401.htm>.

# *Arguing a Position* 6

When you think of your last argument, you probably remember a disagreeable squabble with family, friends, or coworkers; or a television screen full of politicians and commentators waving well-manicured hands and throwing verbal barbs. But reasoned—rather than reactive—argument is something else altogether. Reasoned argument is more thoughtful, less melodramatic, and in fact enjoyable and challenging. In writing a reasoned argument, you choose and support a position on an issue while anticipating other positions, accommodating those you find plausible, and refuting those you find flawed or weak. Reasoned argument is always addressed to particular readers—Thomas Beckfield addresses drivers, appealing especially to those who encounter preoccupied cell phone users in heavy traffic, while Keely Cutts addresses the hunters and ranchers who oppose the gray wolf reintroduction she supports. Whomever you address, you can assume, like our student writers, that they are an audience of informed, intelligent readers who can understand and empathize with a reasonable, informed argument that challenges their thinking without ridiculing their values and beliefs.

More effective than the ranting of some TV commentators, reasoned argument has the potential to convince an audience to take your point of view seriously. This achievement makes you a more active participant in American life and culture. And isn't that what all sides of an argument want? Taking part in the conversation that sustains our diverse, contentious democracy is your fundamental right and opportunity. Inserting your views into the debates that swirl around contested issues is one of the most valuable and satisfying contributions an educated person can make.

Reasoned argument fosters change and makes you an active participant in the world your college classes are preparing you for. As you gain knowledge of your issue, you will move beyond what you have always thought about it, expanding your perspective in order to understand its advantages, drawbacks, and ambiguities.

The student writers in this chapter use facts, statistics, process narration, and personal anecdotes to present their arguments. Jennifer Moore portrays the land and fragile beauty of the Arctic National Wildlife Refuge in order to insist that drilling would threaten the ecosystem and the indigenous Americans and animals that inhabit it. In an essay cleverly titled "Always Low Standards, Always," Matt Sulentic employs statistics and reports of gender and racial discrimination to attempt to convince readers that Wal-Mart exploits its workers. Alex Carstensen's essay challenges readers to think rationally— rather than just emotionally—about same-sex marriage.

When you have strong feelings about an issue, it is easy to overlook or dismiss positions different from your own. In reasoned argument, however, you demonstrate that it is possible to respect those who hold different views, even if every cell of your being aches to rebuke and change them. In both using well-supported reasons to justify your position and thoughtfully considering opposing positions and your readers' likely questions or objections, you stand forth confidently as an informed and responsible citizen.

Arguing a position forces you to overcome complacency or indifference in order to influence your fellow citizens' thinking. Writing an argument may surprise you by making you question your own beliefs and assumptions, but this uncomfortable confrontation will expand the boundaries of your thinking and communicating. Stepping out of the status quo, you gain a productive, public voice and a larger role in the complicated and shifting world. So take a position. Study the issue. Consider likely differences between you and your readers. Speak out reasonably. Your fellow citizens are waiting to hear from you.

# Banning Cell Phone Use While Driving

**Thomas Beckfield**

*Mt. San Jacinto College, Menifee Valley*
*Menifee, California*

"Study after study concludes similarly: it is the talking, the cognitive distraction of conversation, that leads to accidents, not the dialing," writes Thomas Beckfield, challenging the cellular industry's claim that more public safety training, not a ban on cell phone use while driving, will resolve the problem of cell-phone-related accidents. With supporting evidence that demonstrates that talking on the phone while driving limits field of vision and affects focus — whether or not a hands-free device is used — Beckfield argues for turning cell phones off before turning vehicles on. After reading this essay, you may think twice about heading out of the garage or parking lot while talking on your own cellular device or about riding with a friend who is on the phone while driving.

---

On February 4, 2002, a driver of a Ford Explorer lost control of his vehicle while commuting on a Washington highway and hurtled over a guardrail into oncoming traffic. The driver of the SUV and four unsuspecting passengers in the minivan with which it collided were killed ("Car Accident"). Until this accident, federal investigators with the National Transportation Safety Board (NTSB) had never "identified use of a cell phone as a possible factor" in a fatal automobile crash ("Car Accident").

Most of us, as either a driver or a passenger, have been behind someone who is driving erratically as he or she tries to use a cell phone. Living in Los Angeles, I have seen countless drivers dangerously weave and zigzag in and out of traffic, fight to stay in their lane, and almost lose control of their vehicles as they talk on their cell phones. Such recklessness can be terribly scary, made all the more sobering by the sight of a young child or infant seated in the back of the wayward vehicle. With many lives put at risk each day by drivers who disregard their own safety and the safety of others, cell phone use while driving a vehicle should be banned.

Exactly how dangerous is it to use a cell phone while driving? Opinions differ. On the one hand, safety advocates insist that cell phone use in cars should be banned completely. A California Highway Patrol report found that "[s]ome 4,700 accidents in 2001 could be traced to cell phone use while driving.... Of those accidents, 31 people died and nearly 2,800 people were hurt" (Bell). Federal investigator Dave Rayburn, the NTSB agent in charge of the February 4, 2002, case, reported, "Some of the issues we are looking at are the fact that the (Explorer) crossed the median and overrode the barrier. The other is cell phone use. Witnesses said the victim was on a phone conversation two or three minutes at the time of the crash" ("Car Accident"). 3

Ever since cell phones became a part of our national culture in the 1990s, scientists and researchers have debated their impact on driving. The most notable research to date was a 1997 study published in the *New England Journal of Medicine*. The study found, in part, that cell phone users were four times more likely to have an accident than those same drivers when they were not using their phones. To clearly convey the findings' seriousness, Redelmeier and Tibshirani, the study's authors, equated the increase to "driving with a blood alcohol level at the legal limit" (456).[1] Redelmeier and Tibshirani also noted that personal characteristics, such as age and driving experience, did not have a significant "protective effect" against the dangers of cell phone use while driving (455). In short, the study provided significant evidence that the driving skills of different groups of people are seriously affected when using a cell phone while behind the wheel of a car. 4

Other studies have also linked cell phone use to poor driving or increased accident rates. Researchers at the University of Rhode Island (URI)—Manbir Sodhi, professor of industrial engineering, and Jerry Cohen, professor of psychology—demonstrated a correlation between cell phone use while driving and reduced field of view. Funded in part by the URI Transportation Center, the researchers chose to concentrate on a specific attribute to measure one's driving skill: the breadth of the visual field to which the driver is paying attention. The subjects in Sodhi and Cohen's experiment wore a head-mounted tracking device that recorded—approximately fifty times per second—where the drivers' eyes were focused (McLeish). 5

Sodhi and Cohen concluded that a considerable decrease in driver alertness occurred when the participants conducted cognitive 6 tasks, such as remembering a list of items, calculating math in one's head, or using a cell phone, while driving (McLeish). The URI researchers discovered another interesting finding: tunnel vision caused by cell phone use continues well after the conversation ends. This dangerous occurrence while driving probably occurs because drivers are still thinking about the conversation they just completed on their cell phone (McLeish). Their minds are simply not focused on their driving environment.

While proponents for the cellular industry recognize and acknowledge the relationship between cell phone use and accidents, they believe banning cell phone use while driving to be zealous, that problems associated with driving and cell phone use may be easily corrected with education and training. In 1997, the Cellular Telecommunications Industry Association committed nearly $15 million to educate their customers on using cell phones safely while driving (Koffler). With public service announcements, television commercials, and radio spots, the campaign advocated the use of hands-free devices, such as headphones, earpieces, and voice-activated dialers, as well as common sense when using a cell phone while driving (Koffler). Yet study after study concludes similarly: it is the talking, the cognitive distraction of conversation, that leads to accidents, not the dialing. 7

If we do not change the laws regarding the use of cell phones while driving, countless lives will inevitably be put at risk. In an interview with the *Washington Post*, NTSB spokesman Ted Lopatkiewicz commented, "We expect down the road to investigate more crashes involving cell phones as they come up" (qtd. in "Car Accident"). And while the cellular industry lobby is still advocating the freedom to use a cell phone as an American right, when one's cell phone call made while driving causes another's injury, some restrictions on freedom are warranted. 8

# NOTE

1.   In a survey conducted by InsightExpress, 23 percent of respondents believed that using a cell phone while driving was as dangerous as driving drunk. While 70 percent believed that using a cell phone while driving was dangerous, 61 percent disagreed with proposed legislation to ban cell phone use while driving, and 54 percent disagreed with the idea that cell phone use while driving should be regulated by the government ("Don't Ban").

# WORKS CITED

Bell, Rick. "Time for Drivers with Cell Phones to Hang Up." *San Diego Business Journal* 18 Nov. 2002: 38.

"Car Accident May Be Blamed on Phone." *CBS News.com*. 2002. Columbia Broadcasting System. 24 Mar. 2003 <http://www.cbsnews.com/stories/2002/02/04/national/main328089.shtml>.

"Don't Ban Dialing Drivers." *Fairfield Country Business Journal* 16 Oct. 2000: 11. *MasterFILE Premier*. EBSCO. Mt. San Jacinto College Lib. 24 Mar. 2003 <http://epnet.com>.

Koffler, Keith. "Outside Influences: Speed Bumps for Cell Phones." *Congress-Daily AM* 21 June 2000: 12. *MasterFILE Premier*. EBSCO. Mt. San Jacinto College Lib. 24 Mar. 2003 <http://epnet.com>.

McLeish, Todd. "URI Study on Cell Phone Use Attracts National Attention." *The University Pacer* Sept. 2002. 24 Mar. 2003 <http://advance.uri.edu/pacer/september2002/story2.htm>.

Redelmeier, Donald A., M.D., and Robert J. Tibshirani, Ph.D. "Association between Cellular-Telephone Calls and Motor Vehicle Collisions." *New England Journal of Medicine* 336.7 (1997): 453–58.

# Always Low Standards, Always

**Matt Sulentic**

*Hawkeye Community College*
*Waterloo, Iowa*

Wal-Mart has been the butt of jokes and the subject of criticism for its low wages and its tendency to outshine small, locally owned stores. Nevertheless, it remains a magnet for thrifty shoppers, including cost-conscious college students like Matt Sulentic. Knowing Wal-Mart's benefits from personal experience, Sulentic decided to investigate the claims against the store. What he found changed his shopping habits and reinforced his decision to major in journalism.

"Writing this paper was not an easy task," says Sulentic, who settled on his topic after abandoning another that proved too broad. Having overheard news reports about Wal-Mart's questionable business practices, Sulentic set out "to see if this was just the media blowing things out of proportion or if it was true." He discovered that many of the media's criticisms were well-founded: "I came across startling quotes, facts and figures, and some real-life experiences that made Wal-Mart sound as dirty as their stores," he says. "While writing the paper was time consuming and required effort, it was the first time that I ever had fun while writing a research paper. This was because of what I learned about the issue."

Does the student author ever shop at Wal-Mart today? "I quit shopping there," he says. "Now I usually shop for groceries at Hy-Vee, Fareway, or Target."

---

The name Wal-Mart generates one of two emotions in people: love    1
or hate. Whether you love or hate the store, there is no denying it is a retail giant, with sales of more than $300 billion annually (Drutman). At the heart of Wal-Mart's success is the store's ability to deliver on its promise of "always low prices." But these low prices come at a cost. To keep expenses low, Wal-Mart underpays its employees, stifles attempts at unionization, and exploits overseas workers.

Wal-Mart is currently the largest employer in the nation, employing about one million people in three thousand stores (Peterson 20). In this respect, Wal-Mart seems very positive, providing many with jobs. However, when one looks at the way Wal-Mart treats job takers, the picture isn't so cheerful. Full-time Wal-Mart employees make an average of $9.68 per hour, and at thirty-five hours per week, that comes to an annual salary of $17,600 (Greenhouse). The poverty line for a family of four is $19,157 (Greenhouse). One of Wal-Mart's leading competitors, Costco, pays $16 per hour on average, 65 percent more than the average wage at Wal-Mart (Greenhouse). 2

Not only does Costco pay higher average wages, but it also offers superior heath insurance. At Costco, 82 percent of workers are covered by company health insurance. By contrast, Wal-Mart only insures 48 percent of its employees (Greenhouse). Susan Chambers, Wal-Mart's executive vice president for benefits, said about 46 percent of employees' children are either uninsured or on Medicaid (Halkias). For those without company insurance, the low wages make it difficult to pay for insurance out of their own pockets. LaTasha Barker, a single mother and a cashier at a Wal-Mart in Illinois, said she earned so little she could not afford family health insurance at $1,860 a year (Greenhouse). 3

To keep wages and benefits from improving, Wal-Mart keeps a watchful eye on employees' attempts at unionization. According to *Canadian Business and Current Affairs,* a Wal-Mart store in Jonquiere, Quebec, Canada, was under surveillance to prevent unionization. One former security guard said that he patrolled the store in civilian clothes, watching employees who were sympathetic to the union drive. Under the Quebec labor code, spying on union leaders or sympathizers is illegal ("Wal-Mart"). 4

In April 2005, the Wal-Mart in Jonquiere closed (Austin). Wal-Mart Canada claims the store was closed for economic reasons, but Quebec's board of labor relations feels Wal-Mart had other motives (Austin). Before the store's closing, two hundred Wal-Mart workers had just received union accreditation but did not have time to sign a collective agreement before losing their jobs ("Wal-Mart"). To take the issue further, the labor relations board pointed out that Wal-Mart had made no effort to find another tenant to assume the store's lease, nor had the building been sold or demolished (Austin). This indicated to the board that the store's closing was not permanent, and thus the dismissal of its workers was found to be illegal under Quebec law (Austin). 5

*(margin annotations: stats; compare / contrast; anecdote / ex; anecdote)*

In addition to paying low wages and suppressing efforts to   6
unionize, Wal-Mart is also accused of sex discrimination. In 2000,
Betty Dukes became the lead plaintiff in a suit "filed on behalf of
1.6 million current and past women workers" (DiNovella). The
members of the class-action suit bought strong evidence against Wal-
Mart. For example, payroll data shows that Wal-Mart pays female
employees "an average of 5 percent less than men in comparable
jobs" (Ramey). The retail giant also routinely denies women promotion and training opportunities. Although nearly 70 percent of Wal-
Mart's hourly employees are women, "only one-third [are] salaried
managers" (DiNovella). In her book *Selling Women Short: The Land-
mark Battle for Worker's Rights at Wal-Mart,* Liza Featherstone presents a litany of stories from Wal-Mart's female employees. The
women's stories cover everything from "business meetings at Hoot-
ers restaurants" to being denied "a skills assessment test, which provides vital data for future promotion," because there weren't enough
copies (DiNovella). The court ruled in favor of the women, but
Wal-Mart is appealing the ruling.

While female employees struggle for equal treatment in the   7
United States, Wal-Mart employees overseas are also fed up with the
exploitation they have endured. On September 13, 2005, a class-
action lawsuit was filed by an American labor rights group on behalf of
employees in foreign countries (Barbaro). The suit claims that suppli-
ers in five countries violated workers' rights, denying them a minimum
wage, requiring overtime, and punishing union activity (Barbaro). Liza
Featherstone writes that "at least 85 percent of Wal-Mart products are
made overseas, most of those in China, under sweatshop conditions,
by workers, mostly women, who lack the right to organize" (qtd. in
DiNovella). Wal-Mart has also faced allegations of child labor in foreign factories. Former Wal-Mart CEO David Glass responded in a
*Dateline NBC* interview by saying, "You and I might, perhaps, define   *authority*
children differently" (qtd. in Drutman). Glass continued, saying that
since Asians are quite short, you can't always tell how old they are.

With its many shortcomings, one may wonder why Wal-Mart   8
continues to prosper. The answer lies in the appeal of Wal-Mart's low
prices. A study conducted by Global Insight Inc. found that savings
amounted to $895 per person in 2004 (Halkias). The presence of
Wal-Mart in a community also keeps the competition in check. In
2004, consumers paid just 4 percent over the cost of the items
(Halkias). But while Wal-Mart may keep competitors in check, it does
so by spreading its policy of poor employee treatment. In order to

maintain low prices, "grocery stores across the country are mimicking Wal-Mart's low wages and skimpy benefits" (DiNovella).

Wal-Mart continues to hide behind the yellow smiley face, masking bad business practices by cutting prices. Wal-Mart's critics suggest that the retailer is quite capable of increasing both employee wages and benefits. Spending just $3.50 per hour more on wages and benefits for full-time employees would cost the company $6.5 billion, which is only about 3 percent of its annual sales (Greenhouse). But for Wal-Mart, profit comes before the needs of employees. Thus, foreign labor is still exploited, and domestic workers continue to be underpaid. As Wal-Mart satisfies its need to roll back prices, unfortunately, wages and business practices will roll back with them.

*[margin annotations: "9"; "speculates about future"]*

# WORKS CITED

Austin, Ian. "Quebec Rules against Wal-Mart in Closing of Unionized Store." *New York Times,* 19 Sept. 2005: C7. Lexis-Nexis. 2 Feb. 2006 <http://web.lexisnexis.com>.

Barbaro, Michael. "Suit Targets Wal-Mart's Overseas Operations." *Washington Post* 14 Sept. 2005: D06.

DiNovella, Elizabeth. "The True Cost of Low Prices." *Progressive* 69.1 (2005): 44-46. *Academic Search Premier.* EBSCO 31 Jan. 2006 <http://search.epnet.com>.

Drutman, Lee. "Wal-Mart Is a Little Good, a Little Bad." *Deseret News* 28 Aug. 2005.

Greenhouse, Steven. "Can't Wal-Mart, a Retail Behemoth, Pay More?" *New York Times* 4 May 2005. *International Labor Rights Fund.* 19 Nov. 2005 <http://www.laborrights.org/press/Wal-Mart/walmart_pay_0505.htm>.

Halkias, Maria. "Retail Giant's Impact Mixed." *Dallas Morning News* 5 Nov. 2005.

Peterson, Eric. "Wal-Mart's Fans and Foes: Towns May Be Ready or Not for Retail Giant." *ColoradoBiz* 1 Nov. 2002: 18–22.

Ramey, Joanna. "Wal-Mart Disputes Class-Action Filing." *Women's Wear Daily* 190.28 (2005): 16. *Business Source Premier.* EBSCO. 31 Jan. 2006 <http://search.epnet.com>.

"Wal-Mart Hired Security Guards to Spy on Sympathizers in Quebec." *Canadian Business and Current Affairs.* 2 Dec. 2005. Lexis-Nexis. Canada Press Newswire. <http://web.lexisnexis.com>.

# Wolves in Yellowstone

## Keely Cutts

### The Catholic University of America
### Washington, D.C.

As usual, conservation and commerce are at loggerheads—this time over the reintroduction of gray wolves into Yellowstone National Park. In this essay, Keely Cutts takes conservation's side, offering both a moral argument for reintroduction (since we humans killed the original Yellowstone wolves, we should take responsibility for restoring the endangered species to its habitat) and a practical one (a wolf reintroduction will improve the park's ecology). But she is careful to consider the concerns of hunters and ranchers, too. She raises and responds to their objections in a tone that is neither aggressive nor dismissive, and she builds bridges between the two sides, both acknowledging that her opponents share her concern for the park's ecology and making clear that she cares about the economic security of states and ranchers. As you read, notice the words and phrases Cutts uses to calm rather than inflame—such as those she uses to describe her opponents' emotions.

———————

Yellowstone National Park, part of the states of Wyoming, Montana,     1
and Idaho, is the center of a controversial issue. From the park's
founding in 1872 until the 1920s, the gray wolf was an integral part
of Yellowstone ecology. By 1926, however, the U.S. government
had successfully eliminated all the wolves in the park. Now legislation
has been proposed to reintroduce the wolf to Yellowstone. The legislation would allow for a limited reintroduction of several packs of the
Canadian gray wolf, which is very much like the wolf that was part of
Yellowstone's original environment. The total number of wolves is
not to exceed one hundred. There is a fierce debate about this reintroduction, but once one scrutinizes its advantages and disadvan-
tages, there is little reason to continue questioning the benefits of
returning gray wolves to Yellowstone National Park.

One of the most compelling reasons for the return of the wolf to  2
Yellowstone is that human intervention led to the wolf's disappearance. Since human beings created the ecological void, we have a responsibility to return the endangered animal to its original habitat.
As a member of the federal government's endangered species list for
twenty-four years, the gray wolf is the only endangered or threatened
animal indigenous to Yellowstone not to have its own recovery program (Gallagher 39). Wolves were an integral part of the wilderness
of the area now known as Yellowstone National Park for nearly two
million years before the United States government sanctioned the
program to eradicate the wolf population in the lower forty-eight
states (Begley and Williams). Since 1926, when the last pair of indigenous gray wolves in the Yellowstone area was killed, the animal
has not been seen in its ancestral home (Plummer and Shaw 105).
Without the human intervention that resulted from hundreds of
years of misconceptions and biases, it is unlikely that wolves would
have disappeared from Yellowstone.

Another reason it is important to return the gray wolf to Yellow-  3
stone is the ecological imbalance caused by the wolf's disappearance.
While many people near Yellowstone fear that the introduction of a
new set of Canadian gray wolves will create an imbalance in the park's
ecosystem, the truth is that their presence will actually improve the
park environment (Gallagher 37). In Yellowstone, the wolf serves as a
keystone species that maintains diversity and balance in the local
ecosystem (Savage and Campbell 76). According to biologists, without
wolves to prey on the many elk, bison, and deer, the populations of
those groups have expanded to such numbers that they are overgrazing, and many die every winter from lack of food (Begley and
Williams). Similarly, coyotes in Yellowstone have increased dramatically because of a lack of competition from wolves. As a result, the now
prosperous coyotes have decimated the local rodent population, eating
an estimated one-third of all ground squirrels and two-thirds of voles
(Savage and Campbell 72). Returning wolves to Yellowstone will help
keep both smaller predators—like coyotes—and larger animals, such
as deer, elk, moose, and bighorn sheep, in balance and will also remove
old and ill animals from the herds to create a healthier gene pool.

In addition to restoring balance to Yellowstone's animal popula-  4
tions, the reintroduction of wolves should have a positive effect on
the local flora. Since the disappearance of wolves, many plant species
have suffered from the overgrazing caused by increased herd sizes.
The cottonwood serves as one example. After wolves were removed

from the park in the 1920s, elk herds could "browse deciduous woody species unhampered by predation risk" (Beschta 401). This excessive grazing has prevented the reproduction of new cottonwood trees, and over time, it is expected that cottonwoods will no longer exist in portions of Yellowstone's northern range (Beschta 402). A wolf reintroduction would naturally reduce the herd sizes of grazing animals, giving the cottonwood and the rest of the local flora a chance to reestablish themselves.

Opponents to the reintroduction argue that the reduction of herd sizes will have negative effects. Many fear the drop in game will result in less profit from hunting licenses, meaning less revenue for the surrounding states ("NRA"). It is more likely that with the projected one hundred wolves reintroduced into the park, the elk population in particular would drop from 3,329 to 3,165, a difference of only 164 animals (Williamson 58). The wolf predation should only involve the older and weaker of the herds, benefiting the herd population as a whole. The fear that the elk, bison, and deer populations would disappear with the return of the wolves to the park seems to be unfounded. Renee Askins, wolf advocate and founder of the Wolf Fund, notes, "the only time that [I] can recall when one animal did in another with such a vengeance was the great turn-of-the-century wolf hunts" (qtd. in Dawidoff 44).

Because Yellowstone is a natural habitat for wolves, and since other areas in the United States where wolves can be found are few, the return of the gray wolf to the park is essential. A total of only 1,250 gray wolves can be found in the states of Minnesota, Wisconsin, and Michigan. The introduction of Canadian gray wolves to the park could significantly change the status of the endangered animal (Begley and Williams). In the event that some new disease should strike the wolf population in the contiguous United States, it is entirely possible that the only remaining wolves in the country would be found in Alaska (Begley and Williams). Opponents to the reintroduction argue that in Alaska there is a gray wolf population of nearly five thousand and there is therefore no need to expand gray-wolf territory. Those wolves, however, are for the most part cut off from the lower forty-eight states, and even that territory is dwindling, as people continue to develop more and more of Alaska (Begley and Williams). Yellowstone, with 2.2 million acres, or 3,472 square miles (larger than the states of Delaware and Rhode Island combined), would provide the wolves sufficient area to increase and thrive, without infringing on animals outside the park.

The most explosive and emotional aspect of reintroducing    7
wolves to Yellowstone involves the wolves' impact on the lifestyle
and livelihood of people living near the park. Hunters and officials of
surrounding state governments have their concerns, and ranchers
who make a living herding cattle have fears for their livestock. Each
of these issues causes anxiety for all involved, but even with these
concerns, the return of the gray wolf to Yellowstone is still the best
option.

Hunters believe reintroducing the wolves will reduce the popula-    8
tions of the elk, deer, and bison to such low levels that they will not
be able to be hunted. The hunters further believe that because of the
gray wolf's status on the endangered species list, hunters will be unable to hunt the predator as they would a non-endangered predator
under similar circumstances (Williamson 58). Their concerns seem
groundless, for as I mentioned earlier, there is a minimal projected
drop in herd populations; and in other wolf-populated areas, wolves
contribute to only 6 percent of big-game deaths. In addition, once
the wolf population is established, some licenses might be granted
for wolf hunting (Gallagher 41).

People are also concerned with how the reintroduction of wolves    9
will affect those states adjacent to the park, since some states depend
on revenues from hunting licenses. With the reintroduction, the U.S.
Fish and Wildlife Service would require the states around the park to
survey the populations of elk, deer, and bison for two years without
providing funding, and many feel the extra costs would detract from
other wildlife programs already run by the states ("NRA"). While
these concerns are valid, the small projected decrease in game populations would be unlikely to significantly decrease the demand for
hunting licenses, and the nonsubsidized survey would only be required for two years. Most states already conduct these surveys and
would only need to conduct them earlier than they otherwise might.

Objections from ranchers near Yellowstone pose a more serious    10
obstacle to reintroducing gray wolves into the park. Many ranchers
believe the wolves pose a threat of tremendous financial losses. Jim
Magagna says about the situation, "We can lose animals to bears,
eagles, coyotes—and now they want to add one more factor. There
are a few old-timers left who can tell you harrowing tales of wolves"
(qtd. in Satchell). Most ranchers hate the wolf passionately, express-
ing their feelings in comments like, "Why not invite the Mafia to
move in next door?" (Plummer and Shaw 104). This hatred stems
mostly from folklore about the damage caused by the original gray

wolves of Yellowstone before their eradication more than seventy years ago.

The truth is that none of the 392 land allotments for grazing    11 surrounding Yellowstone are directly linked to the park. Wolves rarely attack and kill livestock, except in the absence of their normal prey ("Local Heroes"). The numbers of cattle lost to wolf predation in Minnesota and Montana are one in every 8,000 and one in every 25,000, respectively. In the case that ranchers do have problems with wolves, a wildlife support group, Defenders of Wildlife, is developing a fund to help cover the costs of farmers and ranchers who lose money due to wolf attacks (Skow 13).

Finally, the fear of those surrounding the park that wolves will    12 attack people should not keep the wolves out of Yellowstone. In modern history, there has never been an unprovoked attack on a person by a non-rabid wolf: in the ninety-seven-year history of the wolf in the Algonquin National Forest in Canada, "[o]nly one person has been injured by a wolf—a little girl who shone a flashlight in a wolf's eye and was scratched" (Plummer and Shaw 105–06).

The controversial reintroduction of the gray wolf into Yellowstone    13 is more than just the return of a native animal to its original habitat; it will also involve overcoming misconceptions and releasing the wolf from its mythology (Askins 17). But while people's fears color their perceptions toward the reintroduction, the return of the wolf to the park will help create the environment that existed in 1872, when 2.2 million acres of land was declared Yellowstone National Park.

## WORKS CITED

Askins, Renee. "Releasing Wolves from Symbolism: Congressional Testimony." *Harper's* Apr. 1995: 15–17.

Begley, Sharon, and Elisa Williams. "Crying Wolf in Yellowstone." *Newsweek* 16 Dec. 1985: 74.

Beschta, Robert L. "Reduced Cottonwood Recruitment Following Extirpation of Wolves in Yellowstone's Northern Range." *Ecology* Feb. 2005: 391–403.

Dawidoff, Nicholas. "One for the Wolves." *Audubon* July 1992: 38–45.

Gallagher, Winifred. "Return of the Wild." *Mother Earth News* Sept. 1990: 34–41.

"Local Heroes." *Good Housekeeping* July 1993: 51.

"NRA Questions the Costs of Wolf Reintroduction." *American Hunter* Nov. 1994: 14.

Plummer, William, and Bill Shaw. "Yellowstone's Neighbors Are Howling Mad over a Plan to Return Wolves to the Park." *People Weekly* 24 Sept. 1990: 104–6.

Satchell, Michael. "The New Call of the Wild." *U.S. News and World Report* 29 Oct. 1990: 29.

Savage, Candace, and William Campbell. "The Ripple Effect." *Canadian Geographic* Sept.–Oct. 2003: 68–76.

Skow, John. "The Brawl of the Wild." *Time* 6 Nov. 1989: 13–16.

Williamson, Lonnie. "The Big Bad Wolf?" *Outdoor Life* Nov. 1992: 57–58.

# *Sharing Something Better*

## Jennifer Moore

*Clark State Community College*
*Springfield, Ohio*

Jennifer Moore simply wanted to "write a paper good enough to get [her] an A" when she began to investigate her topic, the "strikingly beautiful Alaskan preserve" known as the Arctic National Wildlife Refuge, or ANWR. But, she says, "As I researched both sides of the ANWR argument, I began to develop a strong opinion on the issue. The reasoning of those supporting conservation seemed strong, and I enjoyed presenting their arguments and pointing out some of the problems drilling posed." Moore decided to argue her position by focusing on three problems associated with drilling in the refuge: the threat to wildlife and the environment, the financial cost, and the perpetuation of the false hope that ANWR would be a permanent solution to the country's energy crisis.

The title of Moore's essay refers to the "something better" that connects us as Americans — not the prices at the pump, but our belief in America's future, which in Moore's mind translates to a commitment to preserve the country's beautiful spaces for generations to come. If you don't agree with Moore's position, perhaps you share her belief in the importance of guarding our future. In fact, you might be inspired to present the other side of this issue from that very premise, arguing that it is only by relying on domestic energy sources like ANWR that we can protect future generations.

---

The United States of America has frequently been called "the Great 1
Melting Pot" for its successful mingling of people of different races, nationalities, and backgrounds. Not surprisingly, America's diversity also means a diversity of concerns, viewpoints, and priorities. But at least one concern reaches beyond the boundaries of culture and philosophy, pushing itself rudely into the life and pocketbook of practically every citizen: the price of gas. Since September 11, 2001, the

already soaring cost of petroleum and crude oil has continued to skyrocket, and today a gallon of unleaded gasoline costs as much as three dollars per gallon. This startlingly steep and virtually universal expense, along with the national aversion to becoming dependent on foreign oil sources, has convinced Congress to approve a plan to begin drilling in the Arctic National Wildlife Refuge (ANWR), a strikingly beautiful Alaskan preserve that may contain billions of gallons of oil underneath its pristine snow. Proponents of the recent decision claim that drilling in ANWR will protect American economic interests without significantly damaging the land and wildlife in the preserve. Opponents are concerned that native flora and fauna will be forced to pay a high price for the oil found beneath the Alaskan soil. Both schools of thought have valid reasons to support their views. But the costs of oil drilling outweigh its benefits, and its benefits are not assured. If ANWR is exposed to oil drilling, wildlife and indigenous groups will suffer, the environment will decline, and the American people will discover that they have unnecessarily sacrificed one of their most beautiful natural treasures.

The Arctic National Wildlife Refuge is home to wolverines, arctic foxes, polar bears, musk oxen, wolves, and 135 species of birds, but one of the most unique and majestic of all of the ANWR animals is the caribou. ANWR is an important resource for these mighty, tawny-colored animals, with broad chests and huge antlers. The third-largest caribou herd in Alaska, the Porcupine herd, depends on the refuge for migration and for a 740-square-mile stretch of fertile and protected coastal plain that has long served as their primary calving ground (Gildart). Although the ANWR drilling administration claims that environmentally friendly procedures will be used and that no more than two thousand acres of coastal plain will be disturbed, wildlife watchdog organizations stress that

> this 2,000 acres would not be a contiguous, isolated spot but instead would represent a spider web of wells, pipelines, processing plants, oil drilling pads, gravel roads, and airstrips. This development would cast a net over the entire coastal plain, altering its landscape, including the central calving ground of the Porcupine caribou herd. (ANWR: FAQ)

The disturbance of this calving ground would be devastating not only to the Porcupine caribou but also to the Gwich'in, an indigenous Alaskan people whose survival and culture depend on the caribou. Jonathan Solomon, a native Gwich'in, voiced his fears about drilling in ANWR: "If caribou numbers fall, it may change the herd's migrational pattern, because smaller groups have different nutritional needs. Caribou won't migrate past our villages. What will we eat then?" (qtd. in Gildart). Gwich'in Donna Carroll calls the caribou her tribe's buffalo (Gildart). Food subsidies for the Gwich'in would not replace the caribou because these majestic creatures make the indigenous Alaskans who they are. As he finished his hunting, Gwich'in Kenneth Frank sadly remarked, "Our culture is thousands of years old. Is just a few years of oil worth all that?" (Gildart).

ANWR drilling would negatively affect not only the preserve's wildlife and indigenous hunters, but every American citizen. There is no question about it: drilling is expensive. The oil drilling project, which requires large machines and massive amounts of raw material, will take a substantial chunk out of the national budget. We should instead direct the money to the research and development of more efficient modes of transportation and industrialization. Charles Clusen, a member of the National Resources Defense Council, points out that "if we required automobile owners to replace their used tires with ones as efficient as the tires that originally came on the car, we would save more oil than there is in the Arctic refuge" (qtd. in Svitil). The authors of the *Environmental Encyclopedia* note that

> [i]mproving the average fuel efficiency of all cars and light trucks in America by just one mile per gallon would save more oil than is ever likely to be recovered from ANWR and it would do so faster and cheaper than extracting and transporting crude oil from the Arctic.

With the United States consumption of oil currently at 16 million barrels of oil per day (Kriz), the oil in ANWR would only satisfy the appetite of American industry for a short time. Even if ANWR could provide an unlimited amount of oil, drilling there would still not be the answer. With huge areas such as China beginning to industrialize and produce more greenhouse gases, it is imperative that the United States begin a serious exploration of energy sources that will not contribute to environmental ills such as global warming.

Dark mumblings about a far-off environmental disaster or loud protestations from tree huggers about the reproduction rates of overgrown deer can seem far removed to the average American worker struggling to meet the demands of his mortgage, minivan, and 2.3 kids. As America struggles to make a comeback from the difficult early years of the twenty-first century, it is easy to push aside long-term environmental concerns in favor of instant financial gratification. Even so, drilling in Alaska is not the answer. One supporter of

ANWR argued that "we need energy at a time when our own supplies are at risk because of the volatile political climates in the Middle East and South America." Yet in the same article, he acknowledged that "it will take years to develop ANWR" (Weyrich). The political concerns used to justify the development of the nature preserve could be obsolete by the time the oil is pumped out of it.

It is understandable that those concerned about the American   7 economy want to take hold of natural resources now, but the damage to native species and indigenous tribes, the money spent on drilling that could be more profitably be spent making industry more efficient, and the time it will take to harvest the oil all serve as convincing arguments that drilling in the Arctic National Wildlife Refuge is not the answer to our energy crisis. By preserving both the domestic oil reserves and the beautiful wilderness of ANWR, the American people would show that they value future generations. They would find that there is something bigger than gas prices that binds them together.

## WORKS CITED

"Arctic National Wildlife Refuge." *Environmental Encyclopedia*. 2003. *Opposing Viewpoints Resource Center*. Ed. Thomas Gale. 13 Apr. 2005. <http://galenet.galegroup.com/servlet/OVRC>.

"Arctic National Wildlife Refuge: Frequently Asked Questions." *National Wildlife Federation*. 21 Dec. 2004. 26 Apr. 2005 <http://www.nwf.org/resourceLibrary/getData.cfm?>.

Gildart, Bert. "Hunting for Their Future." *National Wildlife* 35.6 (1997). *National Wildlife Federation*. 25 Apr. 2005 <http://www.nwf.org/nationalwildlife/article.cfm?>.

Kallen, Stuart, ed. *How Should America's Wilderness Be Managed?* At Issue Series. Farmington Hills, MI: Greenhaven Press, 2005. *Opposing Viewpoints Resource Center*. Ed. Thomas Gale. 13 Apr. 2005 <http://galenet.galegroup.com/servlet/OVRC>.

Kriz, Margaret. "Tapping Pristine Territories." *National Journal* 1 Jan. 2005. *Academic Search Premier*. 25 Apr. 2005 <http://web22.epnet.com/citation/asp?>

Svitil, Kathy A. "Drilling for Controversy in Alaska." *Discover* Feb. 2005.

Weyrich, Paul. "ANWR: America's Untapped Resource." *CNSNews.com*. 27 Mar. 2003. Cybercast News Service. 26 Apr. 2005 <http://www.cnsnews.com>.

## Alexandra Carstensen

*Southwest Minnesota State University*
*Marshall, Minnesota*

Alexandra Carstensen "got personally involved" in the same-sex marriage issue in high school, after her best friend from elementary school told her he was gay. When in 2004 President George W. Bush called for a constitutional amendment that would prohibit same-sex marriage, she found herself becoming "somewhat of an advocate for civil rights."

Carstensen grew up in what she calls a "very conservative" town, one in which most people would support the president's amendment, so she understood that for many supporters, their deeply held beliefs about marriage were rooted in their Christian faith. That understanding helped her form her approach. "I did not want the average person to be immediately offended and assume I was denouncing religion," she said. "I used quotations from the Bible very carefully, and it took me a couple of drafts before I was satisfied with the use of that source."

She also guessed that supporters of the amendment would read her essay with their own arguments in mind, so she decided to spend much of her time on counterargument. "I feel that the best arguments directly refute the opposition," she said, noting that her research and writing process consisted mostly of "looking up arguments in favor of the amendment and then using critical reasoning to refute them."

In this way, she created an argument founded primarily in logic: "I found research sources that would allow me to present my argument as the only clear answer to the question at hand, and I accomplished this goal by bringing logic and constitutional fact into my paper, rather than emotional and religious bias." But she found the limited use of an emotional appeal helpful as well: "I decided in later drafts that some emotion would be beneficial to my essay. This is where the Statue of Liberty came in. Again, however, I wanted neither to be offensive nor to deprecate the meaning behind such a

**103**

symbol. I just wanted to make people think on a different level." By
including a reference to the well-known motto inscribed on the
Statue of Liberty at the close of her essay, Carstensen makes a
convincing emotional appeal after readers have digested her logical
reasons for finding the amendment discriminatory.

---

In February 2004, President George W. Bush officially supported a   1
constitutional amendment that would restrict civil rights: the Federal
Marriage Amendment. The definition of marriage in American culture has always been ambiguous. Its most basic definition is a union
between two people. President Bush sought to make a more specific
definition part of United States law through an amendment that
declares:

> Marriage in the United States shall consist only of the union of a man
> and a woman. Neither this Constitution, nor the constitution of any
> State, shall be construed to require that marriage or the legal incidents
> thereof be conferred upon any union other than the union of a man and
> a woman. ("Marriage Protection Amendment")

This amendment directly prohibits marriage between same-sex
couples. Passing such an amendment—which amounts to state-
sponsored discrimination, a violation of an American group's rights
as guaranteed in the Constitution—would prove to be exceptionally
difficult, since a two-thirds majority of both houses of Congress and
three-fourths of the state legislatures would be needed to ratify it.
But the very existence of an amendment outlawing gay marriage
sends a powerful message of hate and intolerance to gay Americans
that no American—especially those Americans whose faiths teach
tolerance—should abide.

Throughout American history, immigration laws have been used   2
"to widen the embrace of the national community and sometimes as
a barrier to further inclusion" (Edwards and Lippucci 610). Laws intended to "widen the embrace of the national community" led to the
period of rapid immigration in the mid-to-late nineteenth century.
As diversity increased during this time, cultural groups strove to
maintain their identities, and some groups came to view their beliefs
and practices as superior to those of others (Edwards and Lippucci
609). Ironically, such attitudes, which originated in inclusive immigration laws, gave rise to exclusive laws, which discriminated against
and segregated some cultural groups.

Who is justified in defining individuals as members of particular    3
groups, rewarding some groups with rights, and punishing others with
prohibitions? Punishing an individual for belonging to a certain group
is the very definition of discrimination (Edwards and Lippucci 608).
An amendment to the Constitution defining marriage as exclusively
between a male and a female would directly harm homosexuals by
denying them family insurance and health benefits, joint tax returns
and tax breaks, family visitation privileges, and automatic inheritance
rights (Edwards and Lippucci 98). Therefore, such an amendment is
blatant discrimination. Creating laws that forbid homosexual couples
to marry is de jure segregation, no different from the Jim Crow laws,
which, among other things, made it illegal in many states for two people of different races to marry.

Civil rights are "fundamental rights that government (en)acts to    4
protect (citizens) from the unlawful actions of others, including the
government itself" (Edwards and Lippucci 608). The Fourteenth
Amendment—the constitutional amendment that most safeguards
civil rights—holds that "No state should make or enforce any law
which shall abridge the privileges or immunities of citizens of the
United States; nor shall any state deprive any person of life, liberty, or
property" (*Constitution of the United States of America* 22). According
to the Human Rights Campaign, the marriage act would deny "1,100
rights, protections, and benefits" to same-sex couples and is therefore a
direct violation of their constitutionally protected civil rights.

The most persuasive argument of the supporters of the constitu-    5
tional amendment is the religious one. The Bible seems to portray
homosexuality as a sin—"Thou shall not lie with mankind, as with
womankind: it is abomination" (*Holy Bible*, Levit. 18.22)—and require marriage between a man and a woman—"Therefore, shall a
man leave his father and his mother, and shall cleave unto his wife:
and they shall become one flesh" (*Holy Bible*, Gen. 2.24). Citing
these and other biblical passages, many Christians with strong religious convictions oppose same-sex marriage.

The Bible, however, promotes many things that most Christians    6
do not. In the Old Testament, a man is permitted to marry any number of women as long as he can provide for them: "If he take him another wife; her food, her raiment, and her duty of marriage, shall he
not diminish" (*Holy Bible*, Exodus 21.10). According to biblical stories, King David took six wives and many concubines, and King
Solomon had more than seven hundred wives and three hundred
concubines. Jesus supported the rules of the Old Testament, saying,

"Think not that I am come to destroy the law, or the prophets; I am not come to destroy, but to fulfill. For verily I say unto you, Till heaven and earth pass, one jot or one tittle shall in no wise pass from the law, till all be fulfilled" (*Holy Bible,* Matthew 5.17–18). Thus, although polygamy is supported by both the Old and New Testament, it is illegal in the United States today.

The Bible also states, "For the woman which hath an husband is   7
bound by the law to her husband so long as she liveth" (*Holy Bible,* Romans 7.2). This passage claims a woman is forever bound to her husband, therefore forbidding divorce. Again, although divorce is not permitted in the Bible, it is socially permissible today.

The Bible, unlike the Constitution, was not written to prepare   8
for societal changes, especially regarding marriage. As our society evolves, the Constitution must also evolve, leaving behind the Christian scripture written over three thousand years ago. Over the course of American history, the Constitution has changed to reflect more tolerant belief systems, such as the right of women and African Americans to vote. Traditionalists attempting to preserve the rule of the Bible fail to acknowledge that the Constitution can and must adapt to changes in American society.

Moreover, the United States Constitution has always recognized   9
a separation of church and state, which among other things guards against creating laws inspired by religious moral codes. In the secular regulation rule of the Supreme Court, "all laws must have a reasonable secular purpose and they must not discriminate on the basis of religion" (Wayne, Mackenzie, O'Brien, and Cole 96). For example, the Court ruled that states may require all schoolchildren to have smallpox vaccinations, including children whose religions forbid the shots. If an amendment defining marriage was passed based on the religious ideal of marriage, it would be unconstitutional according to this rule.

Supporters of the Federal Marriage Amendment believe that   10
same-sex marriages threaten the very institution of marriage. These supporters define marriage as the "procreation and raising of children, as well as the bonding of a man and a woman in a lifelong relationship" (Stanton and Winn). Supporters of the Marriage Protection Act hold that same-sex marriages do not fall under this definition, and therefore should not be sanctioned by U.S. law.

This argument has no justification. Not all heterosexual couples   11
choose to have children. Nor are all heterosexual couples "together for life." According to the 2000 census, the divorce rate is between

45 and 50 percent for heterosexuals, invalidating the claim that heterosexuality in marriage leads to lifelong commitment (Kreider).

Moreover, heterosexual marriage has evolved. Due to the women's rights movement and subsequent legislation, marriage is no longer essential, but voluntary. Since children are no longer considered a financial necessity—and in fact are prevented from working long hours by child labor laws—couples now choose to have children or remain childless, as they wish. Prescribed "roles" of husband and wife have also changed, or even switched in some relationships. For example, it is now socially acceptable for both husband and wife to work full time; in some relationships, only the woman works while the man cares for the children and the household (Coontz). Stephanie Coontz, the director for public education for the Council on Contemporary Families, reminds us that changes to the institution of marriage are as old as "the Stone Age" and recommends that we give in to the flux: 12

> Marriage has been in a constant state of evolution since the dawn of the Stone Age. In the process it has become more flexible....Many people may not like the direction these changes have taken in recent years. But it is simply magical thinking to believe that by banning gay and lesbian marriages, we will turn back the clock. (Coontz)

According to the Human Rights Campaign, the Constitution was amended first to include the Bill of Rights, and seventeen times thereafter to protect additional rights of the American people. The Federal Marriage Amendment would be the first to reduce Americans' rights. Of those citizens who argue for a constitutional amendment banning gay marriages, most base their claims on religion. The refusal, on religious grounds, to allow same-sex couples to marry breaks down the barrier between religion and government and creates a Christian society oblivious to the views of our ever-diversifying nation. The Statue of Liberty, our most prominent symbol of American immigration and diversity, is inscribed with these words: 13

> "Keep, ancient lands, your storied pomp!" cries she
> With silent lips. "Give me your tired, your poor,
> Your huddled masses yearning to breathe free,
> The wretched refuse of your teeming shore,
> Send these, the homeless, tempest-tost to me,
> I lift my lamp beside the golden door!" (Lazarus)

Liberty does not offer acceptance in America only to Christian heterosexuals but to people of all cultures, races, religions seeking 14 freedom from persecution. Refusing to allow a specific group to marry is direct discrimination and a threat to our constitutionally protected civil rights, and must not be permitted.

## WORKS CITED

*The Constitution of the United States of America.* Bedford, MA: Applewood, 1995.

Coontz, Stephanie. "The Heterosexual Revolution." *New York Times* 5 July 2005. 7 July 2005 <http//:www.nytimes.com/2005/07/05/opinion/05coontz.html>.

Edwards, David V., and Alessandra Lippucci. *Practicing American Politics: An Introduction to Government.* New York: Worth, 1998.

*Holy Bible. King James Version.* Philadelphia: National Bible, 1958.

*Human Rights Campaign.* 2005. Human Rights Campaign. 20 July 2005 <http://www.hrc.org>.

"Introduction to the Court Opinion in the Dred Scott Case." *U.S. Department of State.* 10 Jan. 2006 <http://usinfo.state.gov/usa/infousa/facts/democrac/21.htm>.

Jacobs, Deborah. "ACLU Goes to Court to Protect Religions, Not Undermine Them." *American Civil Liberties Union of New Jersey.* 28 Dec. 2004. 20 July 2005 <http://www.aclu-nj.org/issues/religiousfreedom/aclugoestocourttoprotectre.htm>.

Kreider, Rose M. United States Census Bureau. *Number, Timing, and Duration of Marriages and Divorces: 2001.* Washington: GPO, 2005.

Lazarus, Emma, "Statue of Liberty." *United States Department of the Interior.* June 2005. 20 July 2005 <http://www.nps.gov/stli/prod02.htm#preserving>.

"Marriage Protection Amendment." *S.J. Res. 1, 109th Congress, 1st session.* Jan. 2005. 10 Feb. 2006 <http://thomas.loc.gov/cgi bin/query/C?c109:./temp/~c109R3GtAM>.

Moody, Howard. "Sacred Right or Civil Right." *Nation* 5 July 2004. Rpt. in *The Reference Shelf U.S. National Debate Topic 2005–2006: U.S. Civil Liberties.* Ed. Lara Weibgen. New York: H. W. Wilson, 2005. 109–15.

Robinson, B. A. "Same Sex Parenting: Overview of the Legal Status of Gay-Lesbian Adoption." *Religious Tolerance.org.* 2002. Religious Tolerance. 20 July 2005 <http://www.religioustolerance.org/hom_pare6.htm>.

Stanton, Glen T., and Pete Winn. "Talking Points on State Marriage Amendment Debate." *mfc.org.* 2005. *Minnesota Family Council/ Minnesota Family Institute.* 20 July 2005 <http://www.mfc.org/marriage/talkingpoints.htm>.

Wayne, Stephen J., G. Calvin Mackenzie, David M. O'Brien, and Richard L. Cole. *The Politics of American Government.* New York: St. Martin's, 1998.

# *Proposing a Solution* 7

Problem solving requires a questioning attitude—a refusal to accept things as they are simply because they've always been that way. It invites creative effort—time spent imagining how things might be improved. When you identify a problem that has long existed or notice that old solutions are failing because they're outdated, you take a step toward positive change. As a student, you are in an enviable position to identify and solve problems. Studying and writing, you have been practicing a stance that problem solving requires—thinking skeptically and creatively. And you have the luxury of time to notice problems and think hard about solutions.

Don't be afraid to research problems that are new to you—an outsider's fresh, unbiased point of view is often very valuable. But remember to consider problems from an insider's perspective, too: problems of your town and city, neighborhood and dormitory, athletic team and booster club. If you volunteer time and effort on behalf of political parties, religious and cultural groups, or gender and environmental organizations, this experience with specific groups uniquely qualifies you to examine their limitations. What's more, a proposal to solve a local problem may well have national implications. For example, Jeff Varley's essay about later high school starting times grew from his struggle with early classes as a high school teen, yet his proposal applies to every high school in the nation.

In addition to giving you a say in your community, practice in presenting problems and proposing solutions will expand your professional-writing repertoire. If student writer Susan Ly pursues a career in management, applies for a job directing a nonprofit, or volunteers to work for a local political organization, she will have demonstrated her ability to notice and analyze problems and suggest ways to fix them, while acknowledging the concerns of the people who would have to carry them out—in this case, meatpacking industry managers who create policies to prevent workplace sexual harassment and train employees to follow them.

It can be frustrating to work diligently on a proposal for a problem that you know you have little power to solve; for no matter how well argued, many proposals are never carried out. People who are quite insightful about solving problems may be hampered or thwarted by economic restraints or aggressive opposition from prominent stakeholders. But this shouldn't deter you from proposing a solution to a problem, especially when you choose a local problem in which you have a personal interest. A friend's account of her experience as a long-term-care nurse inspired Kim Spencer Kline and Dana Jordan to tackle the problem of poorly regulated nursing homes in their state. The students interviewed their friend, reviewed newspaper accounts of nursing home violations in Iowa, researched the laws regulating nursing homes in their state and in others, and set out to write "a real proposal, not just an assignment." Their hard work paid off. Kline reports: "Through a friend, we were able to share this paper with a candidate for governor in our state, who was quite impressed with our work and asked to keep a copy of it."

Don't underestimate the power of interviewing people affected by the problem you intend to solve and approaching others who have the power to change it. Interviews with those who have firsthand experience with the problem can help you anticipate objections to your solution and will allow you to test it with an audience directly involved. Scheduling an interview with someone who has the power to solve the problem may help you anticipate and counter resistance to your proposal.

You are ready to add your voice to the conversations about problems on your campus; in your town; at your job; or with college, government, or corporate officials, whose policies affect your life and the lives of your family and friends. If your proposal can convince readers to consider and perhaps implement your solution, you will have succeeded in altering the conditions of your world.

# High School Starting Time

### Jeff Varley

*Western Wyoming Community College*
*Rock Springs, Wyoming*

---

It is the rare student who doesn't find it difficult to get out of bed in the morning. Recent high school grad Jeff Varley strategically directs the following essay proposing later high school starting times to an audience of his peers—fellow late risers—while also offering sound evidence to sway adult readers who make school-scheduling decisions. Varley even shows how taxpayers in communities where high school students live would benefit from later starting times—no one can accuse him of ignoring the greater good! With an attention-getting introduction, an alarmingly long list of the problems caused by sleepiness among high school students, and a solution that's unexpectedly simple—and even accounts for the several obstacles that might stand in its way—Varley's proposal is unlikely to put you to sleep, whether you're an early bird or not.

---

Ah, sweet memories of high school: waking up at 6:30 in the morning, stumbling into the bathroom to get ready for the day, dressing while still half asleep, munching a piece of toast while listening to our parents tell us that if we just went to bed earlier we wouldn't be so sleepy in the morning (or worse, listening to our parents call us lazy), catching the bus as the sun began to top the trees, and wandering into our first-period classes merely to lay our head down on our desks to doze off for the next fifty-five minutes.

We could never seem to catch up on our sleep, especially during the week. And even if we followed our parents' advice and tried going to bed earlier, the earlier bedtime did not make much, if any, difference in how awake we were the next morning. In fact, for those of us who tried going to bed earlier, we generally just lay there until 10:30 or 11:00 before finally going to sleep. The next school morning, we were still as tired as when we had gone to bed later.

1

2

Yet recent studies provide evidence that the sleep patterns for   3
adolescents are significantly different from those of both young children and adults. Studies of sleep patterns by Mary Carskadon, a professor of psychiatry and human behavior at the Brown University
School of Medicine and Director of Sleep and Chronobiology Research at E. P. Bradley Hospital in East Providence, Rhode Island,
revealed that adolescents, as opposed to younger children or adults,
actually function better when they go to bed later and awake later.
Professor Carskadon's research demonstrates that most adolescents'
biological clocks are naturally set to a different pattern from the
clocks of most children and adults.

The timing of the need for sleep also shows biological changes as   4
children reach puberty. Melatonin, a hormone produced in the
pineal gland, is an indicator for the biological clock that influences
wake/sleep cycles. Carefully controlled studies found that "more ma-
ture adolescents had a later timing of the termination of melatonin
secretion" (Carskadon 351). This indicates that post-pubescent teens
have a biological need to sleep later in the morning. The impact of
forcing people to try to be alert when every nerve in their body is
begging for more sleep can only be negative. This discovery has a
major impact on high school students who are required to wake up
early in order to arrive at school early, for asking teens to learn a
complex subject, such as math, science, or English, before the brain
is awake is futile.

Tardiness, poor grades, depression, automobile accidents, after-   5
school on-the-job accidents, and general lethargy have all been identified as the consequences of insufficient sleep among high school
students. Yet school districts persist in retaining high school starting
times that begin early in the morning, usually around 7:30 a.m. But
such an early starting time does not benefit the students for whom
the educational system is supposedly structured. How do we resolve the
conflict of early high school starting times versus sleepy students?

An obvious solution would be to start high school classes later in   6
the morning. A later starting time for high schools can be a controversial proposal if all of the affected parties are not consulted and
kept informed. Kyla Wahlstrom of the Center for Applied Research
and Educational Improvement at the University of Minnesota
pointed out that "changing a school's starting time provokes the
same kind of emotional reaction from stakeholders as closing a
school or changing a school's attendance area" (Wahlstrom 346).
Presumably, if parents and other interested parties knew about

Carskadon's research, they would be more willing to consider changing the start time for high school.

Some schools have recognized the benefits of later starting times    7
and have implemented a new schedule. One such school is located in
eastern Minnesota. In 1996, the Edina Public School District pushed
back the start time for 1,400 high school students from 7:25 to 8:30
a.m. Edina Public School District Superintendent Kenneth Dragseth
reports that the later schedule has led to better grades, fewer behavioral problems, and a better-rested student body (Dragseth).
Dragseth's anecdotal evidence that better-rested students perform
better is supported by research performed by psychologists at the
College of the Holy Cross in Worcester, Massachusetts. Working
with Carskadon, the psychologists "surveyed more than 3,120 Providence [Rhode Island] area high school students and found students
who got A's and B's averaged about 35 minutes more sleep on both
weeknights and weekends than students who received D's and F's"
(Bettelheim 557).

In addition to better grades, other positive effects cited by re-    8
searchers include better attendance, fewer tardies, far fewer students
falling asleep at their desks, more alert students more engaged in the
learning process, less depression, fewer problems at home and among
friends, enhanced school atmosphere, and fewer illnesses (Lawton;
Wahlstrom and Taylor). With so many benefits to starting high
school classes later, why haven't more districts done so?

One of the most common concerns comes from participants in    9
extracurricular activities. If practices currently often run until 8 or 9
p.m. with a school day that begins at 7:30 a.m., what will happen if
school starts an hour later? This is a legitimate concern that would
need to be addressed on a team-by-team or group-by-group basis.
Some practice sessions could be held immediately after class in the
early afternoon. Some activities could convene after a short dinner
break. If these activities began earlier in the evening, they could be
finished sooner in the evening. The one factor every coach or spon-
sor would have to consider is how important any extracurricular activity is in relation to the primary mission of the school, which, of
course, is learning and education, not sports or clubs.

Availability of buses is another concern for many school districts    10
when any discussion of changing schedules begins. School officials in
Montgomery County, Maryland, estimate it would cost $31 million
to buy enough buses to accommodate later start times for high school
without inconveniencing elementary and middle school students

(Bettelheim 557). Minneapolis, which buses 90 percent of the 50,000 students in the school district, solved the transportation problems caused by starting high school classes later by starting the grade school classes earlier (Lawton). This has the added benefits of bringing younger children to school at a time when many of them are most alert and decreasing the need for before-school child care for these students (Reiss; Lawton). With careful planning and scheduling, the transportation tribulations can be addressed in cost-effective ways.

As the world we live in becomes ever more complex, education becomes ever more important. It is important that the time spent on education be spent as effectively as possible. It is time to look at school schedules that provide the best education at times that are most appropriate to the students. James Maas, a psychologist at Cornell University, points out that "people are beginning to realize it doesn't make sense to pay heavy school taxes when the audience you're teaching is asleep" (qtd. in Bettelheim 556).

## WORKS CITED

Bettelheim, Adriel. "Sleep Deprivation." *CQ Researcher* 8 (1998): 555–62.

Carskadon, Mary A. "When Worlds Collide: Adolescent Need for Sleep versus Societal Demands." *Phi Delta Kappan* 80 (1999): 348–53.

Dragseth, Kenneth A. "A Minneapolis Suburb Reaps Early Benefits from a Late Start." *School Administrator* Mar. 1999. 22 Mar. 2003 <http://www.aasa.org/publications/sa/1999_03/lawton_side_research.htm>.

Lawton, Millicent. "For Whom the Bell Tolls." *School Administrator* Mar. 1999. 22 Mar. 2003 <http://www.aasa.org/publications/sa/1999_03/lawton.htm>.

Reiss, Tammy. "Wake-up Call on Kids' Biological Clocks." *NEA Today* 6.6 (1998): 19.

Wahlstrom, Kyla L. "The Prickly Politics of School Starting Times." *Phi Delta Kappan* 80 (1999): 345–47.

Wahlstrom, Kyla L., and John S. Taylor. "Sleep Research Warns: Don't Start High School without the Kids." *Education Digest* 66 (2000): 15–20. *MasterFILE Premier*, EBSCO. Western Wyoming Community College, Hay Lib. 22 Mar. 2003 <http://www.epnet.com>.

# Cracking Down on Lighting Up

**Monica Perez**

*The Catholic University of America*
*Washington, D.C.*

Only people with their heads in a cloud of smoke could have missed the many public campaigns warning Americans about the dangers of tobacco. But in a proposal essay, even the most well-publicized problem bears repeating, and Monica Perez does this well by solidifying the risks of smoking and the benefits of quitting with statistics and expert testimony. Having readied readers for her proposal by refreshing their memories about the horrors of the "nasty habit," Perez outlines a three-part action plan to "help push smoking out of society," and successfully responds to possible objections to her proposal from tobacco companies, states, and bar and restaurant owners. As you read, pay attention to Perez's tone, which reveals both her disgust with smoking and her determination to "crack down" on it. How effective is that tone as a call to action? Does it anger you? Inspire you?

---

On September 29, 2002, more than a thousand young people converged on Louisville, Kentucky—the heart of tobacco country. They brought some cameras; the media brought some more . . . and for what? To drop dead. Where? In front of a major tobacco manufacturer. That's what it looked like, anyway, as the students—recruits from nearby colleges and universities—fell to the ground in unison for the filming of a commercial. The commercial, sponsored by the American Legacy Foundation, is part of an antismoking campaign called The Citizen's Commission to Protect the Truth, which joins a decades-long movement to educate the public about the dangers of smoking. 1

Smoking is a nasty habit that is the leading cause of many types of cancer; these include cancer of the kidney, cervix, bone marrow, pancreas, and stomach, to name a few. Some of the more obvious diseases caused by smoking include lung, oral, and throat cancers, along with 2

**115**

chronic lung disease. Studies have also linked smoking to heart disease, osteoporosis, and cataracts. Secondhand smoke is another side effect of smoking, but this affects not smokers but the bystanders who happen to be around smokers. According to the Environmental Protection Agency, secondhand smoke is a "Class A carcinogen," meaning that it causes cancer and that it is not safe to be exposed to at any level or for any amount of time. One estimate stated that environmental tobacco smoke kills "53,000 Americans every year" (Clark).

Thankfully, many of the harsh effects of smoking can be reversed. 3 By quitting smoking, you can reap the healing benefits. According to About.com, after twenty-four hours of not smoking, blood pressure decreases, body temperature increases, carbon monoxide and oxygen levels return to normal, and the chance of a heart attack decreases. After two days, nerve endings begin to regrow, and there is an improvement in one's ability to taste and smell. Soon, former smokers may have a new lease on life: in as little as a month, there is significant improvement in coughing, fatigue, shortness of breath, and sinus congestion ("Quit Smoking Benefits"). The question isn't, however, why should someone quit smoking, but how do we get them to do so? How do we help change society's mentality on smoking? We should start with continuing prevention and treatment programs, implementing clean-air laws and smoke-free policies, and continuing to increase cigarette sales taxes.

The best way to get people to quit smoking is to make sure that 4 they never start. "Prevention is a far better investment" than treatment simply because it is so much harder to rid people of an addiction than it is to keep them from falling victim to one ("Smoking Kills"). When it comes to prevention, education is key. We must continue to target younger audiences and teach them the risks of lighting up. If we start to educate children as soon as they enter the schooling system, there is a much better chance they will not be influenced later on. We must also focus our attention on teens. As a group, teenagers and young adults have one of the highest growth rates of new smokers, with three thousand young people beginning every day ("Smoking"). To reduce the number of teens who start smoking, we need to change smoking's image. It doesn't help that our society is bombarded by continuous advertisements and positive images of smoking in movies and television shows. An internal tobacco company marketing report from 1989 said, "We believe that most of the strong, positive images for cigarettes and smoking are created by cinema and television" ("Find Facts"). We must teach the next generations to filter out these false images. There are thousands of different organizations, like The Truth, that can help. But it must be a cooperative effort; parents must speak to their kids, and teachers must act as role models and continue to stress the dangers of cigarette smoking. We also cannot forget that young smokers need extra support and encouragement to quit.

Implementing or strengthening clean-indoor-air laws and smoke-free policies state-by-state is another way to help reduce smoking nationwide. These policies include prohibitions against smoking in public places, such as bars, restaurants, and the workplace. It is important that the public know that clean-indoor-air laws "prompt more smokers to try to quit; increase the number of successful quit attempts; reduce the number of cigarettes that continuing smokers consume," and have a strong, documented "positive impact...on preventing children and adolescents from ever starting" to smoke (Barry, "Clean Indoor Air"). The *American Journal of Public Health* reviewed nineteen studies on smoke-free workplaces and found that all reported either declines in daily cigarette consumption by continuing smokers or reductions in smoking prevalence after bans on smoking in the workplace were introduced (Barry, "Clean Indoor Air"). Smoke-free homes and workplaces also significantly lower adolescent smoking rates. And smoke-free policies are also good for nonsmokers. According to Charles S. Clark, "88% of Americans find cigarette smoke annoying." Some people have even developed allergies to smoke, especially those with asthma. Others just plain don't like the smell and certainly don't want to taste the smoke in their food. According to a report by the Campaign for Tobacco-Free Kids, "People are speaking up for their right to breathe clean, smoke-free air" ("Smoke-Free Laws"). Smoke-free policies will help protect nonsmokers and smokers alike, although perhaps for different reasons.

Like implementing smoke-free policies, raising the sales tax on cigarettes is another indirect way to encourage people to quit or to at least cut down on smoking. If you are a smoker, then you know just how expensive packs are becoming these days. As of 2003, the average price per pack, with all taxes, was about $4.12. And that average is rising, with cigarette taxes in many states going up. Virginia raised its tax to 35 cents per pack from 2.5 cents in February 2004. Alabama followed Virginia's lead by increasing its tax by about 26 cents per pack in May 2004. Results from recent surveys conclude that teen smoking decreases by 7 percent and overall smoking goes down by 3–5 percent for every 10 percent increase in the price of cigarettes ("Update from the States").

Opposition can be seen from every corner. The tobacco compa-    7
nies, the states, and bar and restaurant owners all have something to say. Tobacco companies are upset for the obvious reason that if measures such as these are taken, sales will go down and the number of new smokers will decline—which really isn't such a bad thing. One of the biggest misconceptions about smoke-free laws is that they harm business for restaurants and bars. Not only will these laws "help protect restaurant and bar employees and patrons from the harms of secondhand smoke," but there is overwhelming evidence—dozens of studies and hard economic data—that smoke-free laws can do this without harming business (Barry, "Smoke-Free Laws"). In March 2003, New York passed a citywide comprehensive smoke-free law. A year later, the city reported that "business receipts for bars and restaurants have increased, employment has risen, and virtually all establishments are complying with the law." Moreover, the 2004 Zagat Survey found that while 4 percent of New Yorkers surveyed were eating out less often because of the smoke-free law, a whopping 23 percent were eating out *more* often because of the law (Barry, "Smoke-Free Laws"). There will be the occasional bar that hurts because they "relied on customers who spent a majority of their day there smoking and drinking," but overall the positive effects far outweigh the negative effects. States worry about the loss of cigarette revenues and the fate of the tobacco farmer. I say, in this day and age, a health-savvy trend is sweeping the nation and especially the younger generations. It is only a matter of time before the number of new smokers drops so significantly that they cannot support the tobacco industry. States that rely on tobacco revenues should start switching their areas of income now. Tobacco farmers can help this transition by growing soybeans or corn instead. For those wary states, why not at least pursue a trial period of passing smoke-free laws or flat out banning smoking to see the results for yourselves? There will hardly be a "negative economic impact, so there are no valid reasons for…states not to pass similar laws" ("Profile: New Study").

According to Terry Martin, "Smoking remains the leading pre-    8
ventable cause of death in this country." Thousands of lives will be taken this year. Perhaps by implementing these suggested measures, a few may be saved. I can't think of a logical reason not to do everything within states' power to help push smoking out of society. The American community as a whole needs to join together in a collective

effort to rid our country of the maladies smoking brings. Neither one person nor one state can do it alone.

# WORKS CITED

Barry, Matt. "Clean Indoor Air Laws Encourage Smokers to Quit and Discourage Youth from Starting." *Campaign for Tobacco-Free Kids* 1 July 2004. 10 April 2005 <http://tobaccofreekids.org/research/factsheets/pdf/0198.pdf>.

Barry, Matt. "Smoke-Free Laws Do Not Harm Business at Restaurants and Bars." *Campaign for Tobacco-Free Kids* 1 July 2004. 10 April 2005 <http://tobaccofreekids.org/research/factsheets/pdf/0144.pdf>.

Clark, Charles S. "Crackdown on Smoking." *The CQ Researcher Online* (1992). 8 April 2005 <http://library.cqpress.com/> Document ID: cqresrrel1992120400.

"Find Facts." *Seek Truth.* 8 Apr. 2005 <http://thetruth.com/index.cfm?seek=facts>.

Martin, Terry. "The Health Consequences of Smoking." *Smoking Cessation.* 8 Apr. 2005 <http://quitsmoking.about.com/od/tobaccostatistics/a/SGR2004.htm>.

McMahon, Katie. "State Cigarette Tax Rates & Rank, Date of Last Increase, Annual Pack Sales & Revenues, and Related Data." *Campaign for Tobacco-Free Kids* 18 Mar. 2005. 10 April 2005 <http://tobaccofreekids.org/research/factsheets/pdf/0099.pdf>.

"Profile: New Study Shows Effect of Statewide Smoking Ban in Massachusetts." *Morning Addition* 5 April 2005. 8 April 2005 <http://proquest.umi.com> Proquest ID: 817341761.

"Quit Smoking Benefits — the Healing Begins…" *After Quitting.* 8 April 2005 <http://quitsmoking.about.com/cs/afterquitting/a/after_quitting.htm>.

"Smoke-Free Laws: Protecting Our Right to Breathe Clean Air." *Campaign for Tobacco-Free Kids.* 8 April 2005 <http://tobaccofreekids.org/reports/shs>.

"Smoking Kills Millions Each Year." *Australian Nursing Journal* 12.7 (2005): 27. 8 April 2005 <http://proquest.umi.com> Proquest ID: 794596611.

"Smoking: U.S. Won't Meet Smoking Goals." *Health Letter on the CDC* (2000): 11. *Proquest.* 8 April 2005 <http://proquest.umi.com> Proquest ID: 218882731.

"Update from the States: Tobacco Taxes and Smoke-Free Policies in Action" 28 Mar. 2005. *American Heart Association.* 8 April 2005 <http://americanheart.org/presenter.jhtml?identifier=3022856>.

# Quality Long-Term Care: Our Elderly Deserve It

**Kim Spencer Kline and Dana Jordan**

*Des Moines Area Community College*
*Des Moines, Iowa*

Kim Spencer Kline and Dana Jordan begin their essay by briefly re-
counting several sad and gruesome incidents, including the choking
death of an elderly Des Moines woman. These stories get readers'
attention and create a framework for the students' proposal, which
aims to protect some of Iowa's most vulnerable citizens: men and
women in nursing homes. But if stories interest and orient, it is
often drier details—laws and regulations, for example—that tip interest into motivation. This is as true for writers as it is for readers:
Kline's friend's experience as a long-term-care nurse got the cowrit-
ers interested in their topic, but it was the students' research into
Iowa's laws and the laws of other states that motivated them to
"write a real proposal, not just an assignment," and address not
only their teacher and fellow students but also lawmakers and lob-
byists. As you read, notice the range of interest- and motivation-
generating strategies Kline and Jordan use to win their audience's
ear—from asking rhetorical questions and telling stories to citing
graphs and legislation.

-----

During your lifetime, you or someone in your family will probably     1
need to be placed in a nursing home. One of your grandparents or
parents may already be in a long-term care facility. Does that facility
neglect or abuse its patients? Are patients' lives in jeopardy simply because the facility is short on staff? Far too often, the answer is yes. For
instance, between March and April 2004, the *Des Moines Register*
printed more than seven articles advising the public of the numerous
noncompliance issues at the Abbey Nursing Home (Kauffman;
Kauffman and Leys). On April 4, 2004, the Department of Inspections and Appeals declared the forty-one residents of the Abbey in
"immediate jeopardy." Indeed, the residents were in jeopardy. In

one recorded incident, a female resident died from choking on food while unattended in the dining area. Former Abbey employee Joanie Grace, a long-term care nurse of fifteen years, recounted another incident in which the Abbey staff could not locate an oxygen tank to resuscitate a patient. Dangerous situations like these stem from inadequate staffing. To prevent similar problems at long-term care facilities across Iowa, we propose that the Iowa legislature implement specific nursing-staff requirements and implement laws to enforce penalties for noncompliant facilities.

## INADEQUATE STAFFING ISSUES

Incidents of abuse, neglect, and accidental death occur all too often     2
in Iowa's care facilities. A shortage of qualified LPN and RN nurses and certified nursing assistants on each shift results in most of these tragedies. And the staffing problem is only getting worse: over the past three years, complaints to Iowa's ombudsman's office have increased (see Figure 1).

Many patients require extensive care from skilled nurses. Joanie     3
Grace reflects, "If I am responsible for fifty-eight patients on a shift and some of them require G-tube feedings, trach care, and vent monitoring,

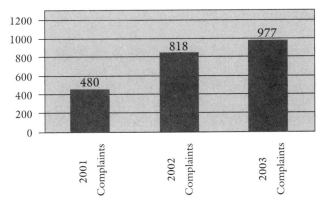

Percent Increase 2002–2003: 19%     Percent Increase 2001–2003: 103%

**Figure 1.**   Iowa State Ombudsman Complaint Activity 2001–2003

a sick patient down the hall may not get assessed until he or she is acutely ill and needing hospitalization. We may have been able to treat the patient at the facility if he or she had been assessed sooner." She continues, "This adds to the burden of financing health care. We need more staff. The inability to provide necessary care is scary for the patient and for the nurse whose license is on the line."

Unfortunately, Joanie's experience in the long-term care field is not uncommon. Understaffing at many hospitals means that most nurses must cover three shifts, including holiday and weekend shifts. When a licensed practical nurse or CNA does not report for work, the staff must scramble to find someone to cover his or her shift, often requiring another nurse to pull a double shift.   4

Inadequate staffing poses risks for patients and nurses alike. Residents may be unattended at crucial times, which can result in falls or choking incidents. Calls for assistance to the bathroom or shower may go unanswered for long periods of time, leaving residents lying in their own waste for hours. Important information in medical charts may be overlooked or omitted by overburdened nurses, resulting in incorrect dosing of medications or improper diets that could lead to serious medical complications. The nurses are directly affected since they are held accountable for any mistakes or oversights in patient care. Proper staff-to-patient ratios could prevent many of these problems.   5

## CURRENT LEGISLATURE

The state of Iowa currently requires "adequate staffing" but does not suggest actual minimums—based on facility size and resident acuity (care) levels—to fulfill this requirement (State of Iowa House File 2990). In fact, none of the regulations are well-defined. The ambiguity of the law's language makes appealing noncompliance fines all too easy. What's more, extended care facilities are excluded from the adequate staffing requirement:   6

> "1. A health facility, *other than an extended care facility,* shall ensure that it is staffed in a manner that provides sufficient, appropriately qualified direct-care nurses in each department or unit within the facility in order to meet the individualized care needs of its patients and to meet the requirements specified in this section." Bill: H.J.259.2, Sect. 4, 135M.4, 5:4–9.

This leaves the staffing requirements for long-term care facilities in the hands of individual facilities. Inadequate staffing has often been the result.

## THE FLAWED PROCESS OF THE DEPARTMENT OF INSPECTIONS AND APPEALS

The Iowa Department of Inspections and Appeals annually inspects care facilities, issuing fines to those they find noncompliant. As stated above, facilities can appeal these fines and be exonerated. In addition to being fined, a facility that has been noncompliant for six months or more can lose its Medicaid/Medicare certification. This means the facility is unable to receive additional Medicare patients until the facility has reached the "reasonable assurance" period and is eligible to apply for recertification (Wood).    7

The use of fines and penalties has proven to be ineffective in most cases because, when faced with thousands of dollars in fines, many long-term care facility owners will voluntarily close their business and sell it to the highest bidder. Some reopen facilities under a new name or declare bankruptcy. Many facilities are owned by corporations or partnerships that, upon being closed down in one state, simply open another facility in another state and proceed to run that facility into the ground.    8

Though fines and penalties are aimed at punishing the owners and administrators of facilities, in the not-so-long run, staff and residents suffer the consequences. A facility that owes huge debts for noncompliance has less money to spend operating the facility efficiently. The result is inadequate staffing, poor wages, inadequate management, or lack of resources, all elements that directly affect patients. A reform in the law regulating long-term care facilities is desperately needed. The health, safety, and financial well-being of the people who live in these facilities is at stake.    9

## GIVING OUR ELDERLY THE QUALITY CARE THEY DESERVE

First, we propose that the law clearly define staffing requirements for long-term care facilities, mandating specific staff-to-patient ratios that    10 take into account the number of residents and level of acuity in a facility, just as staff-to-patient ratios are mandated for other health-care facilities. For example, a reasonable ratio for patients requiring intermediate care would be 7:1, seven patients to one staff member. In addition, each facility should be required to contract with a private nursing pool to provide staffing in emergency situations.

Furthermore, each facility must develop a state-mandated man-    11
agement team that includes not only the facility's administrator and selected staff, but also a state administrator from the Iowa Department of Inspections and Appeals, who interacts with this management team monthly. A state administrator team member should oversee no more than fifteen local facilities to ensure that he or she devotes an adequate amount of time to problem solving in any one facility. The management team would be responsible for overseeing and maintaining proper staffing ratios, ensuring efficient resource management, problem solving for quality-care issues, and implementing incentive programs to encourage good employee attendance and quality work. The state administrator would be responsible for offering alternative solutions to specific problems, such as finding reliable staff.

Next, we propose that the Iowa state legislature implement laws    12
to enforce penalties for noncompliant facilities. Our proposal requires that any long-term care facility that does not meet 90 percent compliance following two consecutive inspections loses its Medicaid/Medicare certification as well as its license to own and operate a long-term care facility in the state of Iowa. Fines based on level of noncompliance would be issued, and the facility would have thirty days to transfer its residents and close its doors.

To prevent chronically noncompliant owners from reopening    13
elsewhere, the existing public registry needs to provide state licensing agencies with a detailed history of all owners/corporations of long-term care facilities, complete with each company's noncompliance issues, penalties, and fines. Serious complaints should be noted in this registry. This registry needs to be accessible on a national scale and should make use of a grading scale for easier deciphering of information. Information should be graded on a scale of 1–4, mirroring the grading scale of the inspections department. Implementation of a complete public registry will help prevent other long-term care facilities from being opened by the same people who ran shoddy, unsafe operations elsewhere.

## THE OTHER SIDE

Some may argue that current Iowa regulations as stated in House 14
File 2290 are sufficient. But the current regulations leave the responsibility for maintaining adequate staffing in the hands of the individual facilities; there is no accountability. The management teams we
suggest would provide the accountability and the resources necessary
to provide quality care in a safe and positive environment.

Other options have been suggested, such as cameras in residents' 15
rooms to monitor the level of care (Huggins). Not only are cameras
an infringement of a citizen's right to privacy, but they also "institu-
tionalize" the atmosphere of long-term care facilities.

The state has considered incentive programs to hire better qual- 16
ity nurses, but this does not solve inadequate staffing problems.

Facility administrators may argue that they cannot afford more 17
nurses, but the management team we have proposed would look at
time-management issues within the existing staff to better allocate responsibilities. Also, funds that are currently spent on the lengthy inspec-
tion and appeals process could be used in the management of facilities.

## THE BOTTOM LINE

With the increase in complaints about elder care in Iowa, the time 18
has come for Iowa lawmakers and citizens to set a higher standard for
quality of life for our elderly generation. Iowa standards in long-term
care should set the example for the rest of the nation. Our proposal
eliminates staffing problems, distributes funds more efficiently, and
encourages quality health care in a positive environment. Happy,
healthy residents are the best advertisers for long-term care facilities,
and a positive work environment promotes loyal and competent employees. The focus in long-term care facilities needs to be directed
back to the residents, where it belongs.

## WORKS CITED

Grace, Joanie. Personal interview. 17 March 2005.
Huggins, Charnicia E. "States Consider Allowing Cameras in Nursing
    Homes." *Slack and Davis.* 1 Apr. 2005 <http://www.slackdavis.com/
    index.php>.

*Iowa Department of Elder Affairs.* State Ombudsman. 28 Nov. 2004 <http://www.state.ia.us/elderaffairs/advocacy/ombudsman.html>.

Kauffman, Clark. "Care Center Investigated Again." *Des Moines Register* 19 Mar. 2004 <http://desmoinesregister.com/news/stories/c4780934/23844434.html>.

Kauffman, Clark, and Tony Leys. "D.M. Facility's Residents Removed over Safety Fears." *Des Moines Register* 3 Apr. 2004 <http://www.desmoinesregister.com/apps/pbcs.dll/article?AID=/20040403/SENDTOPUBLICUS/404030359&SearchID=731917293419>.

*State of Iowa House File 2290, Section 4, 135M.4, H.J. 259.2* <http://www.legis.state.ia.us/GA/80GA/Legislation/HF/02200/HF02290/040217.html>.

Wood, Erica F. "Termination and Closure of Poor Quality Nursing Homes." March 2002. *American Association of Retired Persons.* 28 Nov. 2004 <http://research.aarp.org/il/2002_05_homes.pdf>.

# Sexual Harassment in Meatpacking Plants

Susan Ly

University of California, Riverside
Riverside, California

Susan Ly begins her essay by describing the problem she proposes to solve: In meatpacking plants, the men—both workers and supervisors—are "kissing, groping, and pressuring the women for dates and sex." This startling detail (from a reliable, current source, which Ly cites) establishes the seriousness of the problem and gives her proposal an urgency most readers will find hard to resist. Ly goes on to describe a solution to the problem in enough detail to allow readers to readily imagine its specifics—from the elements of a well-defined harassment policy to the range of delivery options (lectures, videotapes, seminars, e-seminars) for harassment training. Her establishment of the urgency of the problem and her clearly described solution are two of the strengths of Ly's paper, but its biggest strength is its counterargument. As you read, notice the way Ly presents, considers, and judiciously refutes several objections and alternative solutions to her proposal.

---

In the meatpacking industry, the men are grabbing and fondling the women without their consent. They are rubbing their bodies against the women's, knowing that the women are not completely comfortable with it. "Kissing, groping, and pressuring the women for dates and sex" (Schlosser 176) are examples of sexual harassment occurring in meatpacking plants today. The harassment starts at the top: when supervisors, who are mostly men, harass the female workers, the male workers feel that the behavior is appropriate and duplicate it. Moreover, because the supervisors participate in the harassment, the women have no one who can assist them and no one to whom they can report the incidents. So what should be done to end sexual harassment in such an environment?

1

To stop sexual harassment, employers in meatpacking plants    2
should take several steps. First, they should establish a written policy
defining and prohibiting harassment. In this written document, sexual harassment should be defined according to the U.S. Equal Employment Opportunity Commission (EEOC), which states that:

> Unwelcome sexual advances, requests for sexual favors, and other verbal
> or physical conduct of a sexual nature constitute sexual harassment
> when (1) submission to such conduct is made either explicitly or implic-
> itly a term or condition of an individual's employment, (2) submissions
> to or rejection of such conduct by an individual is used as a basis for em-
> ployment decisions affecting such individual, or (3) such conduct has a
> purpose or effect of unreasonably interfering with an individual's work
> performance or creating an intimidating, hostile, or offensive working
> environment. (Hofstra 1–2)

Next, employers should distribute this document to all employ-    3
ees and redistribute it on a regular basis. According to a Web site on
sexual harassment, "Employers must be proactive in order to avoid a
sexual harassment lawsuit" (qtd. in "Steps Employers"). A company
should have a sexual harassment policy that communicates that it is
"taking a 'zero tolerance' approach toward sexual harassment." The
company should "have an attorney review [the policy], and make
sure it gets out to all employees either through the employee hand-
book or in memo form" ("Steps Employers"). If employers do not
take this basic step, harassed victims can sue the company.

In addition, employers should require workers and supervisors to    4
attend sexual harassment training. Training sessions should teach employees how to recognize harassment, how to confront sexual harassers,
and who to turn to for help if they are victimized. Besides lectures,
training sessions should include videos and role-playing activities. Many
companies offer on-site sexual harassment seminars or online seminars.
One such company is Interactive Employment Training (IET), which
describes itself as a "leading provider of sexual harassment prevention
training." IET offers online courses designed by leading industry experts, and sells CD-ROMs and videos that teach about harassment.

By communicating what sexual harassment is and by training work-    5
ers to recognize and report it, employers can prepare employees to recognize and address problems. A good communication and training
program should discourage harassers by making it clear to them—and
their negligent supervisors—that people outside the plant know that
harassment is occurring and are trying to put an end to the problem.

Some wonder whether all employees will be able to read a docu-    6
ment defining sexual harassment, since many workers in the meatpacking industry are immigrants. Having the policies written in a
variety of languages would easily close any language gaps. Others
worry that employees would not read the policies, dismissing them
and throwing them away instead. In fact, it is less important that
each employee read the policy than that the employer takes the initiative to distribute it. The distribution alone will intimidate harassers
by communicating to them that the company is well aware of sexual
harassment and is doing everything in its power to stop it.

One alternative solution that has been proposed is to install video    7
cameras throughout the work site so that the harassment might be
recorded. Even though this may sound like an effective solution, since
employees who know they are being monitored would be afraid to do
anything inappropriate, it is actually a violation of employees' privacy.
Moreover, a monitored workplace might cause workers, especially immigrant workers, to feel self-conscious or nervous. It might actually
slow down the working process, hurting the plant's profits.

Another alternative solution that sounds feasible but is actually    8
not that simple is to create a checks-and-balances system in which pe-
riodic reviews of supervisors by workers, and of workers by supervisors, are submitted to the employer. One reason this may not work is
that the more powerful supervisors may threaten or blackmail the
workers into writing positive reviews.

Sexual harassment is a major issue in slaughterhouses. The victims,    9
mostly women, need as much help as they can get. When workers, supervisors, employers, and outsiders know about the problem, harassers
will think twice before initiating inappropriate behavior. Again, as the
EEOC states, "Prevention is the best tool to eliminate sexual harassment in the workplace" (*Facts*). Also, training can help victims deal with
problems when they arise. Meatpacking plant employers should devise a
written policy to prohibit sexual harassment and hire outside companies
to train their employees about sexual harassment. Their efforts will mean
a reduction in the number of sexual harassment cases across the industry
and much improved working environments in individual plants.

## WORKS CITED

"Creating a Harassment-Free Workplace." *Sexual Harassment*. 6 Feb. 2002
    <http://www.abanet.org/genpractice/lawyer/complete/w96shi.html>.

*Facts about Sexual Harassment.* The U.S. Equal Employment Opportunity Commission. 6 Feb. 2002 <http://www.eeoc.gov/facts/fs-sex.html>.

Hofstra, Patricia S. *Sexual Harassment in the Health Care Workplace* Dec. 1999. Bell, Boyd & Lloyd. 29 Jan. 2002 <http://www.bbl.com/newsletters/sexualharassment.asp>.

*Interactive Employment Training* 6 Feb. 2002 <http://htrain.com/index.html>.

Schlosser, Eric. *Fast Food Nation.* Boston: Houghton Mifflin Company, 2001.

*Sexual Harassment News and Recent Events.* Corporate Training Solutions. 6 Feb. 2002 <http://www.cts-corporatetraining.com/3harass.html>.

"Steps Employers Can Take to Avoid Sexual Harassment Lawsuits." *Sexual Harassment in the Workplace.* 6 Feb. 2002 <http://www.employer-employee.com/sexhar1.htm>.

# *Justifying an* 8
# *Evaluation*

You are already very familiar with evaluations. In fact, if you're like most of us, you depend on them on a weekly or even a daily basis. Before spending more-than-fast-food-money to dine out, you probably ask for suggestions from friends who know the local restaurant scene or read restaurant reviews online or in your local newspaper. And you probably don't watch movies cold; instead, you're more likely to go to the theater on a friend's recommendation or read brief descriptions of what's playing in a free weekly or on a movie-review site before buying a ticket. For a major purchase like a car or truck, cell phone, digital camera, or even a pair of running shoes, you're likely to look for a recent, authoritative review of the product, perhaps in *Consumer Reports*—a magazine whose comprehensive evaluations have catapulted its parent organization, the Consumers Union, into the national consciousness.

Quite clearly, reviews are wide ranging. Student writers in this chapter evaluate quite different subjects: a painting, a magazine, a movie, and an online marketplace. Like any reviewers, these writers judge their subjects, but they go well beyond giving them just a thumbs up or down: they give reasons for their judgments and then support each reason with definitions, examples, descriptions, and comparisons to similar subjects. They may even anticipate readers' reservations or alternative judgments.

Judgments are easy to make—so much so that they are sometimes referred to as "snap judgments." When you evaluate, you test your snap judgments, turning them into reasoned evaluations. In doing so, you develop your powers of attention to details and the ability to discriminate among them. When evaluating some subject and writing up your evaluation of it, you must look closely, attentively (that is, without noisy distractions), look again, think hard and rethink, justify—all the while extending and refining your understanding of subjects like the one you are evaluating. To evaluate, then, is to engage in thoughtful, responsible, discriminating work—work that is worth your time.

# May I Have This Dance?

Robert Nava

Riverside Community College
Riverside, California

We have all had the experience of coming away disappointed from an art exhibition or performance. After attending several "dreary and uninspiring" exhibits at his college's art gallery, Robert Nava was beginning to tire of such disappointments. Then one show—and one painting in particular, *Dance VII* by Gina Han—caught him by surprise. Nava liked the way *Dance VII* evoked movement. Of course, justifying an evaluation means more than just pointing out what you did or didn't like about a work. Evaluative authors should also provide reasons for their opinions and be able to support those reasons, and that means knowing their subject well. Experience helps, as do close or repeated viewings and, in some cases, additional research. Nava is an experienced judge of visual art—he establishes his authority as an evaluator of *Dance VII* by noting his past experience at his college's art gallery. But he has also done his homework. Much of his essay is devoted to an examination of how color and texture work together in the painting to create the impression of movement. That examination required both a sustained viewing of the piece and an understanding of color theory, a concept Nava explains to his readers. We come away from Nava's essay with both a desire to see the painting in person and a new appreciation for color theory and its usefulness as an artist's strategy. It is a gift to the reader when an evaluation combines critique with insight or instruction, as Nava's does. Could your evaluation essay lend itself to such an approach?

---

A visit to the Riverside Community College art gallery can some-   1
times be dreary and uninspiring. Having seen the faculty art show before, I have found that the pieces on display become repetitive and tiresome, with the same artists displaying new pieces with the same style and technique they've used every year before. However, this

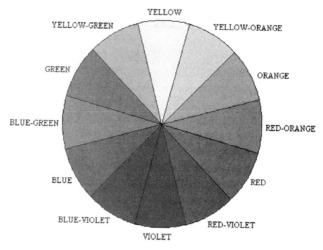

**Figure 1.** The color wheel.

year the faculty artists have produced quite a few surprises, one of which is *Dance VII* by Gina Han. At first glance, I disregarded the oil painting, thinking little or no effort had gone into creating it. What could be so special about a canvas covered in random blotches of color? On a second look, I discovered what was so exciting about *Dance VII:* the creation of movement through color, placement, and texture.

But to better appreciate *Dance VII,* a brief explanation of color theory is necessary. An important tool for any artist is the color wheel, an arrangement of primary (red, yellow, and blue) and secondary (orange, green, and violet) colors that logically blend into one another in a circle, or wheel. From the combination of the primary and secondary colors, all other colors are created. The primary colors, those colors that cannot be created by mixing other colors, are equidistant from each other on the wheel. Secondary colors are those colors created by mixing two primary colors—for example, combining red and blue to create violet. There are also tertiary colors, which are made by mixing a primary color with its adjacent (on the color wheel) secondary color—for example, red (primary) mixed with orange (secondary) will create red-orange (tertiary). The color wheel in Figure 1 shows primary, secondary, and tertiary colors.

With the color wheel, we can also identify different color combinations that, oddly and without any notable explanation, are pleasing

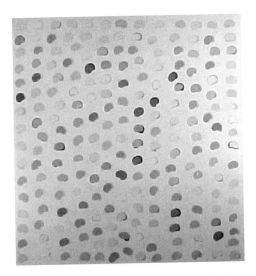

**Figure 2.** *Dance VII* by Gina Han. Oil on canvas (Han).

to the eye. One of these combinations is called *complementary,* which is a pairing of two opposing or contrasting colors—such as red and green, blue and orange, or yellow and violet—that are positioned directly across from each other on the color wheel. These complementary relationships also extend to secondary colors, so that red-orange, for example, is complementary to blue-green. Another relationship on the color wheel involves *harmonious* colors, which are colors in the same section of the color wheel. The closest relationship, however, exists between a primary color and its secondary color.

Initially, *Dance VII* strikes the viewer as merely a colorful piece, but one of its functions is as a testing ground for color theory, creating radical—but acceptable—color combinations. In Figure 2, the majority of the color blotches are purple, violet, pink-violet, and red-violet, all of which are harmonious colors. The complementary color to violet is yellow, hence the background color. Another use of complementary colors is in the color blotches themselves. Each blotch consists of two "disks" of color, one overlapping the other. On occasion, these colors are complementary: green on top of red, violet on top of yellow, etc. On other occasions, however, the complementary colors are implied or less direct. For example, a little bit of green can be mixed into red to produce a new, toned-down version of red that complements green in an interesting and fresh way.

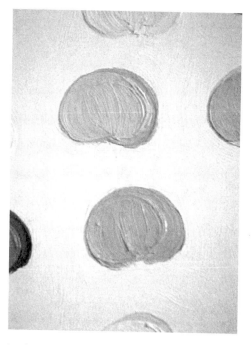

**Figure 3.**   A visual relationship can be found between adjacent blotches (Han).

Another noticeable element in *Dance VII* is that each color blotch is in some way related to one or more color blotches immediately surrounding it. The two blotches in the center of Figure 3 have a color in common: pink. Han uses exactly the same pink for the top "disk" of the lower blotch as she does for the bottom "disk" of the upper blotch. The upper blotch relates to the one above it because Han has used the same greenish color on each blotch's top "disk." The uppermost blotch in Figure 3 is linked to the blotch on the right because Han has used harmonious violet colors for the uppermost blotch's bottom "disk" and the right-hand blotch's top and bottom "disks." The violet-on-violet right-hand blotch is linked to the lower blotch because the lower blotch's bottom "disk" is also a shade of violet. These playful relationships appear throughout the entire piece, creating paths of color for the viewers' eyes to follow.

In addition to the clever use of color, the placement of the individual blotches is key to the painting's composition. Focusing on the perimeter of *Dance VII*, we see that the blotches are, for the most

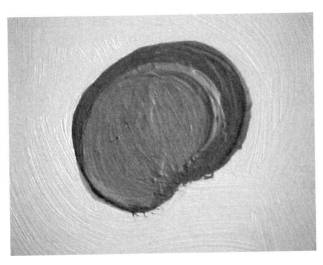

**Figure 4.** Thick applications of paint create texture, adding to the suggestion of movement (Han).

part, lined up neatly. Toward the center of the painting, the blotches begin to break up and "move around," forcing our eyes to wander around without focusing on any single blotch. Once the orderly relationship of blotches begins to break down, the color relationships come into play, bringing order to a largely chaotic environment.

Texture also contributes to movement. The entire piece is 7 smothered in thick applications of paint, and the brushes' bristles carved deep grooves as they were dragged across the canvas. The most noticeable elements of the painting are the blotches, which have the densest application of paint (see Figure 4), but in the negative space, or background, we can see peaks and valleys in the thick layers of paint. These textured strokes intentionally flow around the blotches like ocean currents sweeping against a collection of islands, suggesting movement. The background's fluid-like texture keeps viewers' eyes moving, cunningly redirecting them, again and again.

*Dance VII* is an exciting surprise. The painting disguises itself as 8 an unexciting, effortless piece and then jumps out at the viewers if they dare to examine it more closely. The exploration of color relationships initially draws in the viewers, inviting them to participate. But over time, the viewers will begin to see the relationships between the blotches of color. Their eyes begin to move, and they are swept away in a whirling assortment of color and texture. As suggested by the painting's title, *Dance VII* conveys a fluid, harmonious movement among its colors, well-placed blotches, and textures.

## WORK CITED

Han, Gina. *Dance VII*. Riverside Community College Art Gallery, Riverside, CA.

# Buzzworm:
## *The Superior Magazine*
### Ilene Wolf

*University of California, San Diego*
*La Jolla, California*

There's nothing worse than thumbing through a magazine that bangs you over the head with its one-sided rhetoric. Student author Ilene Wolf introduces readers to one that doesn't: *Buzzworm,* which approaches the controversial subject of the environment from an objective point of view. Wolf begins her essay both by explaining how the title *Buzzworm,* from the Old West term for a rattlesnake, reveals the magazine's purpose — "to create a reaction in its readers" — and by championing *Buzzworm* as a standout among other, less objective environmental magazines. As you read, notice how Wolf moves from a broad political perspective — presenting *Buzzworm* as a vehicle for change, and a better one than its rivals — to a focus on the magazine's technical aspects, including its visual appeal, subfeatures (sidebars), and captions. Does Wolf's attention to these details add to or detract from her evaluation of the magazine's overall effectiveness?

---

Many people today exist within their environment without really knowing anything about it. If this ignorance continues, we will undoubtedly destroy the world in which we live. Only by gaining a better understanding of our planet will we be able to preserve our fragile environment from pollution, hazardous waste, endangerment of species, and ravaging of the land. A new magazine is dedicated to enlightening the general public about these important issues. It is called *Buzzworm.*

What makes *Buzzworm* superior to other magazines dealing with the same subject is that it not only fully explores all of the aspects of the environment but does so in an objective manner. *Buzzworm* effectively tackles the controversial question of how best to protect our planet and conveys the information in a way that all audiences can

1

2

understand. In fact, the term *buzzworm,* borrowed from the Old West, refers to a rattlesnake. The rattlesnake represents an effective form of communication, for when it rattles or buzzes, it causes an immediate reaction in those who are near. Thus the purpose of *Buzzworm* is to create a reaction in its readers regarding the conservation and preservation of the environment.

One of *Buzzworm*'s most striking features is its visual appeal. Excellent photographs complement the articles. Contrasted with the photography in *Sierra,* another environmental magazine, the superb photographs in *Buzzworm* seem more striking. The summer 1989 issue of *Buzzworm* features a dramatic, full-page color picture of a gray wolf, which catches the reader's eye and draws attention to the article concerning the endangerment of the gray wolf's habitat. An issue of *Sierra* from the same year also has a picture of a gray wolf, yet it is smaller and the colors are not as clear—resulting in a less effective picture. Whereas both photographs of the animal pertain to their corresponding articles, it is the one in *Buzzworm* that makes the reader stop and discover the plight of the gray wolf.

A photograph must be of excellent quality and be placed correctly in the layout to enhance the article. The reader should be able to look at the picture and receive some information about the article it corresponds to. *Buzzworm*'s pictures of the East African Masai convey specific information about the tribe. Startling photographs depict the Masai in their traditional dress, focusing on the elaborate beadwork done by the women and the exquisite headdresses worn by the warriors. Looking at one picture of a young warrior wearing a lion's mane headdress, the reader gets a sense of the importance of the ritual and of the great respect that is earned by becoming a warrior. Another picture depicts a mother intently watching her daughter as she learns the art of beading. The look on the woman's face displays the care that goes into the beadwork, which has been an important part of their heritage for many generations. Thus, even before reading the article about the Masai, readers have some understanding of the Masai culture and its traditions.

Another functional and informative aspect of *Buzzworm*'s layout is the use of subfeatures within an article. A subfeature functions in two ways: first by breaking up the monotony of a solid page of print, and second by giving the curious reader additional information. An article entitled "Double Jeopardy," for example, gives the reader an option of learning more about the subject through two subfeatures. The article itself describes the detrimental effects that excessive whale watching and research are believed to have on the humpback whale. To find further information about what might be contributing to the already low numbers of the humpback whale, one can read the subfeature "Humpback Whale Survival." Furthermore, for the reader who is not familiar with the subject, there is a second subfeature, entitled "Natural History," which gives general information about the humpback whale. No such subfeatures can be found anywhere in *Sierra*.

In addition to being an effective way of adding pertinent information to the article, the subfeatures also add to the unity of the magazine. The subfeatures in *Buzzworm* all share a common gray background color, adding to the continuity in layout from one article to the next. This produces a cleaner, more finished, and visually appealing magazine.  6

Once again, *Buzzworm* shows superior layout design in keeping the articles from being overrun by advertisements. I realize that ads do generate necessary revenue for the magazine, but nothing is more annoying than an article constantly interrupted by ads. *Buzzworm*'s few ads are all in the back of the magazine. In fact, not once does an ad interrupt an article. On the other hand, *Sierra* is filled with advertisements that are allowed to interrupt articles, which only frustrates the reader and detracts from the articles.  7

*Buzzworm* is unique in that it focuses on more than just one aspect of the environment. In contrast, *Sierra* devoted its entire September/October 1989 issue to one subject, the preservation of the public lands in the United States. Although it is a topic worthy of such discussion, readers prefer more variety to choose from. The content of *Buzzworm* ranges from the humpback whale to the culture of the Masai to a profile of three leading conservationists. The great variety of issues covered in *Buzzworm* makes it more likely to keep the reader's attention than *Sierra*.  8

*Buzzworm*'s ability to inform the reader is not limited to the information in its articles. Captions also play a large part. Readers who are too lazy to read an entire article will most often look at the pictures and read the captions. Thus *Buzzworm*'s long and detailed captions are like miniature paragraphs, giving out more details than the terse captions in *Sierra*, which usually consist of only a few words. The difference in the amount of information in the two magazines is obvious from a look at a typical caption in *Buzzworm*—"Finding relaxation of a different kind, Earthwatch participants spend a vacation patrolling beaches and assisting female turtles in finding a secluded  9 nesting area"—compared to one in *Sierra*—"Joshua tree with Clark Mountain in background." Both captions give a description of their corresponding pictures, but only the caption found in *Buzzworm* gives any indication of what the article is about. The captions in *Buzzworm* supplement the articles, whereas the captions in *Sierra* only give brief descriptions of the pictures.

Finally, *Buzzworm* is objective, a rare quality in environmental magazines. An article on tourism versus environmental responsibility focuses on both the environmental and economic aspects of tourism, stating that while tourism generates income, it often destroys places of natural beauty that are so often visited. In contrast to this point of view, the article also cites examples where tourism has actually helped to preserve the environment. For every argument presented in *Buzzworm*, the counterargument is also presented. This balance is important, for readers must have all of the facts to be able to make well-informed judgments about controversial issues.

Despite all of its wonderful aspects, *Buzzworm* does have its flaws. Some of its graphics pale next to the color photographs. Also, the photographs should be more varied in size to create a more visually appealing layout. Except for these minor flaws, *Buzzworm* achieves its goal of appealing to its readers. In informing the general public about conservation and protection of our environment, *Buzzworm* is far more effective than *Sierra*.

# A Film Evaluation
# of Garden State

## Anna Marie Cruz

*University of California, Riverside*
*Riverside, California*

Evaluations always start from likes and dislikes—a moviegoer's enjoyment of the chemistry between lead actors, her feeling that the end rings false. But successful writers of evaluation essays move beyond such personal reactions. In her evaluation of *Garden State,* Anna Marie Cruz both considers how her readers might judge the film differently from the way she does—imagining, in particular, an older generation's standpoint—and responds to specific criticisms of the film from published reviews. Using these criticisms to launch her determined defense of *Garden State,* Cruz gets an eye-opening lesson in film that transforms the way she watches movies: "I used to watch movies to enjoy the story line and the special effects, but after writing this essay, I watch movies differently. I tend to pick up more from the film: the use of metaphors and music selections, for example. I also began to understand what the cinematographer and the scriptwriter intended to convey besides the obvious plot." As you read, notice how Cruz's close study of *Garden State,* which arose out of a need to communicate her point of view to critics of the film, leads her to observations and realizations she might not have otherwise had.

———————

Members of every generation have their own signature movies—   1
movies that capture their moment in time. *Garden State* is such a
movie, a sure winner for audiences between the ages of eighteen and
thirty. Written and directed by Zach Braff, *Garden State* is an eccen-
tric coming-of-age comedy that "documents the emotional awaken-
ing of Andrew Largeman (also known as 'Large'), played by Braff"
(Tenenbaum). With Braff's lack of experience on the big screen as an
actor, director, and screenplay writer, many wonder how his movie
did so well; they wonder why so many people are so in love with the

film. The answer is this: The well-written story line, Braff's creativity and expertise in cinematography, and his musical selections all tie together to create a "hilarious and heartfelt" movie that many viewers, especially viewers of my generation, love and relate to (Travers).

Braff's story line is wonderful, full of metaphors for the journey 2 that Braff's character, Largeman, goes through in the movie. Although some people may find the story line unrealistic, many people of my generation would disagree. In her review of the movie in the *London Times,* Wendy Ide claims that the film is rather "episodic, a little patchy and not as true to life as Braff clearly hoped it would be." Although some events seem surreal, such as the fact that the nine-year-old Largeman was responsible for his mother's becoming paraplegic, *Garden State* does portray the real world in ways that people of my generation do in fact relate to. They relate to the feeling of "alienation," the feeling of being "a young adult with no idea where life is headed," and they understand Braff's portrayal of "the awkward relationship with home" (Yuan).

In the movie, Largeman has returned home to New Jersey to at- 3 tend his mother's funeral. During his four-day stay, he finds himself, and he finds a purpose to live. Through his growing relationship with Samantha (Sam), played by Natalie Portman, he discovers his emotions. A review of Braff's *Garden State* in the *Warsaw Voice* claims that the movie spends "too much time scuffling around with its hands in its pockets before [Braff] seems to panic in the last twenty minutes and [finally] unearths the most unwieldy symbol." But that "scuffling around" is essential. The slow pace allows Braff to build the relationship between the two main characters, Andrew Largeman and Sam. Allowing the audience to become acquainted with Andrew and Sam gives viewers the chance to feel along with the characters their times of sorrow, love, and happiness.

The important metaphor that Braff reveals near the end of the 4 movie is the infinite abyss as a metaphor for life. When Large says, "Have fun exploring the infinite abyss" to his friend Albert, and Albert responds, "You, too," the audience understands that Albert's infinite abyss is the quarry, while for Large, it is life. The quarry is unknown, the way life is unpredictable: no one knows the quarry, and no one can tell the future. Large aspires to a life like Albert's, a life of happiness and contentment spent with the one you love. When Large screams at the quarry, it signifies that he is almost finally sure of himself, that he is almost at the point where Albert is; he just hasn't fully realized it. In fact, he doesn't realize it until his plane is about to leave for Los Angeles. One of the important turning points is the scene in the tub. As Large shares an intimate moment with Sam (they are wearing clothes but soaking wet), his numbness begins to disappear. Once Large is able to feel real emotions, he can begin to deal with reality's challenges. After the tub scene, Large goes to his father for permission to live his life. He asks that his father be content with life and OK with who they are. He also forgives his father for ruining his childhood with his yearning for the perfect happy family, which kept Large from having emotions.

*Garden State*, Braff's film debut, displays his creativity and skill in directing cinematography. Braff's use of color and composition and his creative use of camera techniques greatly influence the way the story is presented to the audience, giving them "clever visual cues" (Yuan). For example, Braff uses a color motif—a movement from dull tones such as blue and gray to warm lively tones such as yellow and orange. This color transition suggests Largeman's evolution from an empty, meaningless existence to a purposeful one, full of emotions such as love. In one of the early scenes, Largeman lies in his white bed with a straight, stiff, lifeless body. The color white symbolizes Largeman's numb, almost robotlike personality. Similarly, Large's father's office and bedroom are monotone, with beige as the prevalent color, and are also very orderly, with cold, contemporary architectural elements. The same goes for Largeman's bedroom; the only difference is that the monotone is blue instead of beige. The dark color scheme in Largeman's bedroom, so different from the beige scheme in the rest of the house, shows that Largeman is set apart even from his own family. Braff uses green and complementary colors in Largeman's best friend Mark's house. The use of green and its complementary tones conveys the transition from cold colors to warmer ones. Visiting the doctor's office, Largeman waits in a cold, monotone waiting room. When he is finally called into Dr. Cohen's office, he steps into a wood-paneled room, which is in sharp contrast to his father's office (his father is also a doctor). Dr. Cohen's office is more homey and warm, and less orderly, than Dr. Largeman's office. Dr. Cohen, who is more open and less stiff than Dr. Largeman, also acts more like a father to Largeman than his own father. Another example of Braff's use of color is Sam's home, where warm shades like orange and yellow predominate. Sam's home is much less orderly than Largeman's; it's basically organized chaos. It's also random, with mismatched furniture and decor. The changes in color tones from cold to warm—from white, beige, and dark blue to green, orange, and yellow—signify the change in Largeman, from being disconnected to being human. This is also apparent in the change in Largeman's skin tone. In the beginning of the movie, Largeman is a pale, almost powdery white, blending into his empty apartment. When he finally changes, becoming a person who can feel and be open, his skin color looks flushed and lifelike.

Braff also uses composition in meaningful ways. For example, he 6 centers the characters only occasionally, for emphasis. In particular, he centers Sam and Large during significant moments in the development of their relationship. The first time he centrally frames Sam and Large is when they are sitting together near the fireplace, when Large finally opens up and tells Sam the truth about his mother. The moment when Large protects Sam is the second time Braff frames them in the center. In that scene, Large finally takes a stand; he is finally active instead of passive. The third time Braff centers them is when they are in Albert's ark, when Albert says that all he needs is his wife and beautiful baby. Braff centers Sam and Large because Albert and his wife's happiness is something that Large and Sam are trying to achieve with one another. The centering hints to the audience that Large and Sam are approaching that kind of love with one another. The fourth and final scene in which they are centered is at the end, when they kiss, because that is the climax of their relationship, the achievement of the love they were developing throughout the film. Braff also uses nature to focus and isolate events and characters. In two scenes, for example, Braff uses fog to isolate the characters from their environment: in the scene in which Kenny—Large's high school friend who has become a cop—pulls Large over, and in the pool scene.

Braff also uses creative techniques such as camera speed and 7 imaginative transitions. During the ecstasy party, for example, he slows and stops the camera to focus on some moments, and speeds it up through less important moments. He also uses zoom instead of moving the camera. Little camera movement and more zoom helps the audience see the bigger picture. More camera movement might have distracted viewers. Braff also uses interesting transitions. In one, Large reaches to adjust the air nozzle above his seat on an airplane, and the nozzle becomes the phone in his apartment. In another transition, from the Vietnamese restaurant where Large works to the rest room in the airport, Large's earpiece feeds him the order for his next table and then switches to announcements in the airport. In yet another scene, as Large waits for his plane to take off, he is mindlessly thinking while everyone else is moving around the plane. He then hears a bell ring. The ring signals his epiphany: he realizes that he no longer has to search for anything; everything he has ever wanted and needed is with Sam.

*Garden State* features music from the Shins, Iron and Wine, Nick Drake, Simon and Garfunkel, Colin Hay, and Frou Frou. Braff's musical choices are excellent, and he uses his selections in unique and creative ways. As Longanecker writes, "the soundtrack is incredibly fitting and the songs are integrated into the film in a way that subtly but powerfully enhances [the film's] mood and message." Some people feel that the "selections are a bit too obvious" and that they were chosen to attract a certain kind of viewer. Those things may be true, but Braff's musical selections do contribute to the movie—for example, by heightening the emotion of a scene, or communicating something about it. One exception, in the opening section, is the song that is a prayer to Ganesh, an important Hindu God. Many people will not understand Braff's use of that song because it is not a well-known piece and there is no obvious explanation for its placement, as there is for his other selections.

Some songs are used mostly for the mood they convey, such as Colin Hay's "I Just Don't Think I'll Ever Get Over You," played after Jelly's funeral in Sam's backyard; the song "Blue Eyes" by the Cary Brothers, played during the scene in the bar when Largeman and Sam get to know each other; the song "Fair" by Remy Zero, played when Large sits near the fireplace while Sam tap dances for him; and the version of "Such Great Heights" by Iron and Wine, played in the short scene when Sam and Large are in bed.

In other cases, it is a song's lyrics that stand out most. For example, the song "Don't Panic" by Coldplay is used to illustrate Largeman's condition as he lies, stiff and lifeless, on his bed. Words like "bones sinking like stones" echo Largeman's corpselike state. Similarly, when Largeman takes his motorcycle out for a ride and "Caring Is Creepy" by the Shins plays in the background, the lyrics "I think I'll go home and mull this over" are a good representation of his contemplative state of mind. And in the scene in which Largeman sits on the couch at the house party, the lyrics of "In the Waiting Line" by Zero 7 explain Largeman's isolation and stagnation. His feeling of seclusion from reality and society is best explained by the words, "There doesn't seem to be anybody else who agrees with me." Throughout the party, he stays motionless, absorbing the environment around him, and the words "motionless wheel, nothing is real, wasting my time in the waiting line" further demonstrate that.

Some songs are used for both their lyrics and their mood. Simon   11
and Garfunkel's "The Only Living Boy in New York" is playing when
Large, Sam, and Mark scream on top of the bulldozer. It is still playing
when Large and Sam kiss for the first time, and the words "let your
honesty shine" play when the sun shines on them as they kiss. The
song "Let Go" by Frou Frou, played at the end of the movie when
Large returns to Sam at the airport, explains Large's final transforma-
tion. Large finally lets go of his "tragedy" and accepts the fact that
"there's beauty in the breakdown"—in other words, he realizes that
he will not mess up his relationship with Sam if she witnesses him
breaking down. During the credits, the song "Winding Road" by Bon-
nie Somerville plays, basically summing up the entire film.

Throughout the movie, the music "weaves in and out of the film   12
as naturally as music does in real life" (Tenenbaum). Sometimes the
music even plays a part in the movie, as when, in the doctor's office,
Sam offers Large her headphones to listen to the song "New Slang"
by the Shins, claiming it will change his life forever. The song does
open up his mind, especially the words "I'm looking in on the good
life I might be doomed never to find," which describe Large's journey toward a better, truer life.

Although it is not a film for everyone, *Garden State* still draws   13
people in, as evidenced by the movie's massive ticket and DVD sales.
Zach Braff's well-written story line, creativity and expertise in cinematography, and musical selections all contribute to the movie's success, especially among viewers of my generation.

## WORKS CITED

Ide, Wendy. "*Garden State.*" *Times (London)* 11 Dec. 2004.

Longanecker, Mindy. "Zach Braff Stuns with Feature Film Debut." *Cava-
lier Daily* 7 Sept. 2004.

Tenenbaum, Sara. "*Garden State* a Stirring, Sweet Film Wise Beyond Its
Years." *Justice* 1 Sept. 2004.

Travers, Peter. "*Garden State.*" *Rolling Stone* 27 July 2004.

"World of Movies—Film Review—*Garden State.*" *Warsaw Voice* 5 Dec.
2004.

Yuan, Xiao-Bo. "*Garden State* Is Too 'College' for Its Own Good." *Johns
Hopkins News-Letter* 13 Sept. 2004.

*Zach Braff.* 1 March 2005 <http://www.zach-braff.com/gardenstate.html>.

# eBay: The World's Finest Online Marketplace

## Duc Do

University of California, Riverside
Riverside, California

Right away, student author Duc Do's confident tone and detailed observations signal to readers that he is an expert navigator of the eBay marketplace. His knowledge of the online auction site allows him to inform without ever threatening to confuse. The most timid Internet shoppers—readers who hesitate to send their credit card information through cyberspace, or who wonder if they will ever receive the items they purchase—will find comfort in Do's detailed explanation, peppered with thoughtful anecdotes of his own experience. Do's thoroughness and choice of a topic he knows intimately serve not only his readers but also the writer himself. As the veteran Internet jockey notes, his research for this essay "actually made [his] experience on eBay even better."

---

Have you ever strolled through the mall and thought to yourself, "There are so many things on display, but I don't have enough time to look at them all"? Now imagine this: Take everything you see at the mall and multiply it by ten thousand. That will give you a rough idea of how many items are for sale on The World's Online Marketplace, eBay (www.ebay.com). eBay is a Web site, but not any ordinary one. It started out in 1995 as a place for the wife of former CEO Pierre Omidyar to trade Pez dispensers with other collectors (Adler). Today, eBay is where over 95 million registered buyers and sellers from across the globe gather to trade goods through online auctions (Conhaim). It is a marketplace unlike any other, and interestingly enough, access to this huge market is but a mouse-click away. No walking is required—except for the occasional trip to the post office or to your own door to greet the mailman. It may seem remarkable that so many people use a single Web site, but look more closely at the site and you'll understand why.

In this essay, I will evaluate the eBay Web site based on the criteria    2
for an e-commerce site: (1) Is it well designed? (2) Is it user friendly
(convenient, easy to use, and helpful to new users)? and (3) Is it reliable and secure? Since the Web site is very large, I will concentrate on
evaluating the site's most commonly used pages and features. Although this Web site has been upgraded several times over the course
of the four years that I have used it, I will evaluate only the current version of the site. Overall, I am truly impressed with this Web site; it is
very well designed, extremely user friendly, very convenient and easy to
use, and also very reliable, although in a few ways, the Web site could
be better—especially in the placement of some links.

As with any Web site, the visitor's first impression of the eBay    3
Web site comes from the front page. The design of this page immediately meets my criteria of being visually appealing. The color
scheme is aesthetically pleasing—the combination of yellow boxes
and blue-colored links on a white background is neither too gaudy
nor too plain and also offers great contrast. The design also uses a
combination of smooth and sharp corners such that the page does
not look like a stack of plain boxes on the screen—an aspect I find
displeasing on many amateur, and even some professional, Web sites.

Besides these attractive visual aspects, the front page is above all    4
very useful. At the very top of the page, as on every other page on
this site, are the most important links: buy, sell, help, sign in, register,
and search. (Having these links in the same place on every page
makes navigation easy and convenient—busy shoppers never have to
flounder through multiple clicks of the browser buttons or retype the
URL in the address bar to return to the main menu.) The rest of
the front page contains many links neatly partitioned into groups on
the left-hand side of the page, starting with links to eBay's specialty
pages (among them eBay Motors for car enthusiasts and Half.com
for books and other types of media), followed by categories of items
listed in alphabetical order. The center of the page displays an ad that
links to auctions in an interesting category, and the right side of the
page offers more catchy pictures linking the user to even more featured auctions. These links, while numerous, are organized in a very
orderly fashion and are illustrated with pleasing visuals, giving users a
variety of options without sacrificing convenience or clarity. (Interestingly, according to a psychological study of item placement on
e-commerce sites such as eBay, many links—especially merchandise,
help, home, and log-in links—are placed where most people would
expect them [Bernard]).

A scroll down the page reveals more links: those to other sites,   5
including twenty-five international eBay sites, as well as other options
such as PayPal—used to pay for the auctions—and downloads for
tools to aid in buying and selling. At the very bottom is a small button
that says "e-trust" and some copyright messages about the site and
company. The "e-trust" button assures users that the site is legitimate
and trustworthy, which is especially important because the company
deals with a very precious commodity—money. The copyright message informs users that this Web site is the official site of eBay, Inc., a
company that owns stocks and is also on the list of the fastest growing
technological companies—a company we can trust. Traverse the
many other pages on the site and it becomes even more apparent that
this site believes in trust and honesty—warnings against fraud and
links to customer support pages in case of fraud are plentiful. Therefore, this Web site clearly conveys that it is very reliable, a fact that I
have also confirmed through repeated use over the past four years.

From the home page, users can link directly to many other   6
pages. For those who cannot find a certain link, a site map link at the
top leads to a page with a very clearly organized and categorically al-
phabetized list of links. I find it very easy to search within this site
map, although for novice users, the categorization methods may take
some getting used to. However, for both new users and current users
exploring new options, the help page on this Web site is one of the
most useful ones I have seen. Links to the help page (easily distinguishable by their blue color) are available at the top of every page as
well as in places where clarification might be necessary. Within the
help page, users can find clear directions to every step in the
processes of buying, selling, paying. An even more appealing option,
which I do not often see on other sites, is the set of audio/video
step-by-step tours of the processes, which show users exactly what
they can expect to see and do. From the help page, users can also
find links to eBay University, which offers both live and virtual
classes. And for those special questions not answered in the help
pages, there is even a live help feature for real-time assistance—
another sign of how dedicated this site is to helping its users have the
best possible experience. There has yet to be a question that I have
had for which the help pages did not suffice; those who complain of
not understanding a certain feature simply have not used this excellent help page.

Since this Web site deals with an enormous amount of money,   7
about 15 billion dollars annually (Lynn), it is reasonable that it

requires users to provide identification. The registration process, which is accessible through the register link at the top of every page, requires quite a bit of information about the user, including his or her credit card and checking account numbers (Lynn). Despite this, however, the registration process is actually very simple and free. Throughout the process, eBay emphasizes that all information will be kept confidential. When I first started using eBay, security was a major concern of mine. Having submitted so much information at registration, I worried about identity theft. However, as I came to learn, eBay shared this concern with me, and thus, the password is encrypted and the pages are secure. This is easily verifiable by the "lock" icon on the bottom right-hand corner of the browser—something users much appreciate. There is also no hassle to users regarding massive junk or annoying spam email from advertisers—another drawback of many registration processes—a difference I welcome, as my email is already inundated daily with such messages. I should also mention that there are no annoying pop-ups or spyware on this site, a problem that many Internet users constantly complain about with other sites.

For me and many other users, another obvious concern is how well the auction system can manage the over 16 million items that run on any given day (Muller), not to mention the several-month backlog of completed auction records. How the site accomplishes this, I still cannot say for certain, but the results are very clear. The auctions are handled extraordinarily well. Auctions never become lost in cyberspace, and they always end precise to the second (the official time is listed at the bottom of every page). It also might seem that to find the auctions that one is interested in among millions might take a very long time, but in fact, a search usually takes only two or three seconds (at least on my DSL connection) and no more than ten seconds—even on a standard 56k connection (which I was using during my first year or so of using eBay). The search system is simply extraordinary. It is comparable to that of the major search engines, such as Yahoo! or Google, and can be conveniently accessed through the search field at the very top-right corner of every page. Not only can it search the titles of auctions, but it can also give the user the option of searching the descriptions within the auctions. But what makes it even better than the normal search engine is the advanced search option. Here users can narrow down their search in almost every thinkable way: not only in regard to the category of the item, but also in regard to the location of the seller, the name of the seller, the price of the auction, the format of the listing, and even the number of bids on the item. With so many search options, not to mention many easy-to-use ones (most are as simple as marking the box next to the desired option), narrowing a search with thousands of results to less than a hundred is no difficult task. Part of this magic lies within the categorization of auctions; with 31 main categories and 35,000 subcategories for items (Conhaim), this Web site is extremely orderly. Compared with other databases where even a narrowed advanced search gives a multitude of irrelevant results, this system is far more efficient and user friendly. With it, a user can easily find almost anything he or she wishes to buy, given someone is selling it (Adler).

In addition, the search results are also listed in an easy-to-browse 9 table format, with alternating white and gray backgrounds for each successive auction listing. Next to the title of each auction is the most important information: a thumbnail of the picture provided, the price, the number of bids, and time left. The user can also select an option to show the listings with larger pictures next to each title, or sort the results based on the amount of time remaining, distance, price, or paying method. This flexibility is very helpful and convenient because different search methods are useful at different times. Another very helpful feature is the red coloring of the time left on auctions that end within an hour, which serves as a reminder to users as to how much time they have left to bid on the item—especially useful for procrastinating bidders like myself, who prefer waiting until the last minute to bid. This page indeed is very user friendly; even when I first started using eBay, I found nothing confusing or difficult to comprehend, and have always appreciated the many extremely convenient and helpful features.

The detailed auction page can be easily accessed by clicking on 10 the auction title wherever it is displayed, whether it be the search results page, the home page, or another page. The quality of the page varies by seller because of different listing methods that each seller uses, but the main layout set up by the eBay Web site is always a very user-friendly one. At the top, as I would expect, is the most important information, including the title of the auction, its price, the amount of time remaining, the number of bids, the high bidder's ID, the seller's ID, and the seller's feedback rating (number of positive transactions the seller has made). Many useful links are also located in this area, including those to bookmark the auction, read the seller's feedback comments, place a bid, or go back to the search results. The links are all very clearly listed and colored blue to distinguish them from the rest of the text, making them very easy to locate—even for the most inexperienced users. The information and links also give the user quick access to the most important areas on the page, as well as a chance to see who is actually selling the item and whether the person is trustworthy. This minimizes confusion for the user about anything related to the auction. And for more information regarding the item's description, the buyer can click a link to send the seller a question, another feature I have used very often and found most handy.

Once the user is ready to bid on an item, the "place bid" button 11 at the top will move the user to the "submit bid" field at the bottom of the page. The bidding system used on this Web site is also "tremendously easy" to use (Brown). All the user needs to do is enter a maximum bid and the proxy bidding system will automatically bid the minimum amount needed to keep the user in the highest bidder position (Boyd). In such a way, the user need not sit in front of the computer all day to monitor an auction and bid on it in case someone else does. Although I enjoy micromanaging my bids as if it were a game to see who can throw a bid in at the last second and win, I realize many people cannot spare more than a few minutes, and thus this automated system couldn't be more convenient.

Another thing on the eBay Web site that I have found most use- 12 ful is the My eBay page. All the user's activities on the site are organized onto this one page in a clear table format that categorizes everything from auctions that are being watched to items the user has bought or those he or she is selling. This page allows the user to manage his or her entire account from one place. Any important information that the user needs is neatly organized onto this one page: the time remaining on auctions on the watch list, the final price on items won, reminders to pay for items, questions from others interested in the user's items for sale. With a quick scan of this page, I can easily determine what needs to be done—there is no need to jump back and forth between pages to check on the status of an auction, make sure an item I received was the correct one, or find a link to pay for an item. This, too, makes users' experience every bit more positive, as it helps save them time and trouble.

The previously mentioned feedback system also adds tremen- 13 dously to the trustworthiness of the site. Users accumulate feedback points through good transactions, both as sellers and as buyers. Studies show that buyers are willing to pay "strong-reputation sellers 8.1% more on average than a new seller" (Resnick et al.). While this might work against new sellers, it also assures sellers that they can build trust by being honest (and can also lose it very quickly by suddenly becoming dishonest). It therefore discourages "low-integrity sellers from joining the market" (Resnick et al.), making eBay a reliable market—one that confers many more benefits than risks to its users.

The eBay Web site has much to offer its users, and presents its features not only in a very organized and aesthetically pleasing manner, but in one of the most user-friendly and reliable ways as well (Lynn). The pages and features I have described are probably the most often used ones on the Web site, but they are but a sample of what the site has to offer. Dedicated sellers will discover even more help files and features to aid their businesses. Many other guides exist, including those that teach users how to ensure their privacy as well as what can be done in case of identity theft. Having read through these during my leisure time, I have found them very informative and understandable. 14

At the same time, this Web site is not without its weaknesses. While the pages on privacy are very important, they are not well advertised, and are often only stumbled on by accident (possibly when a user is reporting an incident to the eBay security center). In most cases, it is likely that many users may not be armed with the preventive knowledge provided in these pages because they simply don't know it exists. 15

Another weakness I have found is that despite the many items that are sold on eBay, the Web site's "sell item" submission page seems rather troublesome and somewhat hard to use. Trying to find the correct categories for the item one wants to sell and upload the correct picture and write a good description turns out to be a rather long and hard task. Sellers need to go through and fill out many fields, which may take them a considerable amount of time and effort, especially if they have many items to list. The site makes up for this shortcoming somewhat by having an option to "sell similar item" in which the fields are prefilled with the information from the last time, making the listing process somewhat easier. A better solution is the listing programs that are available through the downloads page, accessible from the front page. However, these—like some of the pages I mentioned previously—are not very well advertised, and their existence is not readily apparent to many users, making selling a bit troublesome for inexperienced users. 16

I have, through the course of my use, also encountered some minor inconveniences with server troubles. The site did experience a twenty-two hour outage in 1999 (which I did not experience myself), 17 which was very detrimental (Dembeck), but that has not happened since (except for a brief ten-minute shutdown that I experienced once a few years ago). However, there are some instances when several of the lists, including the watch list on the My eBay page, do not function properly. While these problems are often repaired within a few hours, they are sometimes rather inconvenient, especially if an auction is about to end and the user cannot easily find the link.

Overall, however, my experience with this Web site has been a very positive one. I have used it to buy and sell over a thousand items from many different categories (everything from plants to music CDs to LEGO pieces and other hobby miniatures), and I continue to do so today. The idea behind the Web site is indeed a very innovative one; a decade ago, few people would have thought that online auctions to connect buyers and sellers across the globe were a possibility in the business world. However, it takes much more than just an innovative idea for such a Web site to be successful, and this is where the eBay Web site prevails. Its superb design, high level of user friendliness, and reliability have helped to attract and keep many users like myself. What the site has to offer me is very well worth the time I have spent browsing it.

## WORKS CITED

Adler, Jerry. "The eBay Way of Life: For Sale: a Castle in Tucson, a Bridal Gown, Tickle Me Elmo and Anything Else You Could Name. *Newsweek* Spent 24 Hours in the World's Biggest Online Marketplace, Hoping to Learn What Makes America Click (Company Profile)." *Newsweek* 17 June 2002. *Expanded Academic ASAP*. Gale. U of California, Riverside Lib. 24 Feb. 2005 <http://www.infotrac.galegroup.com>.

Bernard, Michael. "Examining User Expectation for the Location of Common E-Commerce Web Objects." 1 Apr. 2002. 1 Mar. 2005 <http://csg .chcsolutions.com/csg/research/usability.webobject_placement.pdf>.

Boyd, Josh. "How eBay Controls Auctions without an Auctioneer's Voice." 2002. 1 Mar. 2005 <https://www.cerias.purdue.edu/tools_and_ resources/bibtex_archive/archive/2002-18.pdf>.

Brown, Andrew. "Boot Camp Internet (eBay)." *New Statesman* 129.4469 (1996). *Expanded Academic ASAP*. Gale. U of California, Riverside Lib. 24 Feb. 2005 <http://www.infotrac.galegroup.com>.

Conhaim, Wallys. "Where Buyer Meets Seller." *Information Today* 21.5 (2004): 2. *Expanded Academic ASAP*. Gale. U of California, Riverside Lib. 24 Feb. 2005 <http://www.infotrac.galegroup.com>.

Dembeck, Chet. "Yahoo! Cashes In on eBay's Outage." *ECT News Network* 18 June 1999. 1 Mar. 2005 <http://www.ectnews.com/>.

Lynn, Jacqueline. "Let the Bidding Begin: An eBay Business Could Be Your Entry to the Online Marketplace: Find Out How to Get Started Today (Be Your Own Boss)." *Entrepreneur* 31.9 (Sept. 2003). *Expanded Academic ASAP.* Gale. U of California, Riverside Lib. 24 Feb. 2005 <http://www.infotrac.com.galegroup.com>.

Muller, Lynn. "Risk Free Enterpreneurship and Marketing Via the Internet: Ooh!!! It's So Easy!" *South Dakota Business Review* LXII.II (2003). 1 Mar. 2005 <http://ksghome.harvard.edu/~rzeckhauser/postcards.pdf>.

Resnick, Paul, et al. "The Value of Reputation on eBay: A Controlled Experiment." *Experimental Economics* 9.2 (2006): 79–101.

# Speculating about Causes 9

Beginning your day, you wonder why your car is increasingly hard to start. Driving to campus, you puzzle over why you seem unable to make better use of your study and homework time. Arriving on campus, circling the parking lot looking for a space, you fret about what could be holding up ground breaking for the promised multistory parking structure. This kind of thinking is so natural that your brain does it for you, without any urging or pushing. You couldn't really stop yourself from thinking about the whys and hows of things—even if you wanted to.

But fretful and even obsessive as this kind of thinking may be sometimes, you wouldn't want to shut it off because it could save you time if it inspires you to remove some obstacle; it could make you wiser if it leads to new understanding about yourself, other people, or the world at large; it could make you happier if it results in reaching a long-sought goal or finding romance. Nevertheless, this daily causal thinking—about how something you notice came to be the way it is, or why something happened or continues to happen—is idle and unsystematic.

Yet this kind of thinking is the basis for a more demanding, sustained kind of causal thinking, the kind you will find in the essays of this chapter—essays that speculate about the possible causes of phenomena or trends. (To *speculate* means to conjecture, wonder, or guess, or even to hypothesize or theorize. It can imply risk, play, uncertainty, and chance. A *phenomenon* is something noticeable that occurs or happens. This kind of essay can also speculate about a *trend*—something that has changed or is changing over time.) The student essay writers in this chapter speculate about these phenomena: Why are more people right- rather than left-handed? Why would an immigrant to the United States choose not to learn English? What could motivate a person to commit serial murder? Why are ads for pharmaceuticals so prevalent? These phenomena are the students' subjects, which are well defined and described in the essays. But that's usually the easy part.

The hard part is the speculation about the causes of these phenomena, which is a challenge because you are no longer idly speculating. Instead, you are trying to convince readers that your speculations—your proposed causes—are plausible or likely. The causes you propose may come from your own experience, from research, or both. The writing engages you in sustained, systematic thinking to answer a significant social, cultural, or political question—sustained because it's going to take you awhile; systematic because you will need to select the most likely of many possible causes, sequence them logically, and support them so that they seem plausible, all with the aim of convincing particular readers to take your speculations seriously.

The rewards are great. Along with the other kinds of argument writing in this book, speculating about causes enables you to become the kind of person who confidently inquires deeply into events. You expect there is usually more to know than first appears. Adopting this stance, you join a new culture of debate, reflection, initiative, and knowledge seeking. Gaining confidence, you shake off old constraints and limits.

# Left Out

**Virginia Gagliardi**

*Lebanon Valley College*
*Annville, Pennsylvania*

Being ambidextrous herself, Virginia Gagliardi found herself easily drawn into speculating about why people tend to favor one hand over the other, and why most favor their right. While doing research on this subject, Gagliardi uncovered some surprising answers. "Probably the area that I learned from the most was the area of parental influence," she says. "Nurture really *does* play an important role in the development of handedness."

Her biggest challenge was incorporating all the causes she had discovered during her research. She solved the problem by organizing the causes into three main subject areas: genetics and physiology; general influences, such as religion and language; and local influences, such as childhood training from parents who are right-handed, or the availability of only right-handed tools in school and at home. "These ideas were the ones I wished to convey to my unmindful, right-handed audience and to those people who question the origin of handedness," Gagliardi says.

As you read, notice that Gagliardi relies on research for both her proposed causes and her support for those causes. Altogether, she makes good use of six different sources, all of which are books published between 1981 and 2002, their dates confirming the continuing fascination with handedness, its causes and results. Instead of merely patching the sources together, she imposes her own plan and selectively paraphrases and quotes the sources only as they are relevant to the three main causes she addresses.

--------

Behavioral differences that cause one limb or sense organ to be preferred for certain activities, despite the apparently insignificant differences in their morphology, constitute a problem that...has fascinated scientists and laymen for centuries. (Coren 2)

Opening a can, drawing a straight line, and writing a sentence are 1
three basic activities that display our handedness, the "differential or
preferred use of one hand in situations where only one can be used"
(Coren 2). Handedness presents itself in two well-known categories
—right- and left-handedness. But what causes each of us to be either
right- or left-handed? Why are there so many fewer left-handed people than right-handed people? For years, scientists thought handedness was genetic; however, no genetic theory accounts for the ratio
of right- to left-handers, and the exact contribution of factors to predisposition to one side remains unknown. Genetic models propose
many different ideas about the roles of genes in handedness, but as
McManus writes in *Right Hand, Left Hand: The Origins of Asymmetry in Brains, Bodies, Atoms and Culture,* "what they cannot do
is tell us exactly what it is that *makes* us right- or left-handed"
(163). A combination of factors in physiology, history, and society
explains why genetics plays only a minor role in a Western bias toward one side—the right side—of the body.

Perhaps the most basic explanation of handedness is the initial 2
genetic theory, which states that genetics determines handedness
through a specific gene inherited from parents. If both parents have
the right-handed gene, the children will all become right-handed; in
contrast, if both parents have the left-handed gene, the children
would all become left-handed. Since there are fewer lefties in the
world than right-handed people, the model appears to fulfill conceptions for why handedness occurs and why left-handedness occurs less
often than right-handedness. In the book *Left Brain, Right Brain,*
however, Sally P. Springer and Georg Deutsch elaborate on the extensive biological studies of this genetic model. The biologists who
conducted those studies quickly discovered that in comparison with
obtained data about handedness, "this [genetic] model cannot account for the fact that 54 percent of the offspring of two left-handed
parents are right-handed" (108). So how does this possible cause fail?
If the genetic model were accurate, reported data would show that
two left-handed parents would only have left-handed children.
Therefore, new studies began in an attempt to repair this theory with
a complementary, yet more complex, model.

After many studies attempting to salvage this basic genetic theory, 3
the idea of "variable penetrance" arose. Variable penetrance means
"that all individuals with the same genotype [pattern of genes] may
not express that genotype in the same way" (Springer and Deutsch

108). Simply put, the statement suggests that although the genes make the parents left-handed, the combination that passes to the child may not cause left-handedness in the child. This speculation provides the explanation for two left-handers having right-handed children; however, "even with variable penetrance built into the [allele] model, the [variable penetrance] model's 'goodness of fit' to actual data is less than satisfactory" (Springer and Deutsch 108). The probability of left-handedness increases as the number of left-handed parents increases. However, the real-life data does not coincide with the theory. According to McManus, the fact that handedness "runs in the family" (156) remains distinguishable, but exactly how remains a mystery.

A third theory suggests that nurture determines handedness, not nature—or genetics—itself. Scientists base the theory on how handedness appears, not on which side it appears. In this case, genetics would determine handedness, just not a particular side to the handedness. Simplified, the design suggests, "If your mother and father are strongly handed [very reliant on one side], although we can't predict on the basis of their handedness whether you will be right- or left-handed, we can predict that you will be strongly handed. It is the strength...that is genetically variable" (Coren 91). Of all the theories, this idea proves the most plausible. 4

While genetics undoubtedly participates in determination of handedness, the suggestion that nurture more likely decides the side of handedness continues as the most logical "genetic" explanation. As McManus explains, "there are many things that run in families that are not inherited through genes" (157), such as parents' influence on their children in the development of handedness. The explanation lies in the fact that parents "convey basic pattern[s] of behavior to children" (Porac and Coren 108). Probably the most fundamental behavior learned is in the use of utensils. Parents "teach them [children] to use their first tools, such as spoons, knives, and pencils ..." (Porac and Coren 108), so if the child's predisposition favors left-handedness but he continually learns right-handed motions, he will essentially develop into a right-handed child. This situation provides yet another example of the formation of handedness and how right-handedness forces itself into culture. The most easily defined reason for handedness presents itself every day in society: many people adopt right-handedness for ease of life and teach their children to do the same. This thought about the influence of nurture extends into the fact that handedness incorporates history into its origins. 5

Religion, which tends to be derived from nurture, is one of the    6
most controversial historical justifications for handedness in Western
culture. This idea is obviously seen in biblical illustrations. Followers
of many Christian religions resort to right-handedness as a result of
beliefs or traditions. The notion that left-handedness engages the
devil explicates this fact. Passages from the Bible further reinforce
these principles, such as the verses found in Matthew 25:34–41 in
the New Testament:

> Then shall the King say unto them on His right hand, "Come ye blessed
> of my Father, inherit the kingdom prepared for you from the founda-
> tion of the world."...Then shall He say also unto them on the left
> hand, "Depart from Me, ye cursed, into everlasting fire, prepared for
> the devil and his angels."...And these shall go away into everlasting
> punishment; but the righteous into life eternal. (qtd. in Springer and
> Deutsch 105)

The Creator being associated with the right hand strongly biases
Christians toward the right hand, or the right side in general. Thus,
this preference flows into other aspects of Christian culture. The
most prominent example is in the sign of the cross, performed only
with the right hand; using the left hand is sacrilegious. Another example appears during Communion, when the communicant receives
the wafer in the left hand so that the clean, right hand can transfer
the wafer to the mouth (Fincher 32).

The bias, though, does not limit itself to the church; it also ex-    7
tends into portraits concerning religion. Why, then, does a "marked
tendency in classical renderings of the Madonna and child" (Fincher
30) illustrate Mary holding Jesus on her left side? Analysts proposed
several reasons. According to Fincher, some analysts of the portraits
suggest that the cause lies in the idea of freeing the "right hand for
other, better things" (30). On the contrary, Fincher himself distin-
guishes the motive as something else: "Putting the child on Mary's left
puts Him on the viewer's—and the art work's—right, clearly the
place of honor" (31). Essentially, religion provides incentive for left-
handers to become right-handers; however, religion remains just one
aspect of history that influences this partiality for one side of the body.

For those people who lack a religious affiliation, the simple act of    8
speaking holds an effect equivalent to the effect of religion on handedness because language places a stigma on left-handedness. Consistently, favorable connotations referring to right-handedness emerge
in several languages. Fincher illustrates this idea from the word "riht,

Anglo-Saxon for straight, erect, or just" (37). He also uses the "French word for right, droit, [which] also means 'correct' and 'law'" (37), to further demonstrate the point of language as a root of favoritism in handedness. Springer and Deutsch point out that "the French word for 'left,' *gauche,* also means 'clumsy'" and that "*mancino* is Italian for 'left' as well as for 'deceitful'" (104). They also explain that the Spanish phrase "no ser zurdo," which means "to be clever," translates directly as "to not be left-handed" (104). As terrible as those definitions appear, most Western languages have them—including the English language.

In English the term "left-handed" has derogatory classifications. 9 For example, *Webster's Third International Dictionary* lists several definitions of the adjective "left-handed," including the following:

> a: marked by clumsiness or ineptitude: awkward; b: exhibiting deviousness or indirection: oblique, unintended; c: obs.: given to malevolent scheming or contriving: sinister, underhand. (qtd. in Springer and Deutsch 104)

Similarly, analysis of the English language reveals common phrases filled with bias. "For instance, a *left-handed compliment* is actually an insult. A *left-handed marriage* is no marriage at all. To be about *left-handed business* is to be engaged in something unlawful or unsavory" (Coren 2). On the contrary, "to be someone's *right-hand man* means to be important and useful to that person" (Coren 2). Over time, this tainting of a certain handedness carries over into everyday life and remains one of several reasons why left-handers may try to become right-handers or at least ambidextrous. Other motives to switch revolve around the impressions and pressures of social traditions.

One of the largest-scale examples lies in written language. The 10 system of the written English language solely supports right-handed people because "[written] alphabetic languages...were designed for right-handers" (Ornstein 83). Coren explains the differences in the mechanics of left- and right-handed writing as:

> Our left-to-right writing pattern is set up for a right-handed writer. The most comfortable and controlled hand movement is a pull across the body. For the right-hander it is a left-to-right movement, and for the left-hander it is reversed. (230)

Due to the way a left-hander pulls across his body, his hand will rub over words he has already written, whereas a right-hander always moves his hand away from the words he has already written. This problem forces left-handers into unnatural hand positions during writing; most primary school teachers attempt to persuade left-handed children into writing right-handed. In fact, the "Victorians even invented a vicious leather device with a belt and buckles for strapping the left hand firmly behind the back" (McManus 268). Writing, although the most obvious of problems, remains just one of many issues for a left-hander in a right-handed society.

Every day, left-handers encounter issues with common tools that right-handers take for granted. A simple household item, such as a can opener, can become the most complex of items for a leftie. Because a can opener "is designed to be held with the left hand while the cutting gear is operated by rotating a hand with the right hand" (Coren 223), using the instrument left-handed "forces the left-hander into a set of ungainly contortions" (Coren 223). Another example surfaces in the use of knives, typically beveled on only one side—the right side. Having the knife designed as such aids the "right-hander by producing a force which holds the blade upright" (Coren 227), causing the slice to peel outward from the material, rather than toward it. Still other issues outside of household items exist only for lefties. 11

More problems affecting left-handers reside in locations such as school and work. The simple process of using a ruler becomes a difficult task for a left-handed individual. The ruler, designed with right-handers in mind, presents numbers in a left-to-right fashion, much like the written English language. "This [style] makes sense for the right-hander because the motion of drawing the line usually begins at the 'zero inch' location on the far left and continues...until it reaches the mark indicating the desired length, somewhere to the right" (Coren 231). For a leftie, however, this system poses several problems: 12

> [This process] requires the left-hander to cover the numbers while drawing the line with a pulling motion across the body from right to left. The left-hander also covers the end of the ruler...causing a tendency for the pen to suddenly drop off the end of the ruler if the line is drawn too quickly and the unseen "zero inch" point is reached before the pen is stopped. (Coren 231)

Saws create problems by exposing body parts dangerously close to the blade. "When the right hand is used, the arm and elbow flare out to the side, safely away from the saw blade" (Coren 237), protecting a right-handed person from injury. Yet "if a left-hander wants to use this equipment, he must either use his right hand to hold the work...or cross his body with his left hand which places his arm directly in line with the saw blade" (Coren 237). This design forces a left-hander to resort to right-handedness temporarily or even permanently in many factory and workshop settings. However, these mechanical influences cannot solely explain the phenomena of left-handedness.

    The combination of these factors forms a basis for handedness in    13 the world. Right- and left-handedness appear as common expressions in everyday life, but the existence of both presents a misconception. Due to factors in physiology, history, and society, handedness appears in two forms, but not in right- and left-handedness. Rather, handedness categorizes into right-handedness and ambidextrous handedness for the sole reason that "to survive in this right-sided world, left-handers soon learn to do with the right hand many things that the right-hander could never and will never do with the left. The end result is a degree of ambidexterity" (Porac and Coren 95). Perhaps only one form of handedness exists, since, according to Porac and Coren, essentially "the left-hander must become more right-handed" (95). This idea reinforces the reason why right-handedness appears more often than left-handedness. Therefore, even though the exact cause of handedness remains unknown, the residue of known facts points not toward a right- and left-handed world, but in the direction of a world that completely relies on one-sided handedness.

# WORKS CITED

Coren, Stanley. *The Left-Hander Syndrome: The Causes and Consequences of Left-Handedness.* New York: MacMillan, 1992.

Fincher, Jack. *Lefties: The Origins and Consequences of Being Left-Handed.* New York: Barnes and Noble, 1993.

McManus, Chris. *Right Hand, Left Hand: The Origins of Asymmetry in Brains, Bodies, Atoms and Culture.* Cambridge, MA: Harvard University, 2002.

Ornstein, Robert. *The Right Mind.* New York: Harcourt Brace, 1997.

Porac, Clare, and Stanley Coren. *Lateral Preferences and Human Behavior.* New York: Springer-Verlag, 1981.

Springer, Sally P., and Georg Deutsch. *Left Brain, Right Brain.* San Francisco: W. H. Freeman, 1981.

# Hispanic Pride vs. American Assimilation

## Stephanie Cox

*Metropolitan Community College*
*Omaha, Nebraska*

"Why would immigrants want to make their lives more complicated by having to rely on others to communicate for them?" Stephanie Cox asks, after learning that the Spanish-speaking mother whose missing toddler she had helped find—a woman who had trembled and perspired as she tried to communicate her desperate situation— had declined the offer of English lessons from the church where Cox worked. Cox is compelled to discover why. A little research reveals that the woman belongs to a growing group of Mexican immigrants to the United States who are choosing not to learn English. This is no isolated incident—it is a phenomenon, Cox realizes.

After Cox narrates the incident of the lost girl as a way to engage readers' interest, she presents her subject—the phenomenon of acculturation—which she defines as "adapting to American culture" while continuing to "uphold the values and traditions of Latin America." She then forecasts the three causes—the three explanations for the phenomenon—that she will argue for: cultural pride; the proximity of a native country, especially Mexico; and the unwillingness of some Hispanics to help new Hispanics assimilate. Her plan is simple and visible.

Notice that Cox takes a stand on a hot-button social and political issue. Many Americans would be unsympathetic to the woman's refusal to learn English. Cox, too, admits some preconceived ideas on the matter, yet she keeps an open mind. She wants to know more before she judges the woman's decision not to learn English. She is motivated by curiosity.

---

My heart ached for the woman. She was visibly distressed and seemed to grow more agitated by the minute. Tiny beads of perspiration were beginning to form on her brow, and the black purse she carried shook in her trembling grasp. She was desperately trying to tell me something, 1 but I was unable to understand. She spoke Spanish and I didn't. After many awkward attempts at communication, the woman's ten-year-old English-speaking son was located. His translation revealed her worry over her missing toddler. It seems the child had wandered off while her mother was visiting a pastor of the church I work for. With the woman's son's help, we gathered enough details about her daughter's disappearance to locate the child, who had been playing in an empty classroom.

Even though the situation seemed to have ended happily, I was still troubled by it. If only the woman had known some English. The church offered several excellent programs to help immigrants learn about American culture and practice the English language. Had she taken the help offered by the church, she would have been able to communicate effectively enough to convey her message and prevent unnecessary frustration and possibly dangerous delay. When I presented my concerns to one of the church pastors, I was surprised by his response. This woman was at the church to pick up her son from an English class. When she had been given the same opportunity, she quietly refused. While she felt strongly about the importance of English for her son, she herself was proud of her Mexican heritage and had no desire to become an English speaker.   2

I was shocked. Why would immigrants want to make their lives more complicated by having to rely on others to communicate for them? This woman must surely be an exception, I thought, but to my surprise, she is among many Hispanic immigrants in the United States who are acculturating rather than assimilating into American culture (Grow et al.). Many Americans still view the United States as an ideal nation, a model for the world, and assume everyone must surely want to "be like us," but there is a new phenomenon among many U.S. immigrants: active pride in their home cultures. This cultural pride is especially evident among Hispanic immigrants who choose to adapt to American culture without losing the traditions and values of their native countries.   3

Hispanics are one of the fastest growing and largest minority groups in the United States, and they are developing their own version of the "true" American. Nearly nine out of ten Hispanics have accepted the importance of adapting to American culture, while nearly nine out of ten also believe it is extremely important to continue to uphold the values and traditions of Latin America (Artze).   4

This phenomenon of Hispanic acculturation rather than assimilation can be witnessed in several cities and towns in the United States.   5

Perhaps one of the best examples of how Hispanics are striving to maintain their own culture can be seen in Los Angeles. As early as 1950, Los Angeles contained the largest Hispanic population in the country, and the conflict between assimilation and acculturation was already beginning. Immigrants were forced to choose between American cultural traditions and the distinctive values of Latin America. Today, you will find groups of new immigrants along with second- and third-generation Hispanics all with the same goal in mind: to successfully thrive in an ethnocentric culture without losing their own identity (Rodriguez).

While there may be quite a few reasons immigrants are reluctant to assimilate, forgetting old traits and adopting new ones, three are most prominent. First is the strong feeling of pride Hispanics have for their native countries and cultural values, and the security they feel when segregated from American society. Second is the close proximity of Hispanics, especially Mexican Americans, to their native country. Third, and most startling, is the seeming lack of support from many Hispanic Americans to help new immigrants assimilate.

With the ever-increasing number of immigrants from Latin America, it is not uncommon to find entirely Hispanic communities within American towns and cities. These communities help to reinforce cultural traditions and pride, and make it unnecessary for immigrants to adopt new cultural traits or learn the English language. Many Hispanic Americans not only feel comforted by their segregation but also are wary of the negative influences American society may have on their families (Branigin).

The self-segregation of many Hispanic immigrants in America can be compared to that of Americans who live and work abroad but remain quite isolated from their host culture. A classmate of mine described living in Japan while her husband was stationed at a military base there. Day-to-day life revolved around American customs. Her children attended American schools on the military base; she shopped at military stores geared toward the wants and needs of Americans; and her family socialized with a close-knit group of American friends. On the rare occasions that she and her family left the military base, she was startled by the numerous stares and suspicious glances she and her family received from Japanese citizens. While confident that she and her family had done their best to adhere to Japanese societal norms, the reaction of the Japanese left her with the acute feeling that she was still very different, and the isolation of the military base offered her family a feeling of security.

My classmate's experience is mirrored by the experiences of    9
many Hispanics living in the United States. In response to unsub-
stantiated fears of America becoming "Mexicanized," some politicians and government officials are being urged to speak out against
Hispanic immigration. Most notably, border states such as California
and Arizona are openly opposing immigration from Latin America by
developing new anti-immigration bills. California's Proposition 187
and Arizona's Proposition 200 would limit the public benefits received by illegal immigrants, and politicians acting on public support
of these bills and hoping to seek reelection are motivated to develop
even more anti-immigrant legislation (Judis). While these proposi-
tions are much more aggressive than suspicious stares, the message is
the same: if you are different, you must be a threat.

In addition to feeling more comfortable within their own com-    10
munities, many Hispanic immigrants see isolation as a way to hold on
to their cultural values. In California, where bilingual education is no
longer the norm, children from Hispanic families are immediately
submerged into the English language and thus into American culture. Many Hispanics feel that this immersion forces their children to
choose between the values taught by their parents—such as the importance of family—and those of their new country (Rifkin).

Reluctance to assimilate is strengthened even more when tradi-    11
tional, conservative Hispanic families witness their children adopting
negative aspects of American culture. Many Hispanics cite American
gang violence when defending their decision to keep their children
away from American culture. Alarmingly, Hispanic youth may actually be propelled toward gang life by the attitudes and stereotypes of
Americans who mistakenly assume that most Latinos are illegal immigrants (Branigin). A quest for group identity and a sense of belonging can be a strong lure for Hispanic teens trying to find their place
in an unsympathetic society.

Fear of negative influences impacting traditional cultural values    12
is not the only reason Hispanics have hesitated to adopt American
culture. Unlike the majority of immigrants from other locations,
Hispanics—especially Mexican Americans—have the privilege of living fairly close to their native country. It is not uncommon for many
Hispanics to travel between their native and adopted countries on a
regular basis. These frequent visits help reinforce the customs, values,
and language of Latin America (Grow et al.).

This reinforcement of Hispanic customs and values is evidenced    13
not only by immigrants' attitudes toward American society but also by

the many cultural traditions Hispanics bring to the United States. One tradition that is growing in popularity in America is the Quinceanera, the celebration of a Latina girl's fifteenth birthday. Historically rooted in Aztec and Roman Catholic customs, the Quinceanera is a time to celebrate a young girl's entrance into adulthood. While this lavish celebration is primarily a Hispanic one, which begins with a Roman Catholic Mass and ends with a reception in which the girl performs a dance with her father and members of her court, it is also showing signs of adaptation to American society. This can be seen in the celebrations held by Hispanics who are not members of the Roman Catholic Church, and who tend to invite friends of different ethnic heritages (Miranda). Once primarily a closed ceremony for family and close friends, the Quinceanera is expanding beyond its Latin American roots and replanting itself into Hispanic American culture.

Another example of a Hispanic cultural tradition celebrated in   14 the United States is Cinco de Mayo. Celebrated on the fifth of May, this holiday commemorates the 1862 Battle of Puebla, one of the most glorious victories in Mexico's military history. When France attempted to take control of Mexico by force, a poorly equipped Mexican army was able to halt the invasion of the French powerhouse despite being outnumbered by thousands. This celebration, with its message of success despite overwhelming obstacles, inspires Hispanics to be proud of their heritage (Vargas).

Finally, many new immigrants to the United States may feel   15 more comfortable within their own cultural group and hesitate to adapt to American culture because of discouragement from their own peers. Mexican Americans born and raised in the United States, called Chicanos, often humiliate new immigrants who are attempting to learn English. One immigrant teen, who despite three years in an English as a second language course still did not speak fluent English, believed the other students were laughing at her when she attempted to speak English (Branigin). This kind of teasing can lead to feelings of insecurity among newly arrived immigrants.

Not only are Hispanic children and teens experiencing discourage-   16 ment from Mexican Americans, but so are many new immigrant adults who are seeking jobs in the United States. An immigrant named Antonio experienced this harsh reality when he found himself assigned to do one of the most laborious jobs in a meatpacking plant, while his cultural counterpart, a Chicano, was displaying the title of supervisor and taunting immigrant workers like him. In fact, in this particular meatpacking plant, it was quite common to see new immigrants from

Mexico performing arduous tasks while enduring snide comments from their Chicano supervisors, who would make statements such as "Go back to Mexico, wetback!" or "Chicanos numero uno!" (Campo-Flores). Humiliation like this can cause many immigrants to stay within their own communities, where they feel accepted.

The feelings of isolation felt by the immigrant teen and the feelings of frustration felt by the immigrant worker Antonio shed new light on the complexities Latin American immigrants must face every day. Distrust of an unfamiliar culture mixed with strong pride in their own heritage has led to immigrants' longing to maintain the traits of their native country. As I remember the distraught woman who quietly yet proudly refused the pastor's offer to help her learn English, I can now respect her decision. She was quoted as saying, "I was Mexican at birth, I am Mexican today, and I will be Mexican forever."    17

## WORKS CITED

Artze, Isis. "To Be and Not to Be." *Hispanic* Oct. 2000: 32–34. *Academic Search Elite*. EBSCO. Metropolitan Community Coll. Lib. 22 Jan. 2006 <http://www.epnet.com>.

Branigin, William. "Immigrants Shunning Idea of Assimilation." *Washington Post* 25 May 1998: A1.

Campo-Flores, Arian. "Brown Against Brown." *Newsweek* Sept. 2000: 49–50. *Academic Search Elite*. EBSCO. Metropolitan Community Coll. Lib. 25 Jan. 2006 <http://www.epnet.com>.

Grow, Brian, Ronald Grover, Arlene Weintraub, Christopher Palmeri, Mara Der Hovenesian, and Michael Eidam. "Hispanic Nation." *Business Week* March 2004: 58–70. *Academic Search Elite*. EBSCO. Metropolitan Community Coll. Lib. 10 Jan. 2006 <http://www.epnet.com>.

Judis, John B. "Border War." *The New Republic* 16 Jan. 2006: 15–19.

Miranda, Carolina A. "Fifteen Candles." *Time* July 2004: 83. *Academic Search Elite*. EBSCO. Metropolitan Community Coll. Lib. 27 Jan. 2006 <http://www.epnet.com>.

Rifkin, Jane M. "Locked in Conflict with Mainstream America." *Hispanic Times* Dec. 1998/Jan. 1999: 40–41. *Academic Search Elite*. EBSCO. Metropolitan Community Coll. Lib. 22 Jan. 2006 <http://www.epnet.com>.

Rodriguez, Gregory. "Don't Mistake the Parts for the Whole in L.A." *Los Angeles Times* 6 July 2001: B15.

Vargas, Roberto. "Cinco De Mayo: An Opportunity to Inspire Courage." *Hispanic* May 1999: 48. *Academic Search Elite*. EBSCO. Metropolitan Community Coll. Lib. 25 Jan. 2006 <http://www.epnet.com>.

# *What Makes a Serial Killer?*

## La Donna Beaty

*Sinclair Community College*
*Dayton, Ohio*

Chances are there will never be a serial murder in your neighborhood, but there are more serial killers at large in the American population than you might imagine—close to 350, according to La Donna Beaty's research. While there's nothing we can do to avoid serial killers—their lack of telltale physical characteristics makes them impossible to peg—we can speculate about the forces that conspire to make them the monsters they are. Beaty offers several possible triggers that, taken together, might turn a child into a serial killer, including psychological abuse, frequent moves, and genetic abnormalities. As in most essays speculating about causes, Beaty's conclusions must be tentative. And yet speculating about the reasons serial killers develop may be our best approach to the problem: the scientists and psychologists who continue such speculative work may one day find a humane way to treat them or, even better, keep potential killers from becoming violent in the first place. As you read, notice how visibly Beaty signals her move from one cause to the next as the argument progresses.

---

Jeffrey Dahmer, John Wayne Gacy, Mark Allen Smith, Richard Chase, Ted Bundy—the list goes on and on. These five men alone have been responsible for at least ninety deaths, and many suspect that their victims may total twice that number. They are serial killers, the most feared and hated of criminals. What deep, hidden secret makes them lust for blood? What can possibly motivate a person to kill over and over again with no guilt, no remorse, no hint of human compassion? What makes a serial killer? 1

Serial killings are not a new phenomenon. In 1798, for example, Micajah and Wiley Harpe traveled the backwoods of Kentucky and Tennessee in a violent, yearlong killing spree that left at least twenty— 2 and possibly as many as thirty-eight—men, women, and children dead. Their crimes were especially chilling, as they seemed particularly to enjoy grabbing small children by the ankles and smashing their heads against trees (Holmes and DeBurger 28). In modern society, however, serial killings have grown to near epidemic proportions. Ann Rule, a respected author and expert on serial murders, stated in a seminar at the University of Louisville on serial murder that between 3,500 and 5,000 people become victims of serial murder each year in the United States alone (qtd. in Holmes and DeBurger 21). Many others estimate that there are close to 350 serial killers currently at large in our society (Holmes and DeBurger 22).

Fascination with murder and murderers is not new, but re-    3
searchers in recent years have made great strides in determining the characteristics of criminals. Looking back, we can see how naive early experts were in their evaluations: in 1911, for example, Italian criminologist Cesare Lombrosco concluded that "murderers as a group [are] biologically degenerate [with] bloodshot eyes, aquiline noses, curly black hair, strong jaws, big ears, thin lips, and menacing grins" (qtd. in Lunde 84). Today, however, we don't expect killers to have fangs that drip human blood, and many realize that the boy-next-door may be doing more than woodworking in his basement. While there are no specific physical characteristics shared by all serial killers, they are almost always male, and 92 percent are white. Most are between the ages of twenty-five and thirty-five and often physically attractive. While they may hold a job, many switch employment frequently, as they become easily frustrated when advancement does not come as quickly as expected. They tend to believe that they are entitled to whatever they desire but feel that they should have to exert no effort to attain their goals (Samenow 88, 96). What could possibly turn attractive, ambitious human beings into cold-blooded monsters?

One popular theory suggests that many murderers are the prod-    4
uct of our violent society. Our culture tends to approve of violence and find it acceptable, even preferable, in many circumstances (Holmes and DeBurger 27). According to research done in 1970, one out of every four men and one out of every six women believed that it was appropriate for a husband to hit his wife under certain conditions (Holmes and DeBurger 33). This emphasis on violence is especially prevalent in television programs. Violence occurs in 80 percent of all prime-time shows, while cartoons, presumably made for children, average eighteen violent acts per hour. It is estimated that by the age of eighteen, the average child will have viewed more than

16,000 television murders (Holmes and DeBurger 34). Some experts feel that children demonstrate increasingly aggressive behavior with each violent act they view and become so accustomed to violence that these acts seem normal (Lunde 15, 35). In fact, most serial killers do begin to show patterns of aggressive behavior at a young age. It is, therefore, possible that after viewing increasing amounts of violence, such children determine that this is acceptable behavior; when they are then punished for similar actions, they may become confused and angry and eventually lash out by committing horrible, violent acts.

Another theory concentrates on the family atmosphere into 5 which the serial killer is born. Most killers state that they experienced psychological abuse as children and never established good relationships with the male figures in their lives (Ressler, Burgess, and Douglas 19). As children, they were often rejected by their parents and received little nurturing (Lunde 94; Holmes and DeBurger 64–70). It has also been established that the families of serial killers often move repeatedly, never allowing the child to feel a sense of stability; in many cases, they are also forced to live outside the family home before reaching the age of eighteen (Ressler, Burgess, and Douglas 19–20). Our culture's tolerance for violence may overlap with such family dynamics: with 79 percent of the population believing that slapping a twelve-year-old is either necessary, normal, or good, it is no wonder that serial killers relate tales of physical abuse and view themselves as the "black sheep" of the family (Holmes and DeBurger 30; Ressler, Burgess, and Douglas 19–20). They may even, perhaps unconsciously, assume this same role in society.

While the foregoing analysis portrays the serial killer as a lost, 6 lonely, abused little child, another theory, based on the same information, gives an entirely different view. In this analysis, the killer is indeed rejected by his family but only after being repeatedly defiant, sneaky, and threatening. As the child's lies and destructiveness increase, the parents give him the distance he seems to want in order to maintain a small amount of domestic peace (Samenow 13). This interpretation suggests that the killer shapes his parents much more than his parents shape him. It also denies that the media can influence a child's mind and turn him into something that he doesn't already long to be. Since most children view similar amounts of violence, the argument goes, a responsible child filters what he sees and will not resort to criminal activity no matter how acceptable it seems to be (Samenow 15–18). In 1930, the noted psychologist Alfred Adler seemed to find this true of any criminal. As he put it,

"With criminals it is different: they have a private logic, a private intelligence. They are suffering from a wrong outlook upon the world, a wrong estimate of their own importance and the importance of other people" (qtd. in Samenow 20).

Most people agree that Jeffrey Dahmer or Ted Bundy had to be "crazy" to commit horrendous multiple murders, and scientists have long maintained that serial killers are indeed mentally disturbed (Lunde 48). While the percentage of murders committed by mental hospital patients is much lower than that among the general population, it cannot be ignored that the rise in serial killings happened at almost the same time as the deinstitutionalization movement in the mental health care system during the 1960s (Lunde 35; Markman and Bosco 266). While reform was greatly needed in the mental health care system, it has now become nearly impossible to hospitalize those with severe problems. In the United States, people have a constitutional right to remain mentally ill. Involuntary commitment can only be accomplished if the person is deemed dangerous to himself or others or is gravely disabled. However, "[a]ccording to the way that the law is interpreted, if you can go to the mailbox to pick up your Social Security check, you're not gravely disabled even if you think you're living on Mars"; even if a patient is thought to be dangerous, he cannot be held longer than ninety days unless it can be proved that the patient actually committed dangerous acts while in the hospital (Markman and Bosco 267). Many of the most heinous criminals have had long histories of mental illness but could not be hospitalized due to these stringent requirements. Richard Chase, the notorious Vampire of Sacramento, believed that he needed blood in order to survive, and while in the care of a psychiatric hospital, he often killed birds and other small animals in order to quench this thirst. When he was released, he went on to kill eight people, one of them an eighteen-month-old baby (Biondi and Hecox 206). Edmund Kemper was equally insane. At the age of fifteen, he killed both of his grandparents and then spent five years in a psychiatric facility. Doctors determined that he was "cured" and released him into an unsuspecting society. He killed eight women, including his own mother (Lunde 53–56). The world was soon to be disturbed by a cataclysmic earthquake, and Herbert Mullin knew that he had been appointed by God to prevent the catastrophe. The fervor of his religious delusion resulted in a death toll of thirteen (Lunde 63–81). All of these men had been treated for their mental disorders, and all were released by doctors who did not have enough proof to hold them against their will.

Recently, studies have given increasing consideration to the ge-    8
netic makeup of serial killers. The connection between biology and behavior is strengthened by research in which scientists have been able to
develop a violently aggressive strain of mice simply through selective
inbreeding (Taylor 23). These studies have caused scientists to become
increasingly interested in the limbic system of the brain, which houses
the amygdala, an almond-shaped structure located in the front of the
temporal lobe. It has long been known that surgically altering that
portion of the brain, in an operation known as a lobotomy, is one way
of controlling behavior. This surgery was used frequently in the 1960s
but has since been discontinued as it also erases most of a person's personality. More recent developments, however, have shown that temporal lobe epilepsy causes electrical impulses to be discharged directly
into the amygdala. When this electronic stimulation is re-created in the
laboratory, it causes violent behavior in lab animals. Additionally, other
forms of epilepsy do not cause abnormalities in behavior except during
seizure activity. Temporal lobe epilepsy is linked with a wide range of
antisocial behavior, including anger, paranoia, and aggression. It is also
interesting to note that this form of epilepsy produces extremely unusual brain waves. These waves have been found in only 10 to 15 percent of the general population, but over 79 percent of known serial
killers test positive for these waves (Taylor 28–33).

The look at biological factors that control human behavior is by    9
no means limited to brain waves or other brain abnormalities. Much
work is also being done with neurotransmitters, levels of testos-
terone, and patterns of trace minerals. While none of these studies is
conclusive, they all show a high correlation between antisocial behavior and chemical interactions within the body (Taylor 63–69).

One of the most common traits that all researchers have noted    10
among serial killers is heavy use of alcohol. Whether this correlation is
brought about by external factors or whether alcohol is an actual stim-
ulus that causes certain behavior is still unclear, but the idea deserves
consideration. Lunde found that the majority of those who commit
murder had been drinking beforehand and commonly had a urine alcohol level of between .20 and .29, nearly twice the legal level of in-
toxication (31–32). Additionally, 70 percent of the families that reared
serial killers had verifiable records of alcohol abuse (Ressler, Burgess,
and Douglas 17). Jeffrey Dahmer had been arrested in 1981 on
charges of drunkenness, and before his release from prison on sexual
assault charges, his father had written a heartbreaking letter pleading
that Jeffrey be forced to undergo treatment for alcoholism—a plea

that, if heeded, might have changed the course of future events (Davis 70, 103). Whether alcoholism is a learned behavior or an inherited predisposition is still hotly debated, but a 1979 report issued by Harvard Medical School stated that "[a]lcoholism in the biological parent appears to be a more reliable predictor of alcoholism in the children than any other environmental factor examined" (qtd. in Taylor 117). While alcohol was once thought to alleviate anxiety and depression, we now know that it can aggravate and intensify such moods; for serial killers, this may lead to irrational feelings of powerlessness that are brought under control only when the killer proves he has the ultimate power to control life and death (Taylor 110).

"Man's inhumanity to man" began when Cain killed Abel, but 11 this legacy has grown to frightening proportions, as evidenced by the vast number of books that line the shelves of bookstores today—row after row of titles dealing with death, anger, and blood. We may never know what causes a serial killer to exact his revenge on an unsuspecting society, but we need to continue to probe the interior of the human brain to discover the delicate balance of chemicals that controls behavior; we need to be able to fix what goes wrong. We must also work harder to protect our children. Their cries must not go unheard; their pain must not become so intense that it demands bloody revenge. As today becomes tomorrow, we must remember the words of Ted Bundy, one of the most ruthless serial killers of our time: "Most serial killers are people who kill for the pure pleasure of killing and cannot be rehabilitated. Some of the killers themselves would even say so" (qtd. in Holmes and DeBurger 150).

## WORKS CITED

Biondi, Ray, and Walt Hecox. *The Dracula Killer.* New York: Simon, 1992.

Davis, Ron. *The Milwaukee Murders.* New York: St. Martin's, 1991.

Holmes, Ronald M., and James DeBurger. *Serial Murder.* Newbury Park: Sage, 1988.

Lunde, Donald T. *Murder and Madness.* San Francisco: San Francisco Book, 1976.

Markman, Ronald, and Dominick Bosco. *Alone with the Devil.* New York: Doubleday, 1989.

Ressler, Robert K., Ann W. Burgess, and John E. Douglas. *Sexual Homicide—Patterns and Motives.* Lexington: Heath, 1988.

Samenow, Stanton E. *Inside the Criminal Mind.* New York: Times, 1984.

Taylor, Lawrence. *Born to Crime.* Westport: Greenwood, 1984.

# *Pharmaceutical Advertising*
## Krista Gonnerman
*Rose-Hulman Institute of Technology*
*Terre Haute, Indiana*

While you may not be a hypochondriac by nature, watching television can make any American doubt his or her kidneys, bladder control, blood sugar levels, and virility. And no wonder: direct-to-consumer pharmaceutical advertising is booming these days, up threefold from a decade ago. What led to this explosion? In this essay, Krista Gonnerman sorts through the causes that have been offered to explain it, calling into question those that are poorly supported or those that smack of drug-company propaganda. (Was the surge in drug commercials really caused by a fit of goodwill among pharmaceutical companies?)

Because they are written to explore interesting phenomena and trends, essays speculating about causes are often very good reads—and Gonnerman's is no exception. By considering possible causes systematically and without bias, Gonnerman achieves one of the main purposes of any cause essay: she helps readers make sense of a puzzling phenomenon.

---

Turn on the television, wait for the commercial breaks, and you are 1 guaranteed to see them: direct-to-consumer (DTC) pharmaceutical advertisements. In fact, "Americans now see an average of nine prescription ads per day on television" (McLean). Allegra, an allergy medication; Celebrex, a medication for arthritis pain; Claritin, another allergy medication; Detral, a pill to help control overactive bladder; Lamisil, a drug to combat toenail fungus; Lipitor, a medication used to lower cholesterol; Nexium, an acid reflux medication; Procrit, a medication meant to increase red blood cell production; Viagra, a medication for impotence; Vioxx, an anti-inflammatory medication; Zocor, another medication meant to lower cholesterol; Zoloft, an antidepressant—the list of drugs currently promoted on television seems endless and overwhelming. Flashy, celebrity endorsed, emotionally appealing, with snappy tag lines and occasionally catchy tunes, these thirty-second sound bites typically show healthy people enjoying life. According to one source, the pharmaceutical industry "has tripled drug advertising since 1996 to nearly $2.5 billion a year.... Of the print and broadcast ads, 60% were for just 20 medications" ("NJBIZ"); industry spending is "up 28% from 1999 and 40 times the $55 million spent on mass media ads in 1991" (McLean); in 1998 alone, the drug companies spent more than $500 million solely on television advertising (West).

The most significant and largely encompassing cause behind this     2 veritable explosion of pharmaceutical advertisements on television occurred in 1997 when the Federal Drug Administration (FDA) relaxed the regulations overseeing pharmaceutical advertising on television. Prior to 1997, the FDA regulations addressing prescription drug advertisements were so strict that few manufacturers bothered to promote their drugs in the media. Those drug manufacturers who sought to advertise on television were restricted to broadcasting "a drug's name without stating its purpose. Or stating a drug's purpose without saying its name. Or stating a drugs [sic] name and medical purpose only if the patient insert was scrolled on the screen" (West). But in 1996 the pharmaceutical industry filed a freedom of speech challenge and won, and in August 1997 the FDA's Division of Drug Marketing and Communications issued the revised regulations that are still in effect today. Currently, "[d]rug companies can now tell viewers...what their drug is used for without reciting or scrolling the entire Patient Insert; a major statement of serious side effects and a phone number or other route of obtaining the rest of the information" is now all that is required of the commercial (West). No longer hampered by restrictions, the pharmaceutical industry began in 1997 and has continued to focus its advertising budget on television: "The National Institute for Health Care Management in Washington reports that $1.8 billion was spent on d-t-c pharmaceutical advertising last year [1999], with $1.1 billion on TV" (Liebeskind).

A second, but debatable, cause may originate in patients becoming     3 more proactive in their own health care. Both Carol Lewis, writing in *FDA Consumer,* and Dr. Sidney M. Wolfe, writing in the *New England Journal of Medicine,* note that beginning in the mid-1980s, there was an increase in the number of individuals (1) seeking more medical information than they were being given by their doctors and (2) making medical decisions affecting their own health care. Lewis and Wolfe suggest that based on the pharmaceutical industry's awareness of this groundswell, the industry may have begun producing ads aimed at such consumers. Yet beyond this anecdotal, undocumented evidence by Lewis and Wolfe, there is little to support the suggestion that greater patient involvement led to the dramatic increase in pharmaceutical advertisements on television.

Other causes for the proliferation of pharmaceutical advertisements have been suggested, but these ideas lack merit. For example, it has been suggested that since many individuals do not want to make the necessary lifestyle changes, such as exercising and eating healthier—changes that would result in true health benefits—the pharmaceutical industry began running commercials, in part, to encourage individuals to seek out their doctors as a first step toward a healthier life. But the pharmaceutical industry is a for-profit industry, and its DTC commercials look to market products for the primary purpose of enhancing pharmaceutical companies' bottom lines, not to encourage consumers to embrace healthier lifestyles that will lead to their—potentially—not needing medications.

In a similar vein, "The Coalition for Healthcare Communication, a group of advertising agencies and medical publications dependent on drug advertising, said that an analysis of leading published consumer surveys provides strong evidence that [DTC] advertising of prescription drugs is a valued source of health care information" ("Drug Industry"). In other words, the pharmaceutical industry began running the ads as a way of providing information-hungry patients with reliable knowledge. But as Maryann Napoli sarcastically notes, "Anyone trying to sell you something isn't going to give you the most balanced picture of the product's effectiveness and risks." Or as Dr. Wolfe writes, "The education of patients...is too important to be left to the pharmaceutical industry, with its pseudo educational campaigns designed, first and foremost, to promote drugs."

The 1997 FDA regulatory revisions on media advertisements provided the pharmaceutical industry the opportunity to inundate television with its products. But as consumers we should not blindly accept what we see in the industry's thirty-second sound bites. While we can use the information conveyed in the commercials to help us make more informed decisions about our own health care or use the information in consultation with our physicians, we must never forget that the commercials are meant to sell products; and if those products improve our health, it is merely a consequence of the industry's primary intention.

# WORKS CITED

"Drug Industry Study Finds Direct-to-Consumer Ads Help Customers." *Health Care Strategic Management* July 2001: 10.

Lewis, Carol. "The Impact of Direct-to-Consumer Advertising." *FDA Consumer* Mar/Apr. 2003: 9. *Master FILE Premier.* EBSCO. Rose-Hulman Inst. of Tech. Lib. 20 May 2003 <http://epnet.com>.

Liebeskind, Ken. "Targeted Ads for New Drugs a Shot in the Arm." *Editor & Publisher* Nov. 2000: 33.

McLean, Candis. "The Real Drug Pushers." *Report/Newsmagazine* 19 Mar. 2001: 38–42. *MasterFILE Premier.* EBSCO. Rose-Hulman Inst. of Tech. Lib. 20 May 2003 <http://epnet.com>.

Napoli, Maryann. "Those Omnipresent Prescription Drug Ads: What to Look Out For." *Healthfacts* June 2001: 3.

"NJBIZ." *Business News New Jersey* 25 Feb. 2002: 3–5. *MasterFILE Premier.* EBSCO. Rose-Hulman Inst. of Tech. Lib. 20 May 2003 <http://epnet.com>.

West, Diane. "DTC Ponders the Twilight Zone of TV Advertising." *Pharmaceutical Executive* May 1999: A4–A8. *MasterFILE Premier.* EBSCO. Rose-Hulman Inst. of Tech. Lib. 20 May 2003 <http://epnet.com>.

Wolfe, Sidney M. "Direct-to-Consumer Advertising—Education or Emotion Promotion?" *New England Journal of Medicine* 346.7 (2002): 524–26. *MasterFILE Premier.* EBSCO. Rose-Hulman Inst. of Tech. Lib. 20 May 2003 <http://epnet.com>.

# *Interpreting Stories* 10

Interpreting a story requires you to make inferences, something you do in your everyday life when you arrive at insights about people and relationships, whether in real life or in fiction. You make inferences when you gossip with one friend about a mutual friend, or judge the motives of a TV or movie character. Rather than being final verdicts, your judgments in these situations are more likely to be invitations to further discussion. The same goes for story interpretations, which can be logical and even insistent without being final or comprehensive. In a classroom in which every student offers a different interpretation of the same story, no one student need be right; sharing and discussing the interpretations will result in a fuller understanding of the story for everyone.

Using your gossiping and character-judging experience as a starting point, interpreting a short story can lead you someplace different and, to be honest, harder to get to. After all, unlike gossiping or discussing a movie, interpreting a short story is a solitary experience, not a social one. It's textual, not conversational. And it is unbending in its demands on your time because it's usually associated with a deadline and requires that you choose every word, shape every phrase and sentence, and visibly and logically connect every sentence to the one before and after it.

Though it may seem daunting, this kind of writing can bring great satisfaction. It teaches you strategies that enable you to deepen and extend any interpretation you wish to make, whether in real life or in the arts, and to support your insights in ways your readers or listeners will find plausible and enlightening. It gives you more confidence in asserting and supporting your insights about anything at all with different kinds of people in various kinds of situations. Most important to you personally, it will help you decide which of your insights are worth keeping—which insights, added to your store of hard-won personal knowledge, will lead you to a place of greater understanding of yourself and your world. Along with the other kinds of argumentative writing in chapters 6–9, thesis-centered interpretations—logically organized and well supported—can take you there.

D. H. Lawrence's story "In Love" was published in *The Woman Who Rode Away and Other Stories* in 1928. You can search for the book in your college library or, better yet, access it online through Google Book Search (http://books.google.com). When you have the book in your browser, simply enter the keyword "Hester" into the search bar to skip ahead to "In Love" on page 138. Or, for a quick orientation to the story, read the synopsis below.

---

"In Love," a short story by D. H. Lawrence, opens with twenty-five-year-old Hester anxiously fretting about a weekend visit to the farm cottage of her fiancé, Joe. On this day a month before the wedding, Hester's younger sister, Henrietta, confronts her and tells her point-blank that she needs to snap out of her pout and "either put a better face on it, or...don't go." Although Hester does make the trip, she is never comfortable with her decision. 1

The crux of Hester's problem is that she and Joe had been good friends for years before she finally promised to marry him. Hester had always respected Joe as a hardworking, "decent" fellow, but now that they are to marry, she finds him changed. What she detests is the fact that, in her view, he seems to have made "the wretched mistake of falling 'in love' with her." To Hester, this notion of being in love, accentuated by all of Joe's "lovey-dovey" attempts to cuddle and snuggle and kiss, is completely idiotic and ridiculous. 2

After she arrives at Joe's farm cottage, Hester avoids his advances by asking him to play the piano. As he concentrates on his fingering, she slips outside into the night air and, when Joe comes looking for her, remains hidden in a tree. Alone in the dark, Hester falls into a fit of internal questioning, doubt, and upset concerning "the mess" her 3 life seems to have become. Then suddenly, in the midst of her anxiety, who should arrive but Henrietta, claiming she is in the neighborhood on a visit to a friend down the road. Hester leaps at the chance to join Henrietta and thus escape her entrapment with Joe. When Joe hears this, however, he responds angrily, accusing the two sisters of playing a "game."

In the confrontation that follows, Hester and Joe, for the first    4
time, speak honestly of their feelings. Hester tells Joe she detests his "making love" to her. Joe responds that she's mistaken, that he was in fact not "in love" with her but was behaving in such a manner only because he thought that "it was expected." In the conversation, Joe goes on to reveal his dilemma and his true feelings about Hester: "What are you to do," he says, "when you know a girl's rather strict, and you like her for it?"

In speaking the truth of their hearts to each other for the first    5
time, the couple is able to reveal the depth of their feelings. They recognize that they've betrayed the intimacy of their relationship because they've acted on the basis of expectations rather than on the basis of genuine emotion. By acknowledging these facts, the couple is able to reach new understanding. Seeing Joe's honest love, Hester feels herself responding to him and, in the end, decides to stay with him. She will accept whatever he does, she says, as long as he really loves her.

# *In Love*

## Sarah Hawkins

*University of California, San Diego*
*La Jolla, California*

By the end of paragraph 3, Sarah Hawkins' interpretation is clear; in the last paragraph, she repeats it. In between, she focuses on details of the relationship between Hester and Joe, with Henrietta speaking for the predictable social expectations and constraints Hester and Joe must struggle against. Hawkins stays extremely close to the story throughout her essay, following through consistently with what is called a "close reading" to support her interpretation. The story offers only a small cast of characters and a small scene, and only a few hours pass; yet Hawkins has more than enough material to select from to support her interpretation.

As you read, notice that Hawkins is not merely retelling the story. Instead, she's organized her essay around the stages of the argument supporting her interpretation. The first sentences of her paragraphs—where readers look for cues to the staging or sequence of an argument—keep readers focused and on track. Notice also Hawkins' careful choice of words to help readers understand the personal and social conflicts at the center of the story. Here is a sample:

game vs. genuine feelings
love game vs. love me really
hypocritical vs. pure and true
wooden vs. intimate
social imposition vs. unique bond of love

---

For most people, the phrase *in love* brings many rosy pictures to mind: a young man looking into the eyes of the girl he loves, a couple walking along the beach holding hands, two people making sacrifices to be together. These stereotypes about what love is and how lovers should act can be very harmful. In his short story "In Love," D. H. Lawrence uses the three main characters to embody his theme

1

187

that love is experienced in a unique way by every couple and that there isn't a normal or proper way to be in love.

Hester; her fiancé, Joe; and her sister, Henrietta, all approach    2
and respond to love in different ways. Hester is unwilling to compromise what she really feels for Joe, but she is pressured by her own notions of how a young woman in her situation should feel. Joe appears to be the typical young man in love. He seems at ease with the situation, and his moves are so predictable they could have come straight from a movie script. But when he is confronted and badgered by Hester and Henrietta, he admits that he was only putting on an act and feels regret for not being honest with Hester. Henrietta is the mouthpiece for all of society's conceptions of love. She repeatedly asks Hester to be normal and secretly worries that Hester will call off the wedding. Henrietta is like a mother hen, always making sure that Hester is doing the right thing (in Henrietta's opinion, anyway).

Hester and Joe are, in a sense, playing a game with each other.    3
Both are acting on what they feel is expected of them now that they are engaged, as if how they really feel about each other is unimportant. It is only when Hester and Joe finally talk honestly about their relationship that they realize they have been in love all along in their own unique way.

Hester, ever the practical one, becomes more and more frus-    4
trated with "Joe's love-making" (650). She feels ridiculous, as if she is just a toy, but at the same time she feels she should respond positively to Joe, "because she believed that a nice girl would have been only too delighted to go and sit 'there'" (650). Rather than doing what she wants, enjoying a nice, comfortable relationship with Joe, Hester does what she feels she ought to. She says that she ought to like Joe's lovemaking even though she doesn't really know why. Despite her practical and independent nature, Hester is still troubled by what society would think.

Lawrence seems to be suggesting a universal theme here. If Hes-    5
ter, with such firm ideas about what she wants, is so troubled by what society dictates, then how much more are we, as generally less objective and more tractable people, affected by society's standards? Hester's is a dilemma everyone faces.

At the heart of Hester's confusion is Joe, whose personality was    6
so different before they became engaged that Hester might not have gotten engaged if she had known how Joe would change: "Six months ago, Hester would have enjoyed it [being alone with Joe]. They were so perfectly comfortable together, he and she" (649). But

by cuddling and petting, Joe has ruined the comfortable relationship that he and Hester had enjoyed. The most surprising line in the story is Hester's assertion that "[t]he very fact of his being in love with me proves that he doesn't love me" (652). Here, Hester makes a distinction between really loving someone and just putting on an act of being *in* love. Hester feels hurt that Joe would treat her as a typical girl rather than as the young woman she really is.

Hester is a reluctant player in the love game until the end of the story when she confronts Joe and blurts out, "I absolutely can't stand your making love to me, if that is what you call the business" (656–57). Her use of the word *business* is significant because it refers to a chore, something that has to be done. Hester regards Joe's love-making as if it were merely a job to be completed. When Joe apologizes, Hester sees his patient, real love for her, and she begins to have the same feelings for him again. When she says, "I don't mind what you do if you love me really" (660), Hester, by compromising, shows the nature of their love for each other.

Lawrence uses Joe to show a typical response to society's pressures. Joe obediently plays the role of the husband-to-be. He exhibits all the preconceived images one may have about a man about to be married. In trying to fit the expectations of others, Joe sacrifices his straightforwardness and the honesty that Hester valued so much in him. Although Joe's actions don't seem to be so bad in and of themselves, in the context of his relationship with Hester, they are completely out of place. His piano playing, for example, inspires Hester to remark that Joe's love games would be impossible to handle after the music he played. The music represents something that is pure and true—in contrast to the new, hypocritical Joe. Joe doesn't seem to be aware of Hester's feelings until she comes forward with them at the end of the story. The humiliation he suffers makes him silent, and he is described several times as wooden, implying stubbornness and solidity. It is out of this woodenness that a changed Joe appears. At first the word suggests his defensiveness for his bruised ego, but then as Joe begins to see Hester's point about being truly in love, his woodenness is linked to his solidity and stability, qualities that represent for Hester the old Joe. Once Joe gets his mind off the love game, the simple intimacy of their relationship is revealed to him, and he desires Hester, not in a fleeting way but in a way that one desires something that was almost lost.

Henrietta serves as the antagonist in this story because it is through her that society's opinions come clear. In almost the first line of text, Henrietta, looking at Hester, states, "If I had such a worried look on my face, when I was going down to spend the weekend with the man I was engaged to—and going to be married to in a month—well! I should either try and change my face or hide my feelings, or something" (647). With little regard for Hester's feelings, Henrietta is more concerned that Hester have the right attitude. Although Henrietta herself is not married, the fact that Hester, who is twenty-five, is soon to be married is a relief to her. Not wanting her sister to be an old maid, Henrietta does all she can to make sure the weekend runs smoothly. She acts as though Hester were her responsibility and even offers to come with Hester to take the "edge off the intimacy" (648). Being young, Henrietta hasn't really formed her own views of life or love yet. As a result, she easily believes the traditional statements society makes about love. When Hester says that she can't stand Joe's being in love with her, Henrietta keeps responding that a man is supposed to be in love with the woman he marries. She doesn't understand the real love that Joe and Hester eventually feel but only the "ought-tos" of love imposed by society. It is unclear at the end of the story if Henrietta really recognizes the new bond between Hester and Joe.

What society and common beliefs dictate about being in love    10 isn't really important. In order to be happy, couples must find their own unique bond of love and not rely on others' opinions or definitions. Joe and Hester come to this realization only after they are hurt and left unfulfilled as a result of the love game they play with each other. Hester knew how she really felt from the beginning, but pressure about what she *ought* to feel worried her. Joe willingly went along with the game until he realized how important their simple intimacy really was. In the end, Hester and Joe are in love not because of the games they play but because of an intimate friendship that had been growing all along.

## WORK CITED

Lawrence, D. H. "In Love." *The Complete Short Stories,* Vol. 3. New York: Penguin, 1977.

# Synopsis: Susan Glaspell's "A Jury of Her Peers"

You can read Susan Glaspell's story "A Jury of Her Peers" online at the Electronic Text Center at the University of Virginia Library. Go to http://etext.lib.virginia.edu/modeng/modeng0.browse.html and look under "G" for "Glaspell." Or, for a quick orientation to the story, read the synopsis below.

---

Susan Glaspell's short story "A Jury of Her Peers" begins when three men and two women—Mr. Peters, the county sheriff; Mr. Henderson, the county attorney; and Mr. Hale, a farmer; along with two wives, Mrs. Peters and Mrs. Hale—begin to investigate the death of a farm neighbor, John Wright, who they believe was murdered the previous day by his wife, Mrs. Wright. Although there is no direct evidence linking her to the crime, Mrs. Wright is nevertheless jailed on suspicion of murder.

At the Wright farmhouse, the county attorney asks Mr. Hale, the man who by chance discovered the murder, to recount his experience at the farmhouse. Mr. Hale describes how he found Mrs. Wright sitting in a rocking chair as she calmly told him that Mr. Wright was upstairs dead with a rope around his neck.

As the three men search the farmhouse for evidence that might establish a motive for the crime, Mrs. Peters and Mrs. Hale sit in Mrs. Wright's kitchen. With attentive eyes, they keenly observe domestic details that begin to reveal a pattern of meaning that the men overlook. As they continue to look around, the details begin to speak volumes about the emotional lives and marital relationship of Mr. and Mrs. Wright. Mrs. Peters and Mrs. Hale notice the uncharacteristic dirty pans and towels in the kitchen, neither of which fit Mrs. Wright's character as a careful housekeeper. They note a half-full bag of sugar that, again, is uncharacteristic, suggesting an interrupted task. They find a single square on Mrs. Wright's quilt that is raggedly sewn—just one, amid a field of perfectly sewn pieces—which suggests the seamstress had to be out of sorts with herself.

As these domestic details add up, they gain significance for the women while the men scoff and dismiss their concerns as simplistic and typical of women. Finally, when the women discover a birdcage with its door broken and then—at the bottom of the sewing basket—a dead canary wrapped in silk, its neck wrung, they realize they have stumbled upon the motive for the murder. Bound up in the details of violence and dishonor—the husband killed the wife's canary—Mrs. Peters and Mrs. Hale discover the joyless horror Mrs. Wright endured in her marriage to her hard, uncaring husband. They realize John Wright was the man who killed not only a canary but also the spirit of his wife, a woman who had been a beautiful singer—a songbird—in her youth. Mrs. Peters and Mrs. Hale draw on personal experiences to empathize with Mrs. Wright. Mrs. Peters recalls the raging desire to hurt the boy who killed her kitten when she was a girl, and Mrs. Hale recalls the stillness she felt when her first baby died, likening it to the stillness that Mrs. Wright must have endured in her loveless marriage.

In the end, Mrs. Peters' and Mrs. Hale's empathy for Mrs. Wright is so deep that when the men return to collect them to leave, the women look at each other quickly and Mrs. Hale stuffs the dead bird into her coat pocket. Without concrete evidence to establish a motive for murder, they know a jury will not convict the woman. Mrs. Peters and Mrs. Hale act as Mrs. Wright's first jury—a true jury of her peers, relying on experience, intuition, and empathy rather than legal reasoning to find justice in their world.

# Irony and Intuition in "A Jury of Her Peers"

Margaret Tate

*DeKalb College*
*Decatur, Georgia*

Margaret Tate begins by briefly establishing the historical context and setting of "A Jury of Her Peers"—the early years of the twentieth century in the U.S. Midwest. Her key terms are *intuition* and *irony,* her theme, the differences between men's and women's intuitions. She does not leave you waiting for her thesis: you will find it at the end of her first paragraph. As you read, notice how she selectively and repeatedly quotes and paraphrases the story without retelling it. Instead, she uses the details of the story to support each stage of her argument.

———————

Though men and women are now recognized as generally equal in talent and intelligence, when Susan Glaspell wrote "A Jury of Her Peers" in 1917, it was not so. In this turn-of-the-century, rural midwestern setting, women were often barely educated and possessed virtually no political or economic power. And, being considered the weaker sex, there was not much they could do about it. Relegated to home and hearth, women found themselves at the mercy of the more powerful men in their lives. Ironically, it is just this type of powerless existence, perhaps, that over the ages developed into a power with which women could baffle and frustrate their male counterparts: a sixth sense—an inborn trait commonly known as women's intuition. In Glaspell's story, ironic situations contrast male and female intuition, illustrating that Minnie Wright is more fairly judged by women than by men.

"A Jury of Her Peers" first uses irony to illustrate the contrast between male and female intuition when the men go to the farmhouse looking for clues to the murder of John Wright, but it is the women who find them. In the Wright household, the men are searching for

**193**

something out of the ordinary, an obvious indication that Minnie has been enraged or provoked into killing her husband. Their intuition does not tell them that their wives, because they are women, can help them gain insight into what has occurred between John and his wife. They bring Mrs. Hale and Mrs. Peters along merely to tend to the practical matters, considering them needlessly preoccupied with trivial things and even too unsophisticated to make a contribution to the investigation, as illustrated by Mr. Hale's derisive question, "Would the women know a clue if they did come upon it?" (289).

Ironically, while the men are looking actively for the smoking    3
gun, the women are confronted with subtler clues in spite of themselves and even try to hide from each other what they intuitively know. But they do not fool each other for long, as Glaspell describes: "Their eyes met—something flashed to life, passed between them; then, as if with an effort, they seemed to pull away from each other" (295). However, they cannot pull away, for they are bound by a power they do not even comprehend: "We all go through the same things—it's all just a different kind of the same thing!...why do you and I *understand*? Why do we *know*—what we know this minute?" (303). They do not realize that it is intuition they share, that causes them to "[see] into things, [to see] through a thing to something else..." (294). Though sympathetic to Minnie Wright, the women cannot deny the damning clues that lead them to the inescapable conclusion of her guilt.

If it is ironic that the women find the clues, it is even more ironic    4
that they find them in the mundane household items to which the men attribute so little significance. "Nothing here but kitchen things," the men mistakenly think (287). Because of their weak intuition, they do not see the household as indicative of John's and Minnie's characters. They do not see beyond the cheerless home to John Wright's grim nature, nor do the dilapidated furnishings provide them with a clue to his penurious habits. Minnie's depression and agitation are not apparent to them in the dismal, half-cleaned kitchen; instead, they consider Minnie an inept, lazy housekeeper. Oddly, for all their "snoopin' round and criticizin' " (290), the three gentlemen literally do not have a clue.

The women, on the other hand, "used to worrying over trifles"    5
(287), do attach importance to the "everyday things" (299), and looking around the cheerless kitchen, they see many examples of the miserably hard existence of Minnie Wright. Knowing the pride a woman takes in her home, they see Minnie's kitchen not as dirty but

as half-cleaned, and the significance of this is not lost on them. And, upon discovering the erratic quilt stitching, they are alarmed. Also, they cannot dismiss the broken birdcage as just a broken birdcage. They instinctively know, as the men do not, that Minnie desperately needed a lively creature to brighten up such a loveless home. Upon finding these clues, ironically hidden in everyday objects, the women piece them together with a thread of intuition and create a blanket of guilt that covers the hapless Minnie Wright.

Though there is irony in the fact that the women, not the men, 6 find the clues, and irony in the fact that they are found in everyday household things, most ironic is the fact that John Wright meets the same fate he has inflicted on the poor bird, illustrating that he is perhaps the least intuitive of all the men in the story. John Wright never sees beyond his own needs to the needs of his wife. He does not understand her need for a pretty creature to fill the void created by her lonely, childless existence. Not content to kill just Minnie's personality ("[s]he was [once] kind of like a bird herself. Real sweet and pretty" [299]), he kills her canary, leaving her with the deafening silence of the lonesome prairie. Minnie has endured many years of misery at the hands of John Wright, but he pushes her too far when he kills the bird. Then, ironically, he gets the "peace and quiet" (283) he values over her happiness.

John Wright lacks the intuition to understand his wife's love of 7 her bird, but the two women do not. They understand that she needed the bird to fill the still air with song and lessen her loneliness. After discovering the dead bird, they do not blame her for killing John. The dead bird reminds Mrs. Peters of a traumatic episode from her childhood:

> "When I was a girl," said Mrs. Peters, under her breath, "my kitten— there was a boy took a hatchet, and before my eyes—before I could get there...If they hadn't held me back, I would have...hurt him." (301–02)

The women see the reason for Minnie's murderous impulse, but they know that the men lack the insight to ever fully understand her situation or her motivation; therefore, in hiding the bird, by their silence, they acquit Minnie Wright.

Through the ironic situations in "A Jury of Her Peers," Glaspell 8 clearly illustrates a world in which men and women vary greatly in their perception of things. She shows men as often superficial in the way they perceive the world, lacking the depth of intuition that women use as a means of self-preservation to see themselves and the world more clearly. Without the heightened perspective on life that this knowledge of human nature gives them, women might not stand a chance. Against the power and domination of men, they often find themselves as defenseless and vulnerable as Minnie's poor bird.

## WORK CITED

Glaspell, Susan. "A Jury of Her Peers." *Lifted Masks and Other Works.* Ed. Eric S. Rabkin. Ann Arbor: U of Michigan P, 1993.

# A Note on the Copyediting

We all know that the work of professional writers rarely appears in print without first being edited. But what about student writing—especially essays that are presented as models of student writing? Do these get edited too?

While it's easy to draw an analogy with professional writing and simply declare that "all published writing gets edited," there are some important differences between student and professional writing. For one thing, student writing is presented as student writing. That is, it's offered to the reader as an example of the kind of writing students can and do produce in a writing class. And since most students don't have the benefit of a professional editor, their work may not be as polished as the models they see in textbooks.

For another, unlike professional writers, students rarely have the opportunity to participate in the editorial process. Companion readers like this one are compiled while the main text is being revised, at a time when the authors and editors are immersed in the work of the text and don't have time to also supervise twenty-five or more student writers. For this reason, students are usually simply asked to sign a statement transferring to the publisher all rights to their essays, subject to final editing, and don't see their work again until it appears in print. For these reasons, editing student writing is problematic.

But publishing student essays without editing is equally problematic. Every composition teacher knows that even the best papers, the A+ essays, aren't perfect. But readers of published prose, accustomed to the conventions of edited American English, aren't always so generous. The shift in tense that may be seen as a simple lapse in a student narrative becomes a major distraction in a published piece. Rather than preserve that tense shift in the interest of "absolute fidelity" to the student's work, it is more in keeping with the spirit and purpose of the enterprise to edit the passage. After all, the rest of the evidence indicates that the student is a strong writer and that he or she would likely accede to the change if it were called to his or her attention.

The editing of a student essay is not a violation of the student's work, then, but really a courtesy to the writer. True, some essays require more editing than others—perhaps because the student did not have as much opportunity to revise—but none in this collection has been altered significantly. In fact, every attempt has been made to respect the students' choices.

To give you an inside look at the editing process, we reproduce here the originally submitted version of Sheila McClain's essay "Proxemics: A Study of Space and Relationships," along with the Bedford/St. Martin's editor's changes. You might use this sample as an opportunity to consider the usefulness and necessity of editing. What changes were made, and why? Which of them improved the essay? Were all of them necessary? If you are a writer whose work has undergone editorial revision—perhaps as part of peer review—you might think about how the process felt to you. Did you appreciate your editor's work? Resent it? What did you learn from it? If you're like most of us, you probably realized that it's natural to resist, but necessary to accept, criticism. In other words, you learned to think like a writer.

# *Sample Copyediting*

Proxemics: A Study of Space and Relationships

by

Sheila McClain

Every~~d~~ay we interact and communicate, sometimes
[#]
without even saying a word. Body language, more
**formally**
~~correctly~~ known as nonverbal communication, speaks
volumes about who we are and how we relate to others.
**Lester**
As ~~noted by~~ Sielski, an associate professor at the
**˄writes˄**
University of West Florida, "Words are beautiful,
exciting, important, but we have over estimated them
badly $\frac{1}{m}$ since they are not all or even half the
message." He also asserts that "beyond words lies the
bedrock on which human relationships are built $\frac{1}{m}$
nonverbal communication" (Sielski). ~~As related by~~
**A group of**
~~author Roger E. Axtell~~ psychology students at the
**demonstrated**
University of Texas recently ~~discovered~~ just how

**199**

profound ~~and~~ **an** effect nonverbal communication can have
on people. ~~They~~ **The students** conducted an experiment to test the
unspoken rules of behavior on elevators. Boarding a
crowded elevator, they would stand **facing and** grinning at ~~and~~
~~facing~~ the other people on board. Understandably, the
people became ~~upset and~~ uncomfortable; ~~and~~ one person
~~was~~ even ~~heard~~ suggest**ed**~~ing~~ that someone ~~should~~ call
911 (5-6). Why all the fuss? ~~Normal~~ **Unspoken** elevator etiquette
dictates that one should turn and face the door in a
crowded elevator, being careful not to touch anyone
else and honoring the sacred personal space of each
individual by staring at the floor indicator instead
of looking at anyone else. Although they are not
written down, strict rules govern our behavior in
public situations. This is especially true when
space is limited as on elevators, buses, or ~~the~~ subway
trains (**Axtell** ~~the~~ 5-6).

**Patricia Buhler,** An expert in business management and associate
professor at Goldey-Beacon College, confirms the large
role nonverbal communication plays. She asserts that
as little as 8 percent of the message we communicate
is made up of words. We communicate the rest of our
message, a disproportionately large 92 percent,
~~utilizing~~ **with** body language and other nonverbal forms of
communication (Buhler). ~~According to a professor of~~

~~social work,~~ while researchers have long known that
nonverbal cues play a large role in communication, for
many years they made no efforts to learn more about
**them (Sielski).** ~~this component of language.~~ Amid rising public
interest, several scientists pioneered new research in
the field of nonverbal communication in the 1950s.
Among these experts was anthropologist Edward T. Hall.
He ~~pioneered research~~ **focused** on a specific type of nonverbal
communication called *Proxemics* (ital) (rom). *Proxemics* ~~defined as~~ **is**
the study of how people use personal space to
communicate nonverbally plays a major role in
our everyday interactions with others, whether we are
conscious of it or not, our use of space

**A review of some of Dr. Hall's main terms will help us**
~~Proxemics carries great importance because it~~
**appreciate** ~~affects our relationships with others. To~~ better
**how much our** understand ~~the impact~~ proxemics ~~can have on~~
**use of space** relationships ~~we need to know the meanings of two key~~
**affects** **For example,** **in our everyday interactions, we choose to**
**according to** ~~terms used by~~ Dr. Hall. ~~A professor from University of~~ **position**
~~St. Thomas summarizes Dr. Hall's terms. The first term~~ **ourselves**
**to create**
"Sociopetal space" invites communication. ~~The second~~ **either**
~~term~~ "Sociofugal space" is the opposite ~~of the first.~~ **"socio-**
It separates people and discourages interaction **petal" or**
**"socio-**
(Jordan). ~~For example,~~ a student in a school lunchroom **fugal"**
may ~~choose to~~ sit alone at an empty table in ~~the~~ **a** **space.**
**creating**
corner, away from ~~others~~ **the** students ("Sociofugal space"),

or directly across from a person he would like to befriend (creating sociopetal space"). 

Dr. Hall identifies three kinds of general spaces with which we can create either sociofugal or sociopetal space. These are "fixed-feature space," "semi-fixed feature space," and "informal space" (Jordan). Fixed-feature spaces are hard, if not impossible, for us to control or change. For example, because my college English class is too small for the number of students attending, we have a hard time positioning ourselves so that we can all see the overhead projections. We cannot make the walls of the classroom bigger or the ceiling higher, and the overhead screen is likewise "fixed" in place. We must work within the constraints of these space. A "semi-fixed feature space" is usually defined by mobile objects, such as furniture. The couches and chairs in a living room, for example, may face only the television, thus discouraging conversations and relationship building. But we are able to reposition the furniture to create a more social and conversational environment. "Informal space" is by far the easiest to manipulate. We each ~~have~~ control ~~of~~ our personal "bubble," and we can set distances between ourselves and others ~~which best suit~~ that reflect our relationships with them. ~~To illustrate this~~ Take for example the way that people ~~may~~ approach their bosses, ~~in various ways depending upon how they feel about their boss. If people are~~ A man who is afraid of or dislike**s** ~~their~~ his boss~~, they~~ may communicate with ~~them~~ her from as far away as possible. ~~They~~ He might stand in ~~their~~ her doorway ~~and not enter the boss' office~~ to relay a message. Conversely, ~~people~~ a woman who ~~have~~ has known ~~their~~ her boss for many years and ~~are~~ is good friends with ~~their bosses~~ him may come right in to his office and casually sit down in close proximity to ~~their bosses~~ him. ~~Thus they show by their use of space that they feel comfortable and have a good relationship with their bosses.~~ Individually, we have a great deal of control over our "informal space," and how we use this space can speak volumes about our relationships with others.

~~As one source explains,~~ after observing many interactions, Dr. Hall ~~further~~ broke down ~~this~~ informal space ~~by~~ further, identifying four ~~separate~~ distances commonly used by people in their interactions with others: "intimate distance," zero to one and a half feet;

"personal distance," one and a half to four feet;

"social distance," four to twelve feet; and "public

distance," twelve feet and beyond ~~all distinguish~~

~~zones we use for different interactions~~ (Beebe, Beebe,

and Redmond 231). "Intimate distance," as the name

suggests, is generally reserved for those people

closest to us. Lovemaking, hugging, and holding small

children all occur in this zone. The exception to this

rule comes when we extend our hand to perfect

strangers in greeting, allowing them to briefly enter

our intimate space with a handshake. "Personal

distance," while not as close as intimate, is still

reserved for people we know well and with whom we feel

comfortable. This zone ~~is~~ usually occupies an area

relatively close to us. It can at times be applied,

however, to include objects we see as extensions of

ourselves. For instance, ^while driving^ we may feel ~~that someone is~~

~~being invaded~~

~~invading~~ our personal space ^when we are driving a car^

^by a^

~~if the~~ car (behind us) follows^ing^ too closely. We see ~~the~~ ^our own^

car as an extension of ourselves and extend our

"personal bubble" to include it. "Social distance" is

often considered a respectful distance and is used in

many professional business settings as well as in

group interactions. ~~To, illustrate~~ ^There is a^ "public distance,"

^between a^

~~we might think of the distance used when~~ lectur^er^ing ~~a~~

~~large group or~~ [and a class, or someone] speaking publicly from a podium. ~~This~~ [and his]
or her audience.
~~distance can also include speakers who are not~~

~~physically present, such as watching the President~~

~~address the nation on television.~~

    As we have seen, ~~proxemics, or how we use the~~ [in positioning ourselves in relation]
[to others — $\frac{1}{m}$ especially in choosing nearness or distance — $\frac{1}{m}$ we]
~~space around us, has some impact on the multitude of~~
[communicate respect or intimacy, fear or familiarity⊙]
~~interactions we have with others everyday.~~ We can
improve ~~or damage our social~~ [a friendly] relationships⊙ simply by
using a "warm⌃personable"⊙ distance⌃ ~~with friends.~~ or ~~we~~
~~may~~⊙ drive potential friends away⌃ [by] seeming "cold and
distant,"⊙ or getting quite literally "too close for
comfort."⊙ We⌃ [can] put people at ease or make them
uncomfortable just by our proximity to them. The study
of nonverbal communication, and specifically
proxemics, demonstrates the truth of the old adage⌃
"actions speak louder than words."

# Submission Form

We hope that this collection is one of many, and that we'll be able to include more essays from more colleges and universities in the next edition. Please let us see the best essays you've written using *The St. Martin's Guide to Writing; The Concise Guide to Writing; Reading Critically, Writing Well;* or *Sticks and Stones*. Send them with this submission form and copies of the agreement form opposite (one for each essay you submit) to English Editor—Student Essays, Bedford/St. Martin's, 33 Irving Place, 10th Floor, New York, NY 10003. You can also submit essays online at bedfordstmartins.com/theguide.

**Student's Name** _____

**Instructor's Name** _____

**School** _____

**Department** _____

**Course Text** (circle one)

*The St. Martin's Guide to Writing*          *The Concise Guide to Writing*

*Reading Critically, Writing Well*           *Sticks and Stones*

**Writing Assignment** (circle one)

Remembering Events                     Proposing a Solution

Writing Profiles                       Justifying an Evaluation

Explaining a Concept                   Speculating about Causes

Explaining Opposing Positions          Interpreting Stories

Arguing a Position

Other: _____

# Agreement Form

I hereby assign to Bedford/St. Martin's ("Bedford") all of my right, title, and interest throughout the world, including, without limitation, all copyrights, in and to my essay, ————————————————————, and any notes and drafts pertaining to it (the sample essay and such materials being referred to as the "Essay").

I understand that Bedford in its discretion has the right but not the obligation to publish the Essay in any form(s) or format(s) that it may desire; that Bedford may edit, revise, condense, or otherwise alter the Essay as it deems appropriate in order to prepare the same for publication. I understand that Bedford has the right to use and to authorize the use of my name as author of the Essay in connection with any work that contains the Essay (or a portion of it).

I represent that the Essay was completely written by me, that I have cited any sources I relied on, that publication of it will not infringe upon the rights of any third party, and that I have not granted any rights in it to any third party.

In the event Bedford determines to publish any part of the Essay in one of its print books, I will receive one free copy of the work in which it appears.

Student's signature ————————————————————

Name ———————————————————— Date ————————

Permanent Address ————————————————————

————————————————————————————————

Phone Number(s) ————————————————————

————————————————————————————————

Email Address(es) ————————————————————

————————————————————————————————

*A Note to the Student:*

*When a writer creates something—a story, an essay, a poem—he or she automatically possesses all of the rights to that piece of writing, no trip to the U.S. Copyright Office needed. When a writer—a historian, a novelist, a sportswriter—publishes his or her work, he or she normally transfers some or all of those rights to the publisher, by formal agreement. The form above is one such formal agreement. By entering into this agreement, you are engaging in a modern publishing ritual—the transfer of rights from writer to publisher. If this is your first experience submitting something for publication, you should know that you are in good company: every student who has published an essay in one of our books entered into this agreement, and just about every published writer has entered into a similar one.*

*Thank you for submitting your essay.*